Ordinary Russians

Ordinary Russians

Barry Broadfoot

M&S

McClelland & Stewart Inc.
The Canadian Publishers
481 University Avenue
Toronto, Ontario
M5G 2E9

Canadian Cataloguing in Publication Data

Broadfoot, Barry, 1926—
  Ordinary Russians

ISBN 0-7710-1676-X

1. Soviet Union – Description and travel – 1970- .
2. Soviet Union – Social Conditions – 1970- .
3. Soviet Union – Biography. I. Title.

DK29.B76 1989   914.7'04854   C89-094927-1

Printed and bound in the United States of America

To my children Susan and Ross and my granddaughter Emily

Contents

❁

Preface

What the Soviet Union Is All About

I made my first visit to the Soviet Union in 1967, when as a columnist for *The Vancouver Sun* I visited Moscow, Leningrad, and the Black Sea resort of Sochi.

I recall the grim, winter-weary faces on Moscow streets, the fortress mentality, the never-ending and boring receptions awash with pompous bureaucrats. With good reason our group of Canadian industrialists, bankers, and attendant newspapermen spontaneously cheered when our jetliner lifted off from Moscow. I had seen few, and talked to no, ordinary Soviet citizens.

But I remembered one. As I was leaving one more official dinner out of boredom I passed through an outer dining room and saw a tall man of deeply lined face sitting alone with a bottle of vodka. He hailed me: "Foreigner, hello, and say greetings from me to all the locomotive drivers in your country."

I wished I had stopped. He would have had something to tell me, and in English, but it was illegal for a citizen to talk to a foreigner. It still is; however, the law is rarely observed now. At the time, we all felt an irrational fear and sense of intimidation. But he often came to mind.

I quit newspapering and wrote eight oral histories on Canada and kept up my interest in the Soviet Union. Then, in March 1985, Mikhail Gorbachev was named the General Secretary of the Soviet Communist Party and flung the words *glasnost* and *perestroika* at a world tired of the unending Them-Against-Us posturing and the nuclear arms race.

These were brave new words: *glasnost*, the openness to speak and criticize, to tell no more lies; *perestroika*, the restructuring of the economic systems in order to bring the USSR into the real and competitive world. In New York, Harper and Row published his book, *Perestroika: New Thinking for Our Country and the World*.

Mr. Gorbachev was going public. With broad strokes he bluntly and boldly painted the Soviet Union to the world as a nation in disarray financially, industrially, agriculturally, and socially—with its youth disillusioned and looking to the democracies in the West for solutions as well as for gratification.

Obviously, there were those who would not welcome change. There were an unbelievable 30 million bureaucrats running the country through centralist policies emanating from Moscow. *Perestroika* would hit them hardest of all. The 50 million workers knew they'd be expected to work harder, more efficiently. As for the 55 million passive and politically inactive pensioners living well-subsidized lives, they could be expected to adopt a wait-and-see attitude.

Gorbachev, strong in leadership, highly intelligent, and a diehard Socialist, forthrightly told the Soviet peoples that there were no easy answers and he did what any honest politician would do: he said the road would be hard and long. How hard? How long? No one knew then. They still don't.

In late 1986, I saw my chance to find out how ordinary Russians were coping with these new ideas. I got the name of someone at the Soviet Embassy in Ottawa and wrote him. Would Moscow be interested in having someone come over and poke about? Yes, they were interested. Time passed. Nothing happened. Then, as if to check me out, I was invited to attend the Moscow International Forum for a Nuclear-Free World and Survival of Mankind. It turned out that I was the only Canadian representing our artists, musicians, writers, *et*

al., which made me wonder. Had I just come to their attention
at the right moment? "Let's include a Canadian."

It was first class all the way for the 1,400 of us from eighty-
six countries–and totally orchestrated as a political playground
for Marxist and Leninist ideals. We knew it, they knew it, so
we all ignored it and had a good time.

It was then that I met with executives of Novosti Press
Agency to plan a trip. I said where I wanted to go; the Agency's
representatives would get me from A to B with reasonable
dispatch and arrange any interviews I wanted. It would be hard
work and tough travelling in a country not known for topnotch
transportation facilities, and I insisted that I pay every cent. It
was all agreed: no problem. Five months later I returned bur-
dened down with tape recorders, tapes, camera, film, notebooks, and a few Western treasures like 99-cent pantihose,
cigarette lighters, and cosmetics to hand out at appropriate
moments.

Novosti Press let me down, often failing to set up appoint-
ments in advance, arrange for a car, or provide the best accom-
modations – although my guide went in style the whole time.
But thanks to resourceful field men at the local level, I got
many interviews, ranging from a trapper, a policewoman, and
a poet to fishermen, doctors, farmers, and factory managers.

Few of the official interviews appear in this book, because
the Novosti Press translator was officialdom to them and officialdom, from long experience, meant trouble, or at least problems. Virtually all were from people who approached me in
cafés, on the street, at markets, since I had many free times
and days on my own. They wanted to talk about the outside
world, to practise their English, to just sit with a foreigner and
drink coffee and discuss their lives. They wanted no more of
me than that.

A man who sat opposite me on the Moscow subway followed
me out and we walked for two hours. A knock on the door in
the hotel in Tbilisi: it was a student who had somehow got past
the doorman, and I got a bottle of wine from the dining room
and we talked for an hour. A black market taxi driver with a
drunk passed out in the back seat drove me home from a friend's
home. A woman in the mini-bar in the Hotel Rus at 2 A.M.
wanted to visit Greece, and a journalist, also in Kiev, had a
keener grasp on life in his country than anyone I met.

They all spoke English, and when wound up, it seemed they spoke it better. Only in the presence of my guide did the people look apprehensive. I found myself asking gentle, meaningless questions, just to protect them. Old ways for them die hard.

There was nothing to fear in the Soviet Union and I felt no fear; only the dead hand of officialdom, which did affect my short days there, but then one must consider it affects all the days of all the Soviets, all the time.

They talked freely about food shortages, poor housing, alcoholism, the high abortion rate, the indifferent bureaucracy, the corruption, the briberies, the black market: "It's a way of life. Everybody does it." And everyone loved the Motherland; yes, times had been bad, but things were better, a little better, "we have hope."

According to a Soviet economist, their economy ranks fifty-fifth in standard of living on a world scale. The average Moscow couple with two children pay 59 percent of their combined 380-ruble monthly salary on food, which they wait in queues for up to two hours daily to buy. They survive because their rent, education, and medical services are heavily subsidized – and there are many ways to add a few extra rubles to the income, illegally of course, but "everybody does it." As more than one person told me, "We are a patient people; things have to get better, even if it takes twenty years, maybe not even in my lifetime."

Things *can* get better, but it takes high-tech, sophisticated methods and machinery to produce goods acceptable to Western standards and competitive on the world market. They need to sell these goods to get the hard currency to buy the technology to make the goods. Catch-22? It looked like it from where I stood.

(One must understand the foreign tourist and money. The Soviet Union is truly desperate for foreign currency, dollars, pounds, marks, francs. With it they can buy the foreign technology to lift themselves – so they hope – from their economic morass and mind-boggling inefficiencies.

In April of 1989 the Soviet ruble was artifically priced at $1.19 Canadian, despite the fact that the ruble is not negotiable in the West. Everything they buy must be in hard currency, or by barter, which is virtually unacceptable to the rest of the non-Communist world. International bankers have suggested they devalue the ruble by 90 percent, making it worth about 20 cents Canadian. The black market price is 4 or 5 rubles to the Canadian dollar, thus the black market does its own devaluation.

The Soviets refuse to devalue, thus admitting to the world how bankrupt the nation is, although they have been studying the problem of convertibility for a dozen years and hope for a solution in ten years.

"A Third World country which happens to be a Superpower," as one Canadian Embassy official told me.

A major source of hard currency is the foreign tourist – "the cow to be milked," one frank Soviet official told me. Tour groups get the best rate, but they see little of the real country; but so it is in Canada, too, so what else is new? The lone traveller, such as I, is the real cow, although we are very few. A second-rate hotel with third-rate rooms cost up to $170 a night. U-drives were out of sight. A $30 flight for a Soviet cost $150 and more.

I believe that if the Soviet merely broke even on tourism, they would not want visitors, even for the value of propagandizing them with their endless exhortations of wanting peace, peace, and more peace.

It often came down to the common complaint: the Americans have forced them into these prohibitively expensive arms and space races, thus draining the nation white. Who is preparing to launch Energia, the mightiest Soviet space engine ever? Who has superiority in tanks, aircraft, and nuclear cannon? The Americans are the cause of all their problems, when in truth it is the antiquated and centralized economic policies and the Iron Curtain mentality of the Russian bureaucracy in Moscow – Russians make up half the population of the Soviet Union and decidedly control every aspect of every part of Soviet life.

To use a cliché, if Gorbachev hadn't risen from the pack in 1985, they would have had to invent him.)

The Russian people know this, too. They see the corruption at high and low levels, the abuse of privilege. They speak of the appalling inefficiency on the huge state farms, in outmoded factories. The Chernobyl reactor meltdown has made them more aware of the consequences of a nuclear war – and more supportive of Gorbachev's peace initiatives. *Perestroika*, for many, many Soviets, seems to be the answer.

No one refused to talk to me. I was free to go where I pleased, and wise enough to not ask to go where I knew they'd refuse me. I was never treated rudely, except by waiters. There was not one person I found uninteresting, except for a few bureaucrats I encountered in formal interviews. The ordinary Russian – if there is such a creature – is jolly, loves to gossip, has strong prejudices, and can be very serious about important matters, matters that affect his future and the future of the Motherland. Everyone was open with me; I respected their views and opinions and answered their questions about Canada and the West honestly. For the moments we were together we were friends.

Before I left home in September, after cramming about forty books on the Soviet Union and absorbing a thousand-and-one facts, an old editor said to me, "Don't try to compare. Just listen, be an observor. Let your readers judge for themselves." Good advice, but not always easy to follow. But then good advice never is.

After thirty-two days in the Soviet Union, Aeroflot carried me to Frankfurt, the aerial hub of the world in West Germany. The airport there was as different from Moscow's as day is from night. Here, all was super-efficient, super-cool. Rich and pedigreed. But the first policeman I saw beyond the customs barrier was slung with a mean machine-gun. The only weapon I'd seen carried by a militiaman in the country I had just left was a black-and-white traffic baton. Welcome to the West!

I bought the London *Financial Times* and learned that the bottom had dropped out of the world's stock markets. Panic. Shades of 1929. I wondered if *Izvestia* or *Pravda* would give that news a front-page story. Somehow, I doubted it. There is no stock exchange in the Soviet Union, the banks are at the elementary level. Of course. The state owns everything. That's really what the Soviet Union is all about – except for the people.

As I write this, a year and a half later, that huge country of eleven time zones and 110 languages is still being described as a "dying Colossus" by some Sovietologists. There will always be collective ownership, ownership by the state. There will be one-party rule. But Gorbachev knows that he has forced the nation on an entirely new path, and having come this far, these few steps, will the Communist Party give him time to succeed? Will the people wait? Will the long-smouldering ashes of regional nationalism burst into flame? Riots and deaths in

Armenia and Georgia. Well-organized campaigns for independence in Estonia, Latvia, Lithuania, three tiny but most progres-
sive so-called autonomous republics in the Soviet Union. Even
that slumbering old giant, the Ukraine, is awakening as the
people remember their proud heritage. *Glasnost* out of control?

These enormous problems Gorbachev must deal with fairly
and squarely if he is to keep the carefully built-up respect he
has gained in the West. Machiavellian tactics or raw military
power can destroy him.

If Gorbachev goes, who follows–and what follows?

As Winston Churchill said in the heady days after the Battle
of Alamein, we are not at the beginning of the end but at the
end of the beginning.

An author is only as good as his editor. I wish to thank my
editor, Betty Corson, for her kindness, patience, and extreme
diligence in assembling and editing a great mass of manuscript
to create the book you are now reading. Without her skills,
Ordinary Russians would not have seen the light of day. Thank
you, Betty, dear friend, and also for the four other oral history
books of mine that we have brought forth.

Barry Broadfoot
Nanaimo, B.C.
April 1989

ONE

Welcome to Moscow

ꊺ

*"Do You Have Any Books?"... "No Marriage for Me!"...
Hard Work, Good Times, on the Taiga ... A Pair of Purple
Shoes ... "All We Have Is Hope"... "There Will Be a Statue"
... "New York Is a Jewish City"... Grandmother Made
Moonshine ... Peredishka, a New Russian Word*

*Heathrow Airport. A drizzly English morning after twenty-
three flying, waiting, and time-zone hours from drizzly Vancouver Island. In a grungy lounge Soviet travellers are buying
chocolate bars and American girlie magazines and sixty-two
English girls from spiffy colleges are eyeing fellow passengers
and ooohing and aaahing over the prospect of three months
as exchange students. My seat partner, from Magdalene Col-
lege, assures me, "If you can speak Russian, you can get a
job anywhere." So confident. She expects to have "lots of fun
and meet Russian boys."*

*Moscow. Why do Soviet air terminals look so big and inside
they are so small? It's crowded and noisy as I wait for the
luggage to start appearing. Thirty minutes later, and where
are my bags? Eleven of us are left stranded. A Frenchwoman
stridently declares, "They do this all the time. Just to upset
us! I know our bags are hidden out there somewhere!" No,
this time I'll blame British Airways.*

1

Two hours later—no bags but two forms signed—my cabbie wheels me into Moscow in murderous traffic as he tries to deal: "Dolla'! Ruble! You go?" He wants to exchange money. Illegal. No deal. At the Kosmos Hotel, I tip a dollar. The cabbie grins. That's half a day's wages for him.

My room seems small, I need to stretch my legs. Outside, Yuri Gagarin's curving knife statue looms up out of the smog. Women peddle flowers outside the teeming subway station. Kiosks sell excellent ice cream. Babies are bundled up and it is only a late September Sunday afternoon.

In my room the red phone trills. A Soviet acquaintance from an earlier visit: "Welcome to Moscow!" We meet in the hard-currency lounge for a drink. So how are things in the USSR? He shrugs. "Read the newspapers. They say things are better. We've got glasnost and perestroika." How much better? "Some." How much is some? "They tell us a lot. I say some. A bit. You'll see."

"Do You Have Any Books?"

The lobby of the Kosmos Hotel was designed by a French architect, built by the Finns. It's an international crossroads, with American tourists mingling with Arab sheiks, West Germans talking quietly in the bar with Japanese businessmen, Australians in the big chairs in their daily ritual of writing postcards, English with Oxbridge accents chatting up Greek businessmen, and young Russians trying to buy Western clothes. How did *they* get in the past the doorman?

A young woman in stylish dress approached me. "You are an American?" No. Canadian. "You are visiting our country. What do you think of it?" I replied that I had only just arrived. She smiled and got right to point. "Do you have any books?" She would offer me many rubles for Western books. I said, sorry, I would like to help her but I would need the two I had brought.

She asked what they were and I said a book on the Hudson's Bay Company, written by a friend. No interest in that one. The other? I told her it was trash book, by Harold Robbins. I said I had promised it to my guide, so I could not give it to her, but I told her it was junk–entertaining junk.

"Yes, I know, we know that. Some people will read him, but it is very bad. I have read two of his. I would pay you many rubles, many, many, if you had a book by Robert Ludlum."

Yes, he was very well known, but I had not read him. Spies, espionage, wasn't that his thing? Yes, and that was the kind of reading she wanted. Why? Oh, she would read it and then sell it for a large amount of money to a man she knew. How much? She said 500 rubles. I did some quick thinking: that would be her salary for about three months. Curious now, I asked why he would pay so much. She looked at me. Was this a dumbbell?

"He works in a very large ministry," she said. "It has many departments. Each department has hundreds of workers. I cannot tell you what it is. Very big. He would take the book and cut each page out and then . . . Oh, I should not be telling you this but if you could, if you come back, you could bring back a Robert Ludlum book. I would give you my telephone number. You can buy Mr. Ludlum's books and Mr. Archer's books, spies and this sort of thing, in airports in London and Zurich and Frankfurt, in your own country. Maybe even *Playboy*. He would like to buy *Playboy* too."

"Pretty dangerous, *Playboy*."

"Oh yes. Especially the German edition. It is worse than the American one. Very naughty. Naked girls. People doing these things to each other."

"No, I think you are talking about a magazine called *Penthouse*. *Playboy* really has some excellent reading in it. Naked girls, too, but *Penthouse* is the one you mean."

"Yes, he would like one of those, this man, because he makes good business with books. There is this machine they have in his department. It is from Japan. It makes copies. You put in a page and press a button, and out, out, out, out comes the copies. You can make ten or fifty, a hundred, in three minutes."

"A photo copier, that's what it's called."

"Yes he wants to get as many books like Robert Ludlum and more like him, spies, from the West, because soon the machine will have to go back to Japan. He can make a hundred copies of a book and then he brings them to his apartment and we put the pages together and tie them with string and wrap them up. That is the book. Then he sells them for 40 or 50 rubles. That is easy. There are ten million people in Moscow and everyone wants to read novels from other countries."

"So he'd make, this friend of yours, about 5,000 rubles."

"Maybe twice if it is a good book. Maybe he would make 8,000 rubles. One book. That many moneys and he could buy a new car every week. He has a good one, a new one, and a good apartment, four rooms. Big, and nice. He buys wine from Georgia and there is a butcher . . . when we go there he always has the best meat. Like the bosses have. Cognac from Armenia. In winter he has vegetables. Tomatoes. Oranges. He is an important man. He has two fur coats."

"But where does he get the material, the paper, to print these books? Isn't there a shortage of paper?"

"There will never be a shortage of paper in this country of mine. Meat, all the time. Vegetables, too. Milk, sometimes. Never bread, but sometimes not good bread. But never paper. He just takes it from other departments. People there, they give it to him, enough for a hundred books, and he gives them two books, maybe ten books. He has ninety to sell. Maybe more, just how much paper he gets. But now the machine has to go back soon, too bad. The Japanese company lent it to the department two years ago. They said,'We want you to try it for a while and if you like it, then you can buy more.' They want, you must understand, to sell hundreds of these machines, thousands. They are very good. Fast. Watch them go, whoot, whoot, whoot. Just like that."

"Now what happens?"

"The Japanese will be coming in three months and they will take the machine away. The department, the ministry, it is going to tell the Japanese businessman that the machine is no good. It is a very good machine, but they have used it for two years. They pay nothing. This is the way it is done. You get it and use it and you don't pay for it. You say it is no good. Then you find another foreign company, say in Germany, and you want to try their machine."

How did her friend get away with it? She said it was simple: everybody who had to be bribed, his superior, the night janitor, the doorman, everyone was bribed. A couple of rubles here, once a week, 10 rubles there, 21 to his superior once a week. I asked why 21 rubles? Why not 20 or 25?

"I don't know. He says 21 is the price. Maybe that's what his wife asked him to get. Maybe 21 is her lucky number."

"And if he is caught? If the police find out?"

"He would have to be unlucky. Who would inform on him? If they did they would be doing it to hurt themselves. Then he could say this was his first time and he was sorry and, okay, you are right, he would have to try and pay, you know . . ." She made the gesture, thumb rubbing first finger. "It all is okay. Nothing would happen to him. He has friends. They help him. Maybe they say not to do again.

"Everybody does it anyway. In my job, Intourist, I cash American money for rubles, 4 or 5 to 1 dollar, 100 dollars, I will take 10 rubles. It is not allowed, but many people do that. Nobody watches. I am so small and my friend, 10,000 rubles a year . . ."

"That's pretty big. That's the price of a good dacha, wouldn't it be? A good apartment. A pretty good life."

"Oh, you are misinformed. That much, you say 10,000 rubles, that is nothing. Nothing, I tell you. Many people I know, just friends, they make more. Everybody does it. This is how we make our country work. I will tell you something about it. A long time, very long, it has been this way for so long. Nothing will change it. We could not live if no black market. I change rubles for my tourist group. They are in Moscow four days. Maybe I stay with them. Maybe a new guide takes them on to Leningrad, to Kiev. I make my little 100 rubles profit and that is good, but how do you say it? I am a toothpick and so many others are tall trees in the forest. I think that is the way it is.

"And you have no book by Mr. Ludlum, the American? That is too bad. I would buy for much more than you paid for it. I hope I see you if you come again. Just walk in the lobby with it and people will stop you for it. I must go now. Goodbye. Enjoy our country."

❧ *"No Marriage for Me!"*

"I don't want to marry. Maybe I will at one time but not now. I have known my mother and my aunts; the life they have is not for me. Work and more work. There is no life for them.

My mother is dreaming of the time when she will be fifty-five and then she will be a pensioner. My father says, 'How can you be a pensioner because then how will we live?' This is an argument they have. I know from my friends their mothers have it all the time.

She comes home from the factory and it is one long bus ride to the subway and by then it is so crowded, and then it is six o'clock and she must do the shopping. Another hour and then she comes home and my father and my two brothers, they sit there and ask what is for dinner. She says sausages, some cabbage for soup. Potatoes, maybe. And then she must make the meal for the family. Then she must do what every woman has to do around the apartment. My father says, 'That is the work for women,' and so my brothers do not help and it is nine o'clock by now and she is so tired. If there is washing to do, then she does it.

She says, 'I wish we could get into an apartment in a district where they do the washing. They have laundries in these apartments and for two or three rubles a month the linen and other things are done for them. Not the clothes, the laundry. My mother is a strict woman. She always wants things to be clean.

My mother, her name is Leona, I love her very much. Her father was killed in the war. He was a captain of artillery, fighting there with his men, at Leningrad when it was bad, and then at Voronezh. It was at Kursk where he was wounded and this was when they still were moving the factories to the East and he was put in charge of anti-aircraft guns if the Germans attacked the workers moving the factories. This is when he met my grandmother, who was a young girl working helping to move the factories away from the Germans. I think this is the way it was. He was handsome and so they fell in love. They had my mother and then the fighting got worse and his wounds were healed and he went to the front again and you see, nobody was wasted. When a man was wounded he was still a soldier and when he was healed, he went back to the front to fight the Germans.

My grandmother, after the war, she came to Moscow and she had my mother to look after. She was six years old when they came back to Moscow. This was in 1948. My mother grew up and she married my father. This was in 1963. He was a big man, a strong man, a good Russian man, but he didn't like his job as a supervisor. I don't remember much about those days. I went to school and helped my mother, and my two brothers were born. When my grandmother died, we got her apartment. We already lived with her, you see. The government was very good to the veterans of the war, and her husband, my grandfather, had been given a two-bedroom apartment after the war.

You get an apartment for life and that is why it is so hard on the young people like me. They cannot get apartments in Moscow. In other cities, yes, it is different. There are more apartments, but not too many. They take such a long time to put them up and they never finish them. I have friends who have got apartments out in the districts and they do a lot of the work themselves inside. The authorities say, 'Here is your apartment. You do the rest!'

My mother, she has to get up at five in the morning, she works from eight in the morning, eight hours, in the noise in the mill. She looks after about thirty girls. They are from the country. They are brought in because this is very dull work. It is so much the same it makes people sleepy. Just walking up and down and twisting threads and guiding threads. But they are young and stupid girls. They live in apartments, three girls in a room. Very small. I don't know what they do if one of them wants her boy-friend in. Go out for a walk, maybe. If they can afford the theatre, maybe that is where they go. In summer they can walk along the river. My mother took me to see one of these girls once. The apartments were near her factory and there was a guard on the door, an old babushka woman. Very stern. Like an officer in the army.

This girl was sick with congestion in the head and my mother gave her medicine from the dispensary at the factory and we talked. She was a nice little girl from a village. She thought it was a wonderful place. The apartment, yes, it was nice. It was small, very small, but it was clean. I would have loved to live in it, but only for myself. It was not big enough for three girls. Not big enough really for two, but if you are a girl from a village and lived your life the way they do, this was wonderful. They made about 120 rubles a month, I guess, and I think they only paid a few rubles each for the rent and so it was good. It was new. It was nice. I was surprised.

I told the girl that if I was married I would like this place and my mother said, 'You'll never work in that factory of mine. No daughter will work there, not my daughter.'

The girl asked me if I was married. I told her no, and I said I would never get married. This was two years ago and I was twenty-two, I guess. About that. She said the dearest thing in her life was to get married, but she couldn't meet any boys in Moscow. All the workers in the factory were women, and girls like her. I could see that this one wanted a man. She wanted one much. She was no virgin. These village girls off the state farms, they never are. They start early, those ones do. But she was a nice girl. She will get married. She may be married now. She might have gone back to her village in her new city clothes and found a mechanic or a driver and that would be it. She had her passport to live in Moscow, they get married, they come to Moscow and there is another mouth to feed in this awful city. I hate Moscow and it is the only city I know. They say Kiev is nice. I have been to the South, to Sochi and Yalta, but they are not cities. Yes, yes, yes, they are, but not in their soul. Moscow has a soul. There is no speaking against that. But it is a big grey soul, not much to say in it. Oh yes, in summer it is not so bad and in autumn for three weeks it is nice.

But I will not marry. I live with my boy-friend. I say, 'You will help me with the work.' Man and woman work together, do dishes together, cross-country-ski together, go to parties together, go to bed together. But we work together in the kitchen and cleaning the apartment. It is not our apartment. It is a black market apartment. I can tell you how it is because you will never tell. There is this man, I work with him at the ministry. His wife and he do not live together as she went to live with another man. He has this two-room apartment in a nice district. She says, 'I don't want to see any more of you again.' He says okay, okay, okay, and he goes to his friend's place and says, 'Let me sleep with your family.' That is the way we are. The friend says yes, come, and the man pays 20 rubles a month. That is a lot of money. He is paying his share and he does not eat dinner with the family. He is usually drunk by dinnertime. He asks me if my boy-friend and me want to have his apartment and we say yes. We pay five for the electricity and we pay him 50 rubles for the rent. Yes, that is high. He pays 20 to his friend and he has 30 rubles extra and he also has a place to bring his girl-friend. We let him come twice a week. This is how it is done. He buys vodka from a man and we have a little party. I drink wine, but they have the vodka and his girl-friend always brings little cakes and nice things to eat and we are happy.

So that is my arrangement. No marriage. I have his apartment and I make good wages at the ministry. I am more than just a clerk. I make 300 rubles a month and my work is valuable and this gives me some special things. I can shop for food in the special store and not wait in the queue like my mother for an hour. I order it in the morning and when my work is finished it, these foods, they are ready for me. My boy-friend, he works at a scientific job with plants in the agriculture ministry. He makes 330 rubles, so he is very well paid. So you see, it is easy for us to pay so much for the apartment. Besides, we must give the superintendent another 10 rubles so he won't report us to the authorities. If he did, they would move a family in and where would we be? Maybe I would be sent to Odessa and my boy-friend to some Northern place, to try and make corn grow on the taiga. We must be very careful.

You ask, why no marriage? To marry, a woman must put herself in control of a man. What is this thing, this man thing that he wants babies? It is the woman who has them and it is her pain. I am of the young woman type today who says, 'No, I will not have babies.' I am sorry, I mean, we will have babies if we want them. It will be my decision. The man does nothing.

Many, many women in our country have abortions. There are clinics for these things. Nobody says no, you cannot have them. What meaning is there for to have a baby if it is not wanted in the household? The poor thing could become an orphan. Many girls leave their babies at orphanages at the door at night. They do not want them any more. Oh, I hate these girls. There are a lot of them.

[In its December 12, 1988, issue, *Time* Magazine quoted Soviet figures that 5.5 million babies were born in the Soviet

Union in 1987 and 7.7 million authorized abortions were performed. Soviet officials believe as many as 7 million more abortions were performed outside the hospitals and not reported.]

Some of my friends have four or five abortions, then they
find out, so many and they cannot have babies. Then that is
when they sometimes cry. No babies. I say, 'But you silly
thing, you did not want a baby.' Yes, but now I do. But their
body, it won't have a baby any more. That is the way it is.

I have had two abortions. My first lover paid for them. I did
not go to a clinic. He had a doctor who was a friend. My boy-
friend, he was a doctor and he had this friend, a doctor in
another hospital, a good one. I went to his home one night
and there was a nurse and I had my abortion. My boy-friend
paid him 60 rubles. Then I had another. That was no rubles.
My boy-friend gave the doctor four bottles of vodka. He got
the litres of vodka from a friend. He did something for the
friend. He would not tell me what it was. It was nothing bad,
I think.

No, in answer to your question, I am not a feminist. Of
course I know what that word means. We get the magazines
from West, from you people. We buy copies they make at night
on the ministry copy machines for 5 rubles. We can read. Our
saviour Lenin said everyone would be equal. Men and women.
In jobs, yes, as he wrote it down. In the way it is, no. You see
the old women doing the shopping in the stores. In the stalls.
Sweeping the streets to make a little more. My aunt is a plas-
terer and there are eight women in her crew. In competitions
the women crews always are better than the men. They work
harder. They are better people, you see.

No, the feminist movement is nothing here. The woman
works, the man drinks. Not good, you see. We need something
else. Maybe we don't go to bed with men who drink. You think
that would stop it?

But you speak of marriage. Not for Vera, not for this one.
Yes, maybe someday but I am young now. I have a good job
and the apartment and a man and we have food. Our friends
come to see us and we play jazz records and talk. We laugh.
You stand outside our door and you hear laughing. No eighteen hours of work and six of sleep and eighteen of work again,
pressing the kids' school uniforms, the long ride to The

Centre, work, work, work all day and shopping, making something, ah, sausage again, that awful greasy stuff, and the big fool sits on the chair and reads his newspaper. Not for me. I am a big girl and I know my position in life.

'Why isn't Vera married to a nice boy?' This is what people ask my mother. She says to ask me. Nobody does but if they did I would say I am happy. I have nice clothes. I have a boy-friend and I soon don't like him I will get another. I have an apartment, so I could get a prince. Ha-ha. Couldn't I? Yes. An apartment for one person, me, is like a palace. I am a very rich woman with my apartment. No marriage for me!"

❧ Hard Work, Good Times, on the Taiga

"I was a young man and we had our fun and then it was my time to go in the military, the army, and that was not such a good experience. But it was good for me because the boys and me, we were all the same. Fun, the girls, the drinking, we did a lot of drinking, and my mother, she would cry and say, 'Dmitri, Dmitri, Dmitri, what is going to happen to you? You are going to get in trouble.' And my father had been a soldier in the war against the Nazis and he would say, 'Mama, don't you worry about the boy. He will be going in the army soon and they will make him a man. You will see.'

Then it was time to go and my mother cried because she remembered the war and her two brothers who died in it and no, she said, 'I do not want you going.' But it was the law. I went into the artillery. The big cannons. This was very little good to me because the first year we did nothing but be like servants to the real soldiers, but then we did learn on the guns.

At the end of my two years, I went home to my parents' home in Moscow and my mother said, 'I can see big change in you. You will not end up in jail for doing bad things. You should become a teacher.'

I said okay. I had nothing on my mind. I wanted to go back to girls and drinking but I knew that was wrong, and also, I now respected my mother and would not do what she felt was wrong for me.

There is this university in Moscow. It is for teachers in other languages. English is learned there and German, too. But other languages. Somali, one friend took that. There were students taking, you know, Third World languages. Egypt. Mozambique. Angola. These places in Africa where our country has special interests. I said no, too hot. Too far away. Suppose the Americans come with tanks and guns and there is war. I want to be in my own country.

They said, 'Would you like to go to the East?' I had not thought about Siberia. Cold, I know. They said, 'The pay is good. Would you like to go and teach English? It would be your subject.' I thought to myself, I will ask my girl-friend, Ludmilla. We were not lovers, only friends. I said would she come with me? She said no, she was happy in Moscow, but she would enjoy letters I sent to her. This meant to me, in the old style, that maybe she would be my wife someday. I should have asked her to marry then because in two years she wrote me a letter and said she was married. If she said she was getting married I would have gone home to Moscow and tried to get her to marry me. I should have been forceful in my letters to her. She did not think I cared deeply. This is what she told me later when I was home and she was at her brother's apartment. A sad, sad story in my life.

This was a long time ago in 1974. And they said I could go to Nizhnevartovsk. In Siberia. The taiga, you see. It was what they call a new city. Everything was new. Too new. Some things had been built too fast. They knew how cold it was but they still built schools and apartments and other buildings, too ... okay, I guess they did not know how cold it was. It was very cold and yet it was nice in spring and the autumn. The times I liked best. There were many bugs, the biters, in the summer mostly. The end of July, unless there was a wind. In winter it had snows that fell and fell and the winds were so strong, you could not go out unless you wore many clothes and walked on the streets holding to the ropes they had put up. But oh, it was not too bad. We would get a four-wheel drive

and food, fish and bread and corn and onions and some big
pots and we would drive down away from the city and into
taiga. Lots of lakes. We would make a fire, two big fires, and
we would stand inside the two and boil water and make soup
and boil the fish and onions and carrots and garlic and make
a feast. We ate and drank and we could drink a lot of vodka.
Bottles of it and we didn't feel it. It made us warm and happy,
and when it was night we would sing and laugh and sing about
Siberia, the songs, and drive back to Nizh. It was wonderful
times, those days.

When we'd get into the apartment, then we would be drunk.
It was a good feeling and we didn't have to drink any more.
We just had a lot of good talk and guitar playing and sing the
songs of the Motherland. Nobody got sick. Everybody happy
as hell.

I did not like teaching English. The children, they came
from the parents of Ukrainian people. A lot from there and
other places and they were not good students. Mostly parents
were farmers or truck drivers. People like this worked for two
years in the oilfields, in the gas fields, and they didn't care
about education for their children. The children did not want
to learn. They just wanted to be like their parents and make
a lot of money and go back to the Ukraine to a collective farm.
A house, some land, some cattle and pigs, and have a good
life. Maybe work a bit, but be farmers and sell their meat and
things they grew in the market. They could make a lot of
money.

There was this one party at a place, a lake maybe thirty
kilometres away, and there was a man there and he said, 'Dmitri, you're a big fellow. Why do you teach stupid subjects? How
much do you make?' I said 320 rubles because, you see, you
got much more working in the taiga in the East than anywhere
in Moscow. There it would be 220.

He said, 'I will be back in two weeks after my next period
is over. Are you married?' I said no, and he asked me, 'Where
is your hostel?' I told him Number Five and he said, 'When I
come back I will tell you if there is a job for you. I will tell
the boss you are big, strong, and no wife. You can work with
me on the rig. You will make 600 rubles, 800 if you want, and
listen to this.' I am making . . . saying this as he said it, 'you

will save more money in a month working two shifts, it is not hard, more money in two months than you could ever save. In a year you will be very wealthy. Maybe 8,000 rubles.'

I said yes. I had worked six months in the senior school and it was no good and I had got the very sad letter from Ludmilla and I was unhappy and I told him, 'Yes, if your boss can work the paperwork with the authorities.' He said it would be easy. The oil was more important than to teach dumb country kids; they did not want to learn English anyway. It would do them no good. They were Ukrainians.

In three weeks it was agreed and I went by a truck with other men deep into the taiga. It was spring then and the water was everywhere and the trucks could not get in because of the floods the water caused. Okay. Then a helicopter took us many, many more distances. All the men cheered when they heard it was a helicopter ride. I started around the drilling rig, clean-up. Doing what everyone told me. Then a man got sick and I was put on the second shift. In two weeks the two shifts went out for rest to Nizh and to see their families and kids and get drunk and fuck. Two other shifts came in. Four shifts. So I worked the dark, the night shift. It was very hard and much to learn and I did it. Oleg, my friend at the party, he was my father at first: 'Don't stand there. Grab that wrench. Put it there. Pull that chain over. Watch your head, you fool.' This way I learned.

The summer went by and I worked nine shifts in a row. That is more than two months. A very long time. The doctor, he ordered me to come in. They kept records, you must understand. What is Dmitri doing out there so long? They always wanted an extra man because somebody was always sick. That is how I could work so long. He told the director and the next time the helicopter brought out some special tool we needed, I went back. He examined me, this doctor, and he said, 'You are strong as an oxen. How do you do it?'

It was easy to tell him – work hard, eat big, plenty of meat and milk, sleep eight hours. Don't drink the moonshine they got out there and don't fight. He laughed and said, 'Play some chess. You're turning into an animal. God help the girls when you get back to Nizh for your turnaround. You will, you know. Winter is coming.'

That doctor was right. First autumn, and then winter and the cold. Cold, cold, and more of it. The drill went down and down and we were happy. A bonus when it was over. The noise, even the little winter birds weren't afraid of it. We would throw them food and they would come, happy. We were happy, too. Plenty of food and when we were hungry there was a big box of apples in the room where the television was and things to eat in the fridge. The trucks brought in the food and then it went out to get more mud and fuel for the heating and to keep the mud hot and the pipes and food. Work every day, seven days a week. No holidays for the boys. None. I had the day shift then, but it was dark a lot of the time as it was high up in the taiga.

The cold. It was tough. Trees breaking. It was like a loud gun shooting. You know. Cold. But we worked hard and there was no wind because we were in the woods. We'd laugh and when we pulled up the pipe we'd sing and do it like machines and tell stories and then drill, drill, and the table would shake and we'd know our bonus was coming to us. Then one day the helicopter came in with some specialists and they took the samples and made their chemical tests and said, 'Okay, boys, that's it for this one. You did a good job.' Then we went by plane to Irkutsk for four days and just had a good time and I got more books and took a girl out and loved her. Then they phoned me and I gave my girl a box of chocolates and a sweater and took my new boots and my clothes and some books and I didn't come back for four more months when we had done another well.

It was good there. My own room in the place, a toilet and hot water and the cook. This woman and her daughter, they did us some very good meals, and every Sunday they made a big pot of Siberian pirogies. Ever tasted them? Good pig meat and spices and berries and onions and big, two mouthfuls each, and I could eat twenty and the daughter would say, 'Dmitri, you have an empty barrel inside you.' I remember that. She always said that.

My friend, he had left after six months to go back home and start a little business with his brother. He gave me his new boots and clothes when he left and I said, 'For this, you've made me stay another year.' That was in 1980 by now, and I was the senior, the longest-time man in the camp and they would say, 'How does that guy do it?'

One more year, two times into Irkutsk, but the girl was married now, so I found another for the four days, a nice girl but she had two kids and that wasn't for me. After two years I went to the office and asked them: 'How much have you got for me in the bank? What is charged to me?' I had about 15,600 rubles in the bank and about 500 was charged to me, so I had 15,000 rubles. Nobody in our family ever had 15,000 rubles before and I never knew anybody who had. Even Secretary Gorbachev today, I don't think he has that much. It is not the way in Russia. Get some money, buy a big cake like a wedding cake with fruit and things on it and two litres of vodka, and that is where the hard work is spent. Not Dmitri. He is too smart. This is my story I am telling you.

I came back to Moscow with this big beard of mine and my mother said, 'You go away for years and come back as a professor. What is wrong with the people who work with you? Can they not teach you to be a good man?' She thought I was turned into a hooligan or something, but not a professor.

I said, 'How is my old girl-friend?' and she said she had one kid and was happy.

I said, 'If she is happy I will not bother her.'

I bought this car, this taxi, and I am the black taxi squad leader. We drive at night. There is a kind of licence to it, but we don't drive too much when the legal taxis are running. There is always somebody who has to get home quick. His mama is wondering where he is. See? Or a girl, she has to go home.

I think of the taiga a lot. The good times. I like such hard work. My English is good. I drive lots of people who speak English and they are surprised. I tell them 'English, it is sure easy for me.' Have you got a book you can give me? In English. A good book, with girls in it."

I said no, sorry, as I got out at my hotel and once again I was sorry I hadn't brought a sackful of books. Nobody checked at the airport and everyone wanted books, magazines, in English. I could have made a fortune on *Playboy* magazines. The word was they were worth their weight in gold. A Rambo video movie was worth its weight in platinum, or more. I stuck my head back through the window and asked if he was going back to the oil rigs. "I am happy here, but if the chance is okay, then maybe. They want me. That is a nice thing to know. A man in oildrilling is always a favourite person."

A Pair of Purple Shoes

"I learned to speak English language a little. I did it in the school but it was not enough that I needed, so I have been studying it for four years. I stand in front of the mirror and talk English to myself and it is funny. My mouth, it looks like it makes different shapes than when I speak Russian. I try and my friends, they speak English but they read it from scientific books and magazines that come from England and, I don't know, when they speak it does not seem like I speak. It is a very hard language. It is much different from Russian. Russian is a pure language and the words say what they mean to say. In English, so many other ways. 'Bear' means an animal, like in our forest. 'Bare,' b-a-r-e, means you have no clothes on. B-e-a-r, which means you carry something on your back, but it means an animal. Things like that. English is very hard, you see.

People in this apartment cry like babies too much. Why cry? They are younger, some of them and I say to them it has been bad before. Much more than now. 'I can't buy nice clothes,' Irina, the daughter of the neighbour on this floor, complains, the one with four rooms. A nice little kitchen. A toilet. A washing place. Four rooms! The biggest in this section. Two bedrooms and another room and the room to live in and complaining! 'You don't hear your mother complain,' I say. 'You are a very lucky girl.' And she says she hates this apartment and being so far from the subway and the centre of the city where the nice stores are. I say, 'You have a good school and the birch forest, you have a bicycle, you can go out there and ride around with your friends. Wait until you grow up.' She is fourteen and very beautiful. Have you noticed how beautiful our Russian girls are? How they walk? So proud. Their hair, so yellow and they want to colour it red or orange. That is in the fashion books now, the ones they buy on the grey market, the ones from Germany. 'Why do you complain?' I say. 'You are not on a collective farm, a state farm. You are not working in boots and old clothes. Your clothes are very good.'

'Oh no,' she says. 'They are not as good as the girls I know.' She can't get cosmetics. She wants this stuff they put on their eyes and blacken them. Yes, eye-liner, thank you. That is the word. She wants that and she is a child. 'Mama,' she says, 'I want a pair of purple shoes. Everybody has them.' Her mother says she can't find any.

I go to the GUM store and I see these shoes and I buy them. Forty rubles I pay, but I know they will please little Irina and her mother will pay me for them. She looks at them and says they are not the right colour. She wants purple. I say these shoes are from the GUM shop and they are purple. They are not the right purple. More purple, she wants. I say to myself, 'Little bitch, all right,' and next week I take them on the subway and hold them in my hand and a man comes on and sits beside me and we are talking and why am I holding these shoes. I say because I want to sell them. I cannot take them back. How much will I sell them for? I say 50 rubles and he gives me 50 rubles. I ask him what he wants them for and he says his daughter wants purple shoes. So, you see, they were purple shoes. I hope he does not have as much trouble with his daughter as I had with Irina."

☙ "All We Have Is Hope"

"I will give you three words, and they are about what we dream in the future. They are in Russian. *Nadezhda. Nadezhda. Nadezhda.* That means Hope. Hope. Hope. I have written a poem about them, this word, but it is in Russian and you would not know it. I sometimes have people on my Intourist tours who are from the United States and Canada who speak Russian and I tell it to them and they say it is wonderful. One old woman with a cane and could not hardly see, she said my poem sang like a little bird. That was very nice of her. I wrote my poem out for this old woman and she took it home.

Hope. That is all we are doing. Hoping. We have these words *perestroika* and *glasnost* but they are new. They do not mean a thing to the Soviet people now. You may know that change can come fast but it is not good. There is no planning and organization in change that is fast. These Americans who come, they ask, 'What is this *glasnost?* Where is your *perestroika?*' I tell them these are just words for plans which will come and make us a great country.

There was this professor from the American Columbia University and he said, 'You will never have a great country here. Your history is against you. Russia will always be as it was. Backward.' I am making up his words as he said them, but the other Americans on the tour got angry with him and said he was disrespectful and they said they were apologizing to me and my country for his attitude. It was an unhappy time and when we went along to see other things and parks and monuments on our bus, his friends would not talk to him, this professor.

But this man was right. I went to him and I said that he should not feel unhappy. I said I did not want to see my American tourists treated like this and we had a long talk. I said I could not see what there was to forgive. He had made a statement. He believed in it. He had it from his knowledge of our country and he was a professor. I wish I could have had a very long discussion with this man and learn more.

There are things we do not like, many things we do not understand, about our country. It is of strange ways. So long we have left everything to the bureaucrats and I wonder how a man becomes a bureaucrat of the Soviet kind. They know we do not believe the stories they print in our papers and journals but they continue to say these things and write them.

We are not a stupid people. That is not so. We have a very good education system. It is in every city and region, every republic. Any boy or girl can go to school and then to what you call higher learning. It is free. A poor family making only 140 rubles a month, they can send their daughter to education and she can be a scientist. That is good. Education makes good people. It also makes bad bureaucrats.

I do not think *glasnost* means anything to the people living outside the big cities. It is not for the people in the towns and villages and on the farms. Their lives, they are so black and bruised. They are born there on these places and many of them die there. Now we are told they are making better money, but there is no joy in their hearts. No, you will find they do not have *nadezhda,* hope. Life will always be the same for them. Vodka. Cabbage soup. Potatoes. They get more meat than we do in the cities because there are the farms and the underground market. But there is no theatre, which every Russian loves. They have the circus but the one they see is not the Moscow Circus because that one is for the tourists.

They see things. They are of the land and the cattle and they are smart, they are cunning. They do well for themselves but they come to the city sometimes for something medical and they see Moscow or Kiev or a big city and they say, 'Oh, so this is what is going on.' Then they go back to the farm and they say those Muscovites have got this and that and I saw this and that, but they have no food in the stores and there are thieves to rob you at night everywhere and we can make better ices.

No, I don't think these people have any feelings about *glasnost*.

Our newspaper critics and journalists, they try to explain *glasnost*. How can you explain yellow smoke to a boy who has been blind all his life? I have tried. I can say it is like this but it is not right. This boy said I can smell it. Can anyone smell *glasnost*? No. No, you have to feel it. You have to believe it is there and think you can feel it. It is a good thing, is it not? Everybody has to feel it. Feel that it means something better. So, *glasnost* is just a word and you have to believe.

Our newspapers, now you can write to them and say that this road is so filled with holes that the people are angry. Something must be done. It is all small things, this *glasnost*. I would not like to think that this is all *glasnost* is. That would be no different than before. A woman writes that her daughter died after an abortion and that it was an infection and the doctors did not have clean hands. She wants the hospital made better. The old war veteran, he writes and says there is too much drinking at the football game and the hooligans abuse old men who want to watch. He says the militiamen should do something. Or a factory director is a thief. This is what people call *glasnost*.

I will tell you this honestly. We know all about the factory directors who are thieves. These are things we have heard about and talked about around the table in the kitchen. There is nothing new. There is nothing new about the holes in the road and the young brides who died of abortion when they do not want their first baby. This is the way it is done. It is a scandal we all know, the drinking of spirits by hooligans at the football games. This we all know.

Now, they are putting these letters in the newspapers and everyone reads them and they say, 'We knew that all the time. Why is it important now? The bureaucrats knew all these things for a long, long time, and now they choose to print this letter and that letter.'

We are told at our meetings with the assistant director that tourists will ask many questions about *glasnost*. They do not tell us what it means. This man who has control of our part of the Intourist organization does not tell what to say. Joke with them, laugh with them, move them on to something else and the question will go away. This man earns 300 rubles a month and this is what he tells the tourist guides. This monument is forty metres tall and was built in 1947 and it is in honour of the soldiers of the Great Patriotic War. That is what he wants us to tell the Americans.

I stand up and I tell him Americans and Australians and English are very curious people. They want to know every-thing. It is our duty to tell them if it is possible. We only take them to places where it is possible. Museums, these things. They want to know about our country and we tell them. Most of them are nice. Some old ladies want too much. 'Where can I buy Kodak camera film?' they ask. We say it is not possible. They don't like our film and they get mad. Then I say to myself, 'Why did you not bring enough for your use?'

Some men want to buy rubles for American dollars on the black market. I tell them to see the bus driver. I do not want to do this thing. It is against the law of the Soviet Union. He looks after them. Then he gives me a few rubles that is part of his share of the transaction. Then it is okay. He is giving me a gift.

They don't like our toilets and they all complain about the showers in the bathrooms. I would like to see an American shower someday. They must be wonderful places. I would like to go to America someday. It must be a terrific thing to see.

My tourists say, 'Where do you live?' I say I live with two other guides in an apartment. It is clean and nice and we have a kitchen and a stove and an electric icebox. There is a laundry for all the apartments in the district. The tourists sometimes they ask if they can visit and bring food and cakes and biscuits from the hard-currency store in the hotel and have tea in a Russian home. I would like very much to do this but it is forbidden. This is too bad.

They ask, so friendly, 'Steniya, what is the house like where you were born? Tell us about it.' I say, 'Okay, it is in a little village, maybe 5,000 people. It is an hour's distance on the electric train line out of Moscow. People, some of them work in the city. Some, the most, they work in the factory, and it used to be most of them worked on one of the farms. Now not as many do. There are apartments there now but when I was a little girl it was all houses. Our houses were small. Mine was painted green. My father liked that colour.'

I told them it was not a rich house. There was a big kitchen where we used to do everything and my mother cooked and washed and there was a smaller room and it had two sofas and some chairs and rugs on the walls and there were the pictures of my family. My grandfather and everybody down from him. There was a little . . . a cabinet where there were crystal glasses and some of the medals won by my grandfather. My own father was too young for the war. There were pictures of little lakes with birches by them. There was a picture of Stalin and Lenin and our family Bible. There was a small glass stove in this room.

The house was cool in summer and warm in winter. The thick walls, I think they were made of wood and mortar. There was no bathroom. That was outside. A man would come around with a horse and a cart with barrels for that.

Yes, it is still there, but life in the village has changed. There was a swimming pool. There was a spring and the men dug out a hole long and wide and deep and they put staves, pieces of wood, against the sides to keep the dirt from falling. It was very good, very enjoyable. In winter when it was cold the people would cut ice and store it in straw in their sheds for the summer. It was very satisfactory.

I could have made lots of money taking my tourists to visit my parents; they would see how my parents live and they would pay me. It is not permitted. I told the director this once. 'Let me take my tourists to my village,' and this man yelled at me. 'Not permitted. What are you saying, you foolish girl?

We don't want the tourists to see how you people live.' He was from Moscow and a stupid man. A bureaucrat. Stuffed man.

I told him he should come with me once to see how bored my tourists are with what I have to show them, museums and schools where the children give their little speeches and nobody believes them. Little actors, some of the tourists said. Little propaganda. Little brown skirts and white blouses and blue eyes and white bows in the hair and saying these silly things to the tourists. It makes me sad.

Come to my village. They would welcome you and they would be real Russians. Not little girl and boy actors in the schoolroom, with the teacher standing there and pointing her stick.

An eight-day tour, or a thirteen-day tour, visitors, they don't see our country. They see what they are wanted to see. It is very funny. In Moscow, the Kremlin, not those big rooms behind it where the works get done, the grey men in their black suits who make our lives unhappy. No, the visitors see the jewels and the crowns and the lovely ancient clothes and that is not Russia. Russia is my village and the sewer system they have been making for six years for this little place and they still can not make the apparatus work and you smell the smell. My village is the old women who are widows all dressed in black clothes and pointing to me when I come to visit in my coloured, nice clothes and they are saying, 'That girl, she thinks she is so smart. What does she do to get those smart clothes? Her and her men tourists.' Their old minds like dry peas.

I would like to go to America. I think Canada would be very nice, too, because Canadians are very kind people. Both of these nations, the people smile and laugh a lot and if something turns out badly or if it is just a rainy day, they smile and laugh. The have two drinks of Scotch whiskey in their rooms after the day is done and they come to the dining room and I sit with them. They tell me about their city. They have lots of pictures of their grandchildren and they show them with pride and they don't ask about *perestroika*. This means nothing to them. They have saved their money and they are spending it happily. I would like to be like that when I am a woman of forty and have two sons and two daughters. I see pictures of people having picnics with their children and the man and wife, there they are with a new car. A sporting car, all red. The trees are green and there is a beach of sand. Golden sand. There is a basket with picnic foods in it. Everybody is laughing. Magazine pictures, I know, it is to advertise the automobile or some beer or whiskey but that does not matter. It is life, your way.

I look at all your green property and the little bushes and trees and I think, 'In Russia all that would be in planting to cabbages and potatoes.' No green grass. What is green grass for except cows and cattle and chickens? There are even no grasses around the dachas of the rich people, the politicians and the intellectuals and the military colonels. But in the magazine pictures I see green grass and flowers. I long for that. Someday . . .

I would like to wear furs. Not the hats, but fur coats like the wives of rich men. I would like to marry a man who has a Zil. That is the car the highest officials have for them. A Cheika, maybe. That is a very nice car. I would like to marry a good man who can give me a five-room apartment. That would be my dream. Furs, a car, a good apartment in the middle of Moscow, then children, and a dog. Oh yes, an expensive, a very expensive dog. I am being selfish. I know I am. But we have had seventy years of this government and all we still have is hope. That is what they had in 1917 in the Revolution in Leningrad and we are still waiting. *Nadezhda*, hope, hope, hope."

🐾 *"There Will Be a Statue"*

"A long time ago when Nikita Khrushchev, when he was our leader, he told the Soviet people about what a bad man Josef Stalin was. How millions of people were sent off to the Gulag. You have heard that. The slavery camps in Siberia where a man was sent away to work in coal and ice and maybe he was never seen again. A guard will shoot him for doing the little thing wrong. I was a child then but my father and my mother, they told me they knew people from their district who just disappeared. Then the friends would have to care for the mother and the children. Poor people, we all feel sorry for them. Terrible misery.

I should not be telling you this, maybe, but now we can speak. Not to foreigners. There can be no police now, because we are just walking down this street and we will have some tea. We'll talk. It is such a sunny day, and soon it will be winter and when you get back to Canada you can tell your friends you met a Moscow man who told you these things. My English, you can see, is good. I also speak four other languages and also Egyptian, which I learned because I was to go and work on the dam on the Nile, but then that did not happen.

I will tell you about our Khrushchev. He came to lead us after Stalin's days. He was a peasant. We had nicknames for him and one was 'pig.' Comrade Pig. But a good man, my father said, and he wanted to put up a statue for the many, many thousands of our people who were sent to the East by Stalin for nothing. This was political terror of Stalin. He would say, we need 5,000 more men to work in the woods for making the roads, and the militia, they would get them. They were political enemies, but they weren't. They disappeared, many, many. Khrushchev wanted to put up a statue as a memorial to these poor peoples who died from the cold and the guards' guns. This was twenty-six years ago he said this. He had told the Soviet people about Stalin and then the world knew it. There was a statue, a memorial, to be made, but even if Khrushchev was a good man, he could not get his statue. Too many powerful men said no to this kindly thing . . .

But now, someday soon, with *perestroika*, there will be a statue to these people who suffered from these awful crimes. We have talked it over in our committee (at the ministry) and we will send a letter to the leadership.

Yes, you're right, we have many statues of soldiers, poets, writers, but none of people cutting down trees for roads in the woods in the cold, cold winter of Siberia. Soon will be this statue. Maybe there will be many . . ."

☙ "New York Is a Jewish City"

"I am seventy-nine years old and I don't care. I get treated good. I don't care. It doesn't matter to me. An old man. I saw the revolution when I was a boy, you understand. I know what it was like to be a Jew. Bread, everybody got a little bread when there was not much bread for anyone, but Jews, we got it last. You know what I mean? I never got any bread some time. Not for me, not my family. This was one time when we had a famine in the Ukraine. About 1932, I think. I'm not sure. You're looking at an old man.

I get a pension. Not much, not much, but enough. I give some of it to my nephew and he says, 'Old man, you can stay another month.' I say, 'Okay, Rudy, okay.' It is a little joke I have with him. I'm old, so I don't eat much. I go to the synagogue. The young people, they respect me. 'What was it like in the old days, Grandfather?' I say, 'It was bad and good and good and bad, but you be good fellows, read, come to the synagogue, and don't worry about what's all around. What you read. It has always been lies. I know.' Lies about our people.

In 1937, in March, I go south into Armenia and then across the border and that's where I found myself. Right in Turkey. This was hard times. You see, Stalin, Stalin and his gang, they ran everything and I think, 'Ah, I'm next. Away to Siberia.' So I go to Turkey and then to Egypt. I have money for to pay and I think, 'Did I do wrong?' Leaving my country, my son and daughter with my sister. My wife died. Good one day, dead a week later. God's will.

To New York City. First Barcelona, then New York City, and there is so many Jews there. Are you Jewish? Ah no, I didn't think so. But you've been to New York City, maybe? Ah well, then you know. So many of our people. It is a Jewish city. Every kind, and I get a job and I say, so many Russian Jews here and they all speak English. I got to learn that language. That's what I do. I work in a clothing factory in the day, I go to school at night. At school I learn something but not much. Not much. I learn English at work. I'm young, I'm strong, I'm a good worker. Everyone says so. 'Jacob,' they say, 'you are good worker.' I know that.

Comes the war. All these stories. Killing, killing some more. Everywhere and they don't get me in the army. I got a new wife and a new baby, this boy who is still in New York City and who writes me now and says, 'Okay, come back to America. Come to New York City. You're old. My wife and me, we look after you.'

I forgot to say. In 1950 my next wife dies. She goes shopping, she doesn't see this truck. She dies. I've got the insurance, and that is 3,000 dollars, and I say, this country, New York City, it may be good for my son but not for me. I want to go back to my own country. I've got a cousin, he comes from a village near where I was from, or I mean his father did, so I say to him, 'You take my little boy. He's got no mama. Two wives for me, that is enough. I'm going home.' 'Going home?' they say, 'And Stalin is still killing all those Jews? Don't go.'

Here is me, dumb, but I take my money in the bank, a lot because we don't spend, and I say to my cousin, 'Here is the 3,000 dollars, the insurance. Take it and you be the father for my little boy.'

Then I am back in the Soviet Union. About six months it takes to get my papers and everybody is saying, 'Jacob, you be crazy. They will kill you.'

Look at me. I'm talking to you. This is tea we're drinking. In those years, I don't know how many, I don't talk English to many people. In all my time here I work and I get my pension now and . . . see, how good my English is?

Okay. There's a good American word, 'okay.' Now I'm seventy-nine and young people they come and they tell me they want to go to Israel. Jewish people, young, and they say, life is no good. I say why? Why? They don't like it. Somebody is always making a hard life for these people. I say okay, go. But what is Israel? Always fighting Arabs. They're the ones they should be friendly to . . . With. To be friendly. No, they don't care. They want to go. They apply. I say, 'Okay, you apply to go and you lose your job. How you going to live?' They got money saved. 'Okay, what when your money runs out?' They got friends. Okay, they always got an answer. I say, not an old proverb, but I say, like it is one, 'Life is short, try to enjoy it.'

Then, you see, a letter comes and it says they got to be out of the Soviet Union by ten days, fifteen days. Come and get your visa. Everybody, you see them rushing around. Getting money for the tickets, all this. They get on the airplane. Away they go.

To Israel? You think so? Look, Mr. Canadian, I am going to tell you something. Ready to listen? That airplane flies to Vienna. This is how it works. Someone meets them there. No more Soviet Union. Now it is Vienna. They take another plane and where do you think that plane goes to? Israel? But I will fool you.

They have talked to some man in Vienna and he tells them something and they see somebody else and pay money. Now, you are a smart man. You guess. Ah, you have heard these stories. You are right. In four weeks this young man and his wife, and maybe kids if they got them, they send a letter and it says, 'Here we are in New York City.' How big it is, how happy they are. Maybe they are happy. I don't know, but I see these letters. They do not go to Israel. New York City is always their plan.

This is no place for a young person, a man and his wife. In Moscow you are invisible. Everybody is the same. Same clothes. Look outside there. Same faces. Not happy faces. You think so? They are tired, tired of the underground, all the people, the shopping and all they can get is herring in tins. A few radish. A melon, maybe.

Listen to an old man. I was born before the revolution. I know. I know what New York City is like. For a Jew it is a good place to be. Ah, right, maybe Moscow not so good for a Jew. Okay. But it is our Motherland. You think a Jew should say 'Motherland?' I do. All the old people do. It is our home. We will die here.

If the others want to go, get the papers, lose the job to feed the kids, okay. That is their life. You understand? They will do good in New York City because they are smart. But for me, no. I say no to you. God put me in this place and he told me to go to Turkey and then Egypt and then New York City. Then what did he tell me? I'll tell you. He said go back to your home. Where you were born.

I don't blame the younger people. The smart ones. Far away is better for them than here. But for me, here is okay. Nobody does anything to me and I am okay. I mean I am happy to be a Jew in the Soviet Union. All of the rest of it is nonsense."

❧ *Grandmother Made Moonshine*

"I think it is strange that we call it moonshine and you in Canada call it that, too. Do you think we both made up the name? I don't think so. It seems to me it is an English name. It is only the Armenian and Georgian poets and writers who talk about the moon and it shining. They are that way. The moon shining on Mount Ararat. That sort of thing.

Moonshine. I would say that it is a very bad thing. Do you understand? Alcohol is bad but the people who make it, they don't know what they are making. I read in one of our magazines that they put all kinds of things in it. These chemicals and things, they are bad for people who drink this moonshine.

I remember, and this was before I came to Moscow as a student and before I got my passport to live here, my grandmother on the farm made moonshine. She had a little shed behind our house. This was her place. This old lady, she'd take the potatoes and turnips and other things taken from the gardens at night and she, well, don't they just sort of brew it up and the heat makes the steam and it drips? The drips, that was the alcohol. She'd make a lot and then my father and his brother they'd take this apparatus and bury it further away and then a week . . . no, a month maybe, when there was more stuff, they would dig up this apparatus and she'd make this moonshine again. It was her little business and one big bottle would go to the director, and the commissar in the village, he would get his bottle. Then she would sell some. Maybe she'd make fifteen bottles.

She didn't sell it like you sell in a store. The man in charge of the trucks would be going into the city and she would give him a bottle and my mother would go with him and in the market she'd trade. You'd get clothes for moonshine, good flour, cups and saucers and plates and things we couldn't buy in our store because there was never anything in it. It was easy to trade in the market because nobody was watching you and she would come home on the truck the next day. There would be all these nice things.

She always had some bottles that she kept and we did things with them as like maybe having a party. People would bring food and we'd sit around and eat and sing and talk and the men would drink. This was not the whole of the farm people, you can see that. Our farm was about 800 people and the people who came, they were our relatives and friends. Not many, no. Maybe twenty but that is a lot in a small house because we couldn't have our party outside. People would talk, talk, talk. You know how village people are, don't you? They are the worst gossips, all old women who know everything.

My grandmother, she was a wonderful old woman and she is dead now but the moonshine she made was good. No chemicals in it, no bad things. People trusted her moonshine. Even the director did and let her do it and he drank it, too, but he never came to the big party every month. He always said he was too busy. He was a bureaucrat, you understand. He had to be careful.

Now things are changed. The time I was talking about was nine years ago, more than nine years, and now it is different. You can buy lots of moonshine in The Centre but it isn't good. Many people make it and you can buy it everywhere. This is what they call vodka but it is not real vodka. Good vodka is good, but this moonshine vodka is killing peoples everywhere. I had a friend who died from drinking it and the two boys he was drinking with, they nearly died, too. One boy, his father I met him in the cafeteria in our factory, he told me this boy, when he vomits, it is just like a wolf who has eaten poison. This man was from a place far north of Irkutsk and he knows about poisoning these wolves and he said they go kick, run a bit, kick, and die. He said his son, when he drinks milk with warmth in it, hot milk with honey, he sometimes falls to the floor and kicks. This is a terrible thing, I would say, drinking moonshine that is poison.

Why do they do this? I do not know. Nobody knows.

I was at a party once at a friend's home and a man brought a big bottle of vodka and everybody clapped. Then he turned it upside down and this moonshine vodka turned white. Like a Christmas toy of glass I once had. All white, little pieces of white in it. I said I would not drink it and everybody did and they all said they were sick after that. The man had bought it from an old woman who was selling lottery tickets for a car prize in the subway. She does a big business. I guess she makes this moonshine stuff in her apartment. A lot of them do.

Yes, you can buy it in the subway from an old lady. I know. You bring your bottle and give it to her and she gives you a bottle of this moonshine and you pay, I don't know, 12, 30 rubles, maybe 40. This is a crazy thing, you know.

How many people die? I don't know. It would not be in the newspaper. Thousands. We call them silent deaths. One day a person is alive and joking a lot, laughing, eating, and talking and two days after that, someone tells you he is dead and there will be a funeral. You know, someone who is happy and a funny person and then he is dead. Mostly men. These young men are not most of them. It is the older men, many of them. They do it all the time. Some have drunk since they were boys and now they are getting old. These drunken men and boys, you see them, they are there and the militia, police cars, come along and take them away. What you don't see is the alcoholism in the homes, where it is all the time. This is where it is bad.

The General Secretary's men cannot go into every home but that is where the making of moonshine is going on, and the police agent in every apartment building, he does not know it is going on. Yes, I am wrong. He knows but he cannot look into every one. There is another thing. These agents of the police, how do you know they are not bribed with this moonshine vodka? Every one of them is a thief anyway. In my apartment complex, the group of three, the three agents, we know them. Three black crows, we call them. They steal and take people's things away from them or take money for many things, so if they know someone has this moonshine still in the closet they will take a bottle. Maybe a bottle a week. Our agent, if he gets his bribing, he is selling it and that is why his wife can buy these nice clothes from the dressmaker. Gets them made. She is showing a magazine. Takes cloth and says, 'See this picture? Make me a dress like that. I like this jacket. Make me one like this one. Here is the cloth.'

Bribing all the time. That is what it is like. My uncle who works in a ministry says sometime this moonshine will become like rubles. People will say, 'Don't give me rubles for fixing your car. Fixing this engine, that will cost you two bottles.' The country people on the farms and in the villages, they do it all the time. I told you about our family. But my uncle, he says it will happen a lot more right in the city. I could tell my uncle something. He knows nothing because he is a bureaucrat. Scared as a hare in the forest. He won't even tell my aunt many things. But I could tell him this. You can buy stockings and pants and scarves better with bottles than with money. I can't do it because I have no moonshine but girls at work, they do. They can even buy things you can't buy, like chocolates and books from West Germany.

Oh, it is all so crazy. This is called the Second Economy. Russian peoples have many words for it but the government, that is what they call it. Right under their noses. All the time. If you work in a shop and you can sell anything for moonshine, then you do and then sell that moonshine for a thing you don't have. You wouldn't drink it. It comes like money. It is a crazy thing, we can all say that, but it is happening now. My uncle, he says it could be so. I say, to myself, 'Old man, it is so.' "

☙ Peredishka, *a New Russian Word*

"I will teach you a new Russian word. *Peredishka*. It means 'a breathing space.'

We have to stop the way we are moving, spending so much on arms for a war which will never come. No country will survive that spends nearly 21 percent of its gross national product on arms and hostile actions and defending itself. It cannot survive. It cannot provide a decent standard of living for its people. We cannot buy the technology from, ah, West Germany, England, the Americans, France, the hard-edge material, the technical things, unless we spend more money and that money, it must come from what we spend on our armies and air forces and our missile submarines. We must give something to our citizens. All of them. Not just Russians, but also Estonians. Armenians. Kuzbeks. They must have more meat, more bread. More clothes, but good ones. More shoes, boots, pants, and jackets. More books. More bicycles, more cars. *Peredishka*. That we must have. That is what *glasnost* and *perestroika* is all about. The world must think we are sincere because I believe our leader is sincere. I can see it in his eyes. He has eyes made of steel.

But you know very well, we cannot come and say what we really mean. We cannot say that communism has failed. We know international communism failed long ago. China, that proved it. Cuba, we are keeping communism alive there with billions of rubles a year. We need time now to try and make socialism work. It can work if we give it a chance. Don't you see? It can work. Give us time to fill out our chests and say, ah, and with proudness, 'Look, we are peaceful and we want to prosper, too, and we want our millions of people to have the good things you have in the West.'

Take a message to Canada. Give us *peredishka*. Lots of it."

TWO

Leningrad: City of White Nights

❀

Asta's Story . . . Mafia, an Un-Russian Word . . . To Dacha Country . . . Wild Mushrooms and a Birthday Cake . . . 'We Are Smarter Than Russians" . . . "Glasnost Is Like the North Star"

The midnight express to Leningrad. This coach is for foreigners, the one behind for Soviets. A Japanese electronics engineer tells me, "They just want hard currency. Our yen. I think tell my boss this last trip. Very hard. No more, no more." I think he is cursing in Japanese.

The city will always be a fortress. Battleship buildings: no German army could capture them in house-to-house fighting. Seawater flushes the canals but they still smell. The water in the hotel bathroom bowl is brown.

At the Hermitage Museum the guide tells me it would take a tourist twenty-two years to view all of the three million pieces in its collection. How long does each tourist group spend here? "Two and a half hours," she says with a smile.

The famous Kirov School of Ballet occupies a dusty, cold, and characterless building. In one room a thin girl practises one movement over and over. The thump on the piano calls her back again and again. She runs to a far corner and cries.

35

*When does she dance again? "Tonight," the warm-eyed,
motherly instructor answers.*

*In the Merchants' Market a young woman laughingly helps
me search for a peaked cap; every one in the shop is a size
too small. We go for coffee and she says, "No worry. No good
to worry."*

*Over breakfast one morning a retired English couple, just
off the Trans-Siberian Railway, describe the nightmare journey from Irkutsk: a bone-jarring trip with nothing to eat but
lemonade and chocolate bars for two days. In the lobby later
I order my guide Andrei to cancel our train tickets. We'll fly
to Irkutsk.*

*"Would you like to spend the weekend at my friend's dacha?
It's his birthday and we're having a party." It's an offer I can't
refuse. A long drive into the country, and we arrive. The dacha
is rustic – some might call it primitive – but the people are
warm, generous-hearted. Amid the opening of many bottles of
wine we crowd around the table, dine on steaming bowls of
food. There is much laughter, my guide begins to sing – a magnificent voice – everyone croons the Russian lullabies. A night
to remember . . .*

✎ Asta's Story

"My name is Asta. That is all I can tell you. Nothing is safe
here. Even with our new leader. He is a good man but he has
so much to do and I speak to you honestly with no fear in my
voice, as long as I am just Asta to you. Russians are intelligent
people. Intellectual people. We can do many things of great
importance but we still have to be of great carefulness, so you
must say only that I am Asta. I could say my name was Yulya
or Maria or Natasha, these all are good Russian names, but I
am honest with you, so Asta is my natural name.

When I was a little girl, there I was with my friends in the
school. We were the children of good people, we believed in
our leaders, and we loved our country – and I still do with much

love and joy, but then it was different. We loved Stalin. He was our great leader and that was what our teachers taught us in school. We had our nice brown uniforms and we wore our ribbons in our hair and we walked to parks hand in hand, all the girls in the front and all the boys in the back. Each of us with our friend. We went to school and we were taught many things. Maybe I was seven years old.

I remember our teacher, who I loved very well. She was old and she had a husband who was a superintendent in a metal works factory, and we used to love her clothes. She would sit us on her lap, me and my friend Vera and we would ask her questions about how babies were born and how two people knew they were in love, and she would laugh and tell us that we would have to grow up.

All right, I will tell you that we did grow up and we found out what it was like. Vera married an officer in the navy named Victor and went to Leningrad, and I married a man named Yuri and we found out that things were going to be very different. My Yuri, he told me one day to get out and that was the end of me for a time. I was a translator and during the war I worked translating English and American documents and I never saw him again. He had a new wife, his friends told me.

Vera's husband was a fine officer and one day his submarine sailed out of Murmansk and that was the end of him. The day two officers came and told her he was dead, that was the end of the world for her.

She and me, both good friends and working in the same translating office because she did not go to the North with him and the Germans had stopped bombing Moscow. When the bombers came over, the men would run up to the roof to put out any fires and we would go into the cellar. 'Don't be afraid,' our section chief would say. 'Moscow is a big city and this is a small building. It would take a big bomb to hurt it.' Then after a few months the German air force went away and we thought, oh, they are just showing us what they can do. When they want to do it more, they will come back and do it for good. But then the war in front of Moscow moved back, a big victory for our armies; but people were saying that Moscow was a thing not to be worried about. It was the soldiers that mattered. Kill the Russian armies and Moscow would be captured by the Germans.

This is when, about 1942, when we were moved to the East. We were told to pack two suitcases of things and make sure what you bring is warm clothing. Do not bring your good things. There will be plenty of people, the soldiers, to help keep a good foundation on your possessions in your apartment. There was this big room in this old building and I had half of it. The room was quite big although it was cut in two and I was happy there. I had my little stove and a big table and six chairs and a bed and there was a toilet down the hall and a place to wash and it was good for me. When I got back from Sverdlovsk in 1944 I went to my room and a woman was living in it. She had hid when the militia told us all to leave, but she kept it clean and when I told her she could stay, she got down on her knees and kissed me and cried. She told me what Moscow was like. She said there had been men and women looting the famous apartments . . . the apartments in the good districts where the government people lived. Some had been shot by the militia. They said they were Jews. She said it was the militia who did most of the stealing. But I think that is the way it is in war . . .

Sverdlovsk was a sort of centre. On the map if you look for the Ural Mountains you will see it. It is a provincial city and many of the government people were moved there by the government. That was when they thought the Germans would take our Moscow away from us. Besides, there was no food in Moscow then. You got enough cabbage and maybe three small potatoes and some pieces of salted herring and you made a soup of that and you thought you were rich. There was always lots of vodka, and I don't know how they did it but there was always Armenian cognac and Georgian champagne and people would have parties and say we would win the war. There was talk, too, about Britain not doing anything to help the Russian armies, but we knew different. It was the government way of trying to keep us away from any good thoughts about our Allies.

One night at a party a woman stood up and said, "This is not true about the Americans either. I know. I fly the planes the Americans send us. I was a pilot and they fly the planes to Vladivostok and we fly them to the front. I say, let us drink to the English and the Americans. Drink to our Allies.' We all did, and then something happened. Two days later that woman pilot was taken away and was shot. You see, at our party there was an informer. I don't know what one. Anyone. Or maybe it was not somebody at our party but someone who was there who told a friend or someone in her section and they told and she was shot. This must remind you of stories you have heard. They are true.

We went back to Moscow and then the war was over and it was two years later when the terrible things started to happen. There had been very good opera in Sverdlovsk and ballet, and I got to know some of the people and they moved back to The Centre and these were the ones who were to be cut down by the Stalinists. We had many names for these terrible people but we called them 'The Few' or words like that but there were thousands. They wanted their power and they saw that many had to be killed. Famous generals were killed. I know of some admirals who were taken out of their wives' arms and their children's adoring love and interrogated and tried and sent to labour camps. Five years was a soft sentence. Ten, this is what you expected if you were arrested.

It did not matter if you were guilty. I don't think many were guilty. They were in the way. They said something at a party. They told a friend and someone heard them say, maybe, 'That bastard, he is stealing our bread.' That bastard was someone in a good job. Next thing, two men at the door and saying, 'You are under arrest. You have ten minutes to pack one bag. Pack warm clothing.' Just like they told us to do when we went East to the Urals. Then you knew you were going to a labour camp. If you were arrested, you were guilty. There was nothing easier. You don't like this person in your section. Write a letter to the section head and don't sign your name. Two initials, S.C. or I.L., would do. It happened all the time. There was great fear.

When I say this I mean it. You could not trust your own best friend. I do not talk about workers or farm workers on the big farms. They always were nothing. Not clerks. I talk about the other people. Intelligentsia. Writers. Painters. Authors. Even sculptors, but they did have a better time. They were special because they spent all their time making busts and sculptures of Stalin and Lenin and important bureaucrats and that is the truth. To be a good sculptor, you could be saved.

I do not know how many went to the camps. I only know of the camps she was in, with those thin hands and the varicose veins in her legs and all day, to walk three miles to the bush and cut trees and carry them to the carts and the soldiers stood with guns and said if they stopped they would be shot. In the Siberian winter, many, many miles from Bratsk in the Siberian winter, cold, and they wore the shabby clothes and they did this for five years.

Who is she? I don't understand. Oh, my sister. I forgot. She was arrested and sent to a camp. Every camp had a number. I think her camp was Number 153. You had a name but you had a number and it was sewn on your jacket. A slave, and she had studied to be a ballet dancer. Then because she had too much weight, she loved to eat, she went into the wardrobe and sewed. A young woman who sews costumes, how can she be an enemy of the state?

I sent her parcels of food. Twice a year a prisoner could get a parcel of food, so many centimetres wide, deep, and long, I forget how much, but things like chocolate and other things and warm socks and underwear. I sent four, two in her name and two in the name of her friend who had died. She would sleep with the guard in the mailroom and he would sign her out for the friend's parcels. She lived but she died at that labour camp. You see, labour camps were worse than prisons. Prisons were for killers who murdered and men who stole, and frauds and cheaters and swindlers and politicians who had stolen from the state. The labour camps, many were for women and they were what they called enemies of the state. This was in Stalin days, I must assure you. Then things got better. The Thaw, we called it. Khrushchev, he tried his amnesty program and many of the camps were shut down.

Five years to the day she was sent away, she was put in a vehicle and taken to the railroad. It was our Trans-Siberian. Long before the BAM. The old one. When I met my sister at the station she looked like an old woman. Her hands. Oh, Mother of God, it was awful. But there still was the face. The twinkling eyes, as we used to call her. Twinkle-eyes. Still there. They had broken her body but not her spirit. I took her home and put her in my bed and fed her. I had been saving food for her because I knew when she would be home. I sent her money, a good idea, because she could ride home on the train. With the new order, she was not a . . . how do you say it . . . ? Yes, a convict. She was a victim and everyone was still so scared that she was treated well. Here, one man said, and he gave her part of his lunch and dinner for three days. At every stop he would rush out and buy things and share them with her. He was a bureaucrat and he didn't know which way to button his coat.

Let me explain. There is an old Russian proverb: 'If you get the first button wrong, all the rest of the buttons will be wrong.' So, with the new order after Stalin, that bureaucrat was taking no chances. Maybe these amnesty victims would become powerful someday. I think he wasn't taking any chances, as you say, but I think he was compassionate. He had known what was going on, and this train with a dozen women on it looking like savages, he had compassion. He was a good man, I think. We are a good people, but maybe the worst people to have at a time of the Stalin personality cult are the good ones. They scare more easier and they do what they are told the same way.

But I have not told you what I wanted to. When Vera, dear little Vera, and I were hand in hand at school they used to teach us about the great Lenin. Oh, what a marvellous man he was. Our favourite teacher, the one I told you about, she would tell us what Lenin had said and written. Every child learned it, along with the little rhymes about rabbits and kittens. One I remember was Lenin saying 'The cooks shall be the state.' I always remember that. He meant it will be a government of the people, the workers and the soldiers. That's the way it started, you must understand. In 1917, I mean. Our revolution in Leningrad, that wonderful time. It didn't work out that way. No, it didn't.

The cooks don't run the state. No soldiers either. No dockworkers. No miners. They never have. Not even from the first. Our history is all lies. It always has been lies. The millions they say who died, I think they did because it was the politicians and the bureaucrats who ran the Motherland, our beloved Russia. Work, be honest, don't steal, honour your mother and your father and your church, keep all this in your heart and be true. Think the good things although you don't see them.

You know you are in a whirlpool of lies and you keep reaching for the stone I will call the truth and then, around you go again, more lies, more beatings, more labour camps with beautiful women, writers, good people, our pride, and they come out looking and being old women. Oh, this is so sad.

Money. More money. That is what makes it so bad. Money means everything. I am old now. I was a little girl when my teacher, this lovely lady, told us the cooks will be the state. You ask me how I kept my faith? I will tell you, I don't know. I guess I am just a Russian.

Now we have hope. I am seventy. I will not live to see it, I don't think. Do you? But our new leader and the good men who follow him, they will . . . I know they will make this a good land. It has never been a good land. If you read history, always serfs and kulaks and them. Now the them will be taken care of. Not in labour camps, but they are still out there. Oh yes, why do you doubt me? We know. Russia is just one big place of whisper. Gossip, you call it. We know. But there is fresh air now. I can feel my lungs breathing it in down my long throat. I used to be beautiful. Silver hair, they called it. Better than golden hair. Men looked at me and all I would have to do was smile. If I wanted to. I want Russia to be beautiful someday like that little girl I was.

Yes, get rid of the bastards. That is a first thing. Another thing, food and more heat and newspapers that tell the truth. I think that is coming. We will know the truth when we read it. Some of it is coming now. Old I am, tired I am, but I can see some truth coming through now. Truth is more important than a leg of pork and dumplings with pickles, ice cream and vodka and wine. Truth is a warm house with kind friends when it is a snowstorm outside. I long for truth. It will not come for everyone while I am alive, but it will come.

My daughter is coming for me. It has been pleasant. Not all the time can I use my English and you must be tired. Are you a Christian? Oh, men always say that. My next husband did too. A good man but he would say, 'It depends.' There was a smart one for you. He once brought me a Persian lamb coat when there wasn't one for sale in all of our beloved Moscow. 'Did you steal it from a ballerina?' I asked him that. He said no, he did not steal it, he asked a Georgian where he could get a coat like that. I asked him how much he had to pay and he said 100 rubles. I told him there wasn't a Georgian in the capital who would sell a coat like that for 100 rubles. He said there was, he'd done business with him, and what the Georgian had done was say, 'Give me 100 rubles and sometime I will come back and ask you for the rest.' He meant he would ask for a favour, a something my husband would not be able to do without great risk and discourtesy on his good name. That was the

way it worked in those days. Everyone was a crook. Of course
the Georgian had stolen it. Of course. Do you think I am a fool?
No, the Georgian did not come back. No, not ever. I do not
know what happened to him. I think . . . perhaps you should
ask my dead husband. He might have said something to somebody about the Georgian who stayed at the hotel by the university. That was the way things were done in the days of Stalin.
I got a beautiful coat. Maybe the Georgian got a number and a
padded coat and boots and a trip on a train somewhere. You
see, I am confessing. What happened to the Georgian? I don't
know. In this country nobody knows anything and they know
everything. I am probably a criminal for having that coat. We
make criminals of each other. That is the way our country
worked. It still does, but maybe not much more.

I'm having much faith in our new leader. I trust him. Only
him. I told you the story of the coat. He will know many, a
thousand stories like that. Big things, small things happen. He
will deal with them. God I trust in, and He is my saviour, his
son Jesus. He will make things happy. We have not been happy
for centuries. Read our history.

Now be off with you. I'll say no more. A tiny part of my story,
but enough."

✹ Mafia, an Un-Russian Word

"Our journalists are talking now about Mafia. This is silly to
me and I am good engineer. I know what is the Mafia because
in our office we get North American papers. We get the *New
York Times* and the *Washington Post* and the very good *Time*
Magazine and they write about the American Mafia.

The American Mafia means men with guns and they kill
for narcotics and other vile and terrible things and people are
killed and the police are corrupted and it is a terrible situation.
Italians, men with Italian names, this is what the American
Mafia is about and it is very well organized. Yes, you are right.
It is a business. In this country the newspapers decided that

things were bad among the corrupt officials and they said, 'We must have a name for it, so we will call it Mafia, too.'

Every citizen knows there is crime. How can it be any other way? When goods are in a short supply position and everyone wants automobile tires or very good boots for cold weather or special things. The people who can reach out and get these things, they do this. One says we can steal 1,000 tires from our factory. Just put it down that they were defective, bad, maybe had holes in the tires and they were condemned. The director ordered them to be burned because they would not be acceptable. At night a truck takes them away, 200 a night. That is five nights. They take them to a place and people who can be trusted are told, 'If you go to this place you will be able to buy tires.' What I am telling you is true. A man, maybe he is a doctor, he needs tires and he has to wait a year for two tires. Now he can get them in one night. They cost five times more than if he got a telephone call from the state store and they said to come, his tires are there for him. The doctor does not worry. Why should he? He has plenty of people coming to him at night for special treatment in his apartment and he has so much money he does not know which way to spend it – the extra rubles he gets from people who come to him, the sick ones who want to be healed or use the special medicine. This medicine he gets from his hospital. Nobody is looking and the nurse opens the cupboard and gives him things and he pays her, maybe 40 rubles. He does not care. That is at the bottom.

At the top, this story I am telling you, the man who sells the tires, he gets his profit. The truck driver gets himself enough for some litres of drink. The people in the factory, they know, so they are paid. The clerk who is told to make out the paper saying the tires were destroyed, she gets her 50 rubles. And the director and the others who do this business with him, they maybe have 10,000 rubles in their pockets. It is easy. Nobody tells on anyone. Who is going to tell if everyone is guilty?

This lady wants food. Maybe it is the time of our seventieth anniversary of our Bolshevik Revolution. A glorious day for us. A party with singing and her husband plays the guitar and everybody sings and laughs and gets drunk and there is good food. Now this poor clerk lady can get food. Now she has 50 rubles. All she did was do what her boss told her: 'Do this paper saying the tires were defective. The factory sent 5,000 tires and

1,000 were no good. The people would not buy them.' She thinks, 'I know this is wrong, but I am just a little clerk and I am not at fault.' She does it. The paper, one piece goes to the ministry and one piece goes to the director and one piece goes to the cabinet and that is all she thinks about it. Then there is a party. Everybody says, 'Marina, where did you get this meat for the pies? Where did you get this chocolate for the tarts?' She says she is a good wife and she can save and everybody thinks so, and they say, 'That Marina, such a good wife to save for all these good things.'

Let me explain something to you. She goes to the meat shop and talks to the girl in the white cap with the meat and she shows her a 10-ruble note and makes a little sign like this, see, like this, just with the fingers, and the girl says, in a little voice, 'Go to the back door and I will see you,' and she does and the girl comes and she has meat. Maybe two whole kilos, enough for a big party. So, 20 rubles for the meat and 10 for the girl. I don't know. I am just saying this. Yes, the meat, it was for sale but it was for sale to a certain person. Who is that person? It is for that person who will pay 10 rubles, like, here, take this and give me the meat.

You ask does anyone care about all this? Yes, yes, yes, of course people care. But they are like the shopgirl at the meat market. She says, 'I am not guilty because my friends do it,' she gives her boss 4 rubles of those 10, he pats her on the bum and says she is a good girl. How can you send a little clerk with two babies in the day-care schools off to exile when the big shots do it? Judges would not do it. They would tell her she was a terrible person and the ministry would fire her and it would be put in her workbook and she would find it hard to get a better job.

This is a way of life. I don't know what else to call it. I am being confident with you. It is right because until everything is right, this kind of erroneous behaviour is not wrong. Everybody does it. So the meat clerk has to listen to complaining and mean wives and old women all day, and all she has to sell is this terrible meat that comes in the truck twice a week. And she thinks, 'Yes, my feet are sore and these women are like savages, red Indians, and all right, what is wrong? I have suffered enough.' And then along comes the woman who wants to give the party for the seventieth anniversary and makes the sign. The meat girl, she takes some good meat from the back of the store where the butcher does his cutting. Yes, it is possible half the meat in the store is sold to peoples at the back door. That is the way the little peoples do it. Everyone. Taxis, oh, they are bad. Trucker men, they do it. Waiters. They are bandits, like Armenians and Georgians. Even the old lady who sells the little toys by the subway, she has things hidden in her clothes that people want to buy. The lottery woman, she has things. These are country people, a lot of them. They are cunning.

It is too big to think about. Yes, as you said, I think it is a way of life. I would do it myself if I could.

These little innocent things when peoples try to make their life better. More meat. More chocolate. This is not the Mafia. The Mafia is the big shots. The newspapers, they say it is the bosses, the big guys. I ask you this question: who are these big shots? They write about millions of rubles in bribes and stealing from the state, the people, and I say where do they put this money, these big guys? I say you cannot hide such unbelievable amounts of money. But it happens.

Since *glasnost* it has been in the journals. Our leader says everything must be open. What is happening after that? Stories, articles in the journals, who the bureaucrats were and what they were stealing from the state. It is our money. It is all our money. If you read Lenin . . . no, you do not. He said every one of the peoples would have their right part. What is the word? Yes, share, every peoples would have their right share. But this does not happen.

The journalists write about the trials. They are held every day, I think. How do these journalists know? Somebody told them who had the salary of 460 rubles a month and a little bonus and a big apartment and a big car and a dacha at the Baltic seaside. And his wife, everybody knows his wife. This man is giving her furs, look at her fur hat. It is sable, is it not? How much? I think 500 rubles, maybe. Her jewels. Her clothes. Right in the GUM store there is her clothes, 150 rubles for that and 160 for that and the purse, my wife can tell you it comes from Italy, maybe 400 rubles. Peoples say, "That woman, her husband must be an engineer in a pipe field in Siberia and he brings her diamonds and he sells them for her and makes money. Thousands of rubles.'

No, I know this kind of man. He wears a brown suit like me, a brown shirt like me, an orange tie like me, and he makes 400 or 450 rubles. Not more than me and not smaller than me. He works in a ministry and has a secretary like me and two assistants. I think man like that, he is part of the Mafia. It has to be. Not the little clerk woman who says we will have a party because I have 50 or 100 rubles more. It is very strange.

We Russians like the mystery. Gossip, Talk, talk, talk, even old women in the street going to the stores for bread, they talk and they know. Everybody knows what is happening, but then our leader comes with his new ideas and his speeches on the television and talks about stopping this Mafia business. I never heard him use that word. He would not. It is very un-Russian. But he says our bureaucrats must show leadership. They must be responsible. What this Gorbachev is saying is that the graft and bribery and stealing must stop. The altering of figures on the farms and in the factories, it must be ended and then there will be more food. There will be more automobile tires. I think many people are getting tired of hearing our leaders talk about all this going on.

With our new ways, the journalists write that these people cannot be shot as they used to be, but I can't remember people being shot. They disappeared to a labour camp. Maybe exile if a man talked out hard against the way things were in our country. But they could shoot them, yes, yes, they could. Put things in *Pravda* saying two days ago the director of the wheel factory in Kiev was shot for stealing from the people. He was a thief. A few words like that and his friends who are thieves, too, they will understand.

You don't think so? Why? Because they will think they will never be caught doing this? How do they know the director didn't talk before his trial and call them into the plot and the authorities know and are watching his friends? In our country, you must understand everybody confesses. They are charged and they plead guilty. The trial, that is for to see what the punishment will be.

These other trials. You call it propaganda, I think. They are written up by the journalists. It is usually just so the other ones who are guilty but not caught will see that their crimes are like his crimes. When a man is arrested, he is guilty. The police and the KGB, they are usually right. Not a long time ago, but now they go by what is called evidence . . . That is quite a word, is it not? It means somebody else has told the police all about him. The things in the newspaper are to show the others that they will soon be caught. It is not funny. It is not comical. It is the way justice works and it works out very well. The man is always guilty.

But Mafia, that is a silly word. These journalists, it is my opinion, I think they use that word because it is exciting. Mafia, they say, that is an American word, so we will use it. They talk about guns used for killing. Where would a Soviet citizen get a gun? It is unlawful for a citizen to be in possession of a firearm. It is in our laws. I have never heard of anyone with a gun like a pistol. Shotguns and rifles, yes, but that is for sport. These are on issue permit to the sportsmen. They talk about young hooligans with guns. They would have to come from somewhere else. Maybe in the South they have guns which are brought in over the border from Pakistan, where everyone is a bad person. But pistols, not once have I seen one. Our militia, they do not have pistols.

We Soviets are honest people. We work hard and we may do a bit of a thing wrong, black market maybe, just a little, but it is not evil. We are just trying to make living better, maybe only for one small party with cakes and vodka and singing. That is all."

✿ To Dacha Country

There we were, Andrei and Sergei and me, a Saturday and, as usual, despite many weeks' head start arranging a few interviews in Leningrad, none had been set up.

Sergei, a thoughtful and perpetually worried man of about thirty, was an employee of Novosti Press Agency whose job was to give tender loving care to foreign writers. Now he came up with a suggestion: "Some of my friends are having a birthday party for a friend in the country. Would you like to go to the party at his dacha?"

A dacha, as everyone knows, is the city dweller's refuge, the cottage at the lake, the place in the country, to which he can flee on weekends to escape the everlasting and overpowering dullness of city life. More important, it is a chance to break away from the cramped, tiny apartment, a chance to walk in the woods, an opportunity to see the stars.

I was eager to visit a dacha because few foreigners are allowed off the leash. I had hired an Intourist U-drive with only 1,800 kilometres on it, a fact that amazed Andrei, my guide, and as we started out he kept smacking the heel of his palm on the steering wheel and saying, "A new car, brand-new."

"What is so unusual about that?"

He grunted. This was obviously a question he did not want to answer. Apparently mere writers did not get new cars, as I was to find out later on my travels.

But first, we would visit the Hermitage, the old Winter Palace of the Tsars on the historic Neva River, hard by the site where the 1917 revolution had begun which had set the vast Russian Empire on its roll towards its present state. But why go there? There was a woman, a minor executive of sorts, who worked there and spoke perfect English. I could interview her. About what?

"About her life," said Andrei. "She has done interesting things."

It turned out, of course, that this was an excuse for Andrei to see her. We did find her but Elena was too busy. Clipboard in hand, every inch the Western career-woman type, young, very handsome, and very friendly, she had no time for me. But ah-ha, the visit to the world's most incredible museum was to ask Elena, who actually lived in Moscow, to come with us to the party at the dacha.

The host was a friend of Sergei's, but this did not matter, and I did not care. However, my guide did, and Elena, well, she had better things to do, but she would think it over.

She was friendly, though, and told me that the Hermitage had three million artifacts and if a visitor took one minute to examine each one while the museum was open, it would take twenty-two years.

"How long does the tour-bus visitor, the Westerner, get to visit the museum, Elena?" I asked.

"Maybe two and a half hours." She laughed, realizing the ridiculousness of it all, and as we chatted briefly, she said, "Since *perestroika*, we have these people here all the time," and pointed to an American film crew making a documentary. "They are like mice. They are everywhere."

I looked around me. About thirty Rembrandts in a 3,000-square-foot room can be rather devastating, especially when a tourist group is hustled through at an infantryman's marching pace. We were standing beside an immense marble statue and I casually put my hand on the base and within seconds an old woman had flung herself across the room and was haranguing me, her finger wagging in my face. Elena snapped out some words, the old woman retreated a step, ripped off a short reply and departed. Elena said, "Don't mind that old thing. She is paid to watch that foreigners behave themselves."

We said goodbye and I wished I could have seen her again because she could have told me much about Leningrad from a Moscow point of view. The citizens of the two cities dislike one another. To Leningraders, Muscovites are crude, their city is crude, and there is no greater city in the world than Leningrad. The Muscovites hate Leningraders, perhaps because they know they are right.

Back in the car, we drove and drove, hoping to find a liquor store that was open. There was no queue at the first one we stopped at and I told Andrei it was closed. If there had been booze for sale, the line-up would have been a block long. He went to the locked door anyway. After two more stops, we decided that no grog shops were open that day. I asked why. No reason, said Sergei, these things just happen. Maybe they ran out of vodka and wine the day before. Maybe, maybe, maybe.

We drove back to my hotel and I bought a dozen cans of Lowenbrau beer for 23 dollars in the hard-currency store. By this time it was two o'clock and Andrei said we must have lunch, although I protested. I wanted to see the countryside around Leningrad in daylight. It was late September and the city, by latitude, was about thirty miles south of Churchill, Manitoba, a town so far north that polar bears roam the garbage dump – perhaps the reason it has become a minor tourist centre in summer. Soon it would be dark. But no, a phone call had been made and Sergei's son Paul was preparing lunch.

His apartment block was built on a flat plain at the north end of the sprawling city; Sergei said he liked it because it was close to transportation into the city and it was good for children. There was plenty of room to play.

Even Sovietphiles, those who can see no wrong in the system, have to admit that their apartment buildings, all their buildings, have a most peculiar smell. It is hard to describe. Dust. Old age–although a building might be only ten years old, it has the air of a dowager of seventy. It most certainly has a cabbage aroma. Human sweat. I don't know.

When we entered the tiny kitchen, Paul was at the stove stirring a pot of soup, meat, bones, and vegetables. A polite lad, resourceful, studious but at the same time athletic. He told me in halting English that his passion was soccer, and he loved fishing. He was studying to "be in science" and I wondered, having read in the English edition of the *Moscow News* an irate letter – *glasnost* at work – from a factory official in the hinterland that there were 900,000 scientists working in the Moscow district and the writer wondered what they did. He wondered why they never seemed to do anything to make his factory more efficient and, shifting his attack, claimed that the accountants who visited him every three months only made his job more difficult with their demands that dozens of forms be filled out. He said three or four would do. Perhaps fifteen years down the road, when Paul was a scientific apprentice, *perestroika* would have taken care of this business.

Lunch was good Russian bread and butter and soup, a salad of tomatoes and cucumbers, and tea and apples. I casually asked if a foreigner could take a car outside the city. Weren't there regulations against it? My guides pondered, and decided that yes, some kind of paper was needed. Sergei said he would go back to his office and produce a letter and he and Andrei took off. I talked to Paul, then went out and wandered around the area, drawing the smiles of young mothers pushing prams with smaller children at their side and ignoring the glare of old women whose sisters were custodians at the Hermitage, alert for any foreigners wandering around stealing two-ton marble statues.

Andrei and Sergei returned waving an envelope and I said, "Is it official?" Andrei said it wasn't, not really, but it did have a stamp and a signature and it would do. In other words, it was a forgery of sorts, but they figured it was okay. It was on official Novosti paper.

Sergei's wife came in, dressed in rain clothes and rubber boots, dripping because it had begun to rain. What a nice person!

Her daughter was with her, also wet, and sullen as any fourteen-year-old teenager in the West. The mother was a teacher and her class had been out in the fields digging potatoes that Saturday and she had had a rough time of it. We talked about teenagers, especially those forced to dig potatoes in the rain, and she said all they wanted to do was "get together under the bushes, say foolish gossip, talk, and smoke."

I said, "These teenagers, same as in Canada." She laughed and nodded and I added, "But in my country there would be a revolution if schoolchildren were made to go out and dig potatoes in the rain. Especially on Saturday. That is their holiday."

She said, "Yes, I know, I read about your education. Perhaps you are not so strong with your students and perhaps we are too strong. But this is a poor year, a bad year for the farmers. Too much rain. The potatoes must be picked or they will rot. Then there will be no food this winter."

It was past three by now, and I was getting worried. The skies had turned stodgy grey; would we ever get to dacha country? Soon we left, but not to the country. Back into Leningrad. Andrei was convinced that Elena really did want to come with us – with us? – and she had told him she was going back to her hotel. We drove there, Andrei went in, but no, she wasn't there and she had left no message.

I gave an order: we leave now or I call the whole thing off. I had had it. It was my car, and while I did not want to miss the dacha party, my temper had reached the boiling point. That did it. We would go.

We made one more stop at an outdoor market where Sergei bought a large melon. It was about four o'clock as we finally headed north. Paul, I was told, would come out on his own on a railroad that ran frequently on weekends for dacha owners, hikers, mushroom pickers.

We were in the countryside now on a long two-laned asphalt road leading east and we passed a large sprawling set of low buildings. A collective farm where they raised pigs, Sergei told me. Farther on, we passed a company of young soldiers marching two by two in loose formation on the road shoulder, and I asked what they had been doing.

Sergei said, "I think they have been working in the potato fields."

"They look pretty unhappy, pretty wet."

"They are," said Sergei, and in a rare burst of honesty, he continued: "They are recruits, eighteen years of age. They must serve in the army for two years. Some of these are from good families in the city and some are from the country, but they all don't like it. These boys will work on farms until winter and then they will build military buildings . . ."

Andrei cut in, speaking Russian, and I asked, "Don't they do any military training? Don't they become soldiers?"

"I do not know," said Sergei. "You would have to ask somebody in authority."

"They become soldiers," cut in Andrei. "Can't you see they are wearing uniforms?"

This confirmed what I'd been told in Moscow: that most of the conscripts – compulsory for all except those whose fathers have influence – are used as a type of conscript labour, working on the roads, on the harvests, in construction, digging telephone post holes and working in the woods.

Dusk began to creep over the land, the road was virtually empty, and people stood by the side of the road in small clumps waiting for a bus. I noticed old women standing beside small tables heaped with potatoes, with full bags lying in the ditch. They were, in a way, in the vodka trade: people would buy potatoes by the pail and bagful to make vodka in their kitchens.

Perhaps that was another ingredient in the curious smell that pervaded Sergei's apartment block, but I had seen no still beside the small old black and white television next to the stove in the kitchen. He wasn't in the business, I guess, not even for his own consumption. In fact, he obviously didn't trust the stuff his neighbours made or we wouldn't have driven around looking for an open liquor store. He could have bought moonshine from his local dealer.

The road began to wind through low fir-clad hills, very paintable stuff, and suddenly it happened. Just after I had opened three cans of beer we were flagged down by a militiaman. Andrei told me to stay put, and they both jumped from the car and I thought, "Oh-oh, drinking in a moving vehicle. Trouble." A serious offence.

But no, the militiaman wanted to know why this Intourist car was out of bounds. The letter was produced. He scanned it. There was some banter and he waved us on.

"He was curious," said Andrei. "It is all right. The letter did its work. He was just doing his job." But I noticed he had stopped 100 feet in front of the parked policeman and they had walked back to meet him. He never saw the cans of beer.

"Turn here," said Sergei, and we went down a dirt road for a couple of miles and suddenly, as if a curtain had been drawn, it was dark. The road became a trail, full of potholes, and the going became worse, the potholes deeper, but Andrei didn't reduce speed. It was bone-shaking and I said, "For God's sake, slow down. You'll tear this car apart." The workingman's car is a tough little bit of goods but it wouldn't stand this for long. Nor would we, bouncing around.

"Turn around," said Sergei. "This is the quick way. We will take the long way as it is asphalted." We did, and after half a mile down another side road I began to see lights among the trees. Sergei directed us through the dark, the bottom of the car scraping, then taking off through the air, but we finally came to a halt at the end of a lane.

"This is it. There is my friend's car," and I saw other cars parked under the trees. Somebody opened a door and stood framed in the light. "Here is my friend! The dacha of Boris."

And that is how we came to Dacha Country. We could have been in deepest Siberia. Instead, we were only forty-five kilometres from Leningrad, City of the White Nights.

⚘ Wild Mushrooms and a Birthday Cake

The dacha was ablaze with lights, electric bulbs everywhere, not that they were all needed but perhaps as a gesture of defiance. Deep in the birch forest, you can burn them all day, all night, and no one will knock on the door to accuse you of wasting power.

Several people were in the main room, perhaps eighteen feet by twenty-four, and they stared at me as if I had arrived by parachute from a stray bomber overflying from the West. What in the name of God was a foreigner doing at a dacha, at a party, so far off limits for tourists? Then a woman of about fifty, short and dumpy with twinkling eyes, came up to me, having sized up the situation, and introduced herself as Helena. I never did figure out her role, but I knew I had made a friend and her English was good. Not perfect by a long shot, but what she lacked in words she made up in body language.

She said I was welcome, and this was a party for Boris, and these were some of his friends come to celebrate his fortieth birthday. Boris was an engineer. Others were doctors and professors. We toured the room, navigating around the large table that dominated the room. I knew they all spoke some English, but they preferred just to smile, shake my hand, and then go back to talking Russian with Helena.

Off the room was a kitchen with a large wood stove, not unlike the kind seen in every farm home on the Canadian prairies in the pioneer days. Pots were bubbling, two women tending them. Sergei's melon was resting on a table and he energetically began to slice it, his knife strokes as precise and sure as a surgeon's. Boxes of tarts and cakes were on the narrow bed at the back of the room and clothes hung on hooks. Two sets of shelves held Boris's books.

I had imagined a dacha to be of the type I had read about, where the wealthy Russians, the literati, the professionals, the star athletes, the members of the Communist Party lived in splendour. This dacha was small, without indoor plumbing or toilet, and I could see by the walls that it had been constructed literally piece by piece. It was poorly furnished and everything had a falling-down broken look about it, but it was cheery and warm and filled with the babble of voices and laughter.

Soon we all moved to the big table crowded with bottles of wine and my nine tins of German beer and the parade from the stove to the table began. There were sixteen of us in all: five on one side, three at each end, and five on the other side. I was given a place of honour beside round-faced Boris. Helena explained that he was a professional student. "Ah," I said, "I know them. We have them in Canada: young people who cannot face the challenge of life so, because their fathers are wealthy, they go to university forever." No, no, no, she laughed. "Boris is not like that. He is serious. He does have an engineering job but he can take long periods off to return to university."

With only seven bottles of wine on the table I decided I would drink my German beer; no one accepted my offer to share it. I began a conversation with the pretty young woman on my left and she spoke fairly good English and we were doing fine until she said her boy-friend wanted to change places with her. So he did and for the rest of the evening he did not speak to me. It could not have been jealousy, but what could it have been? On my right, Boris was pleasant but his English was strictly limited. So I listened to the conversation and laughter flowing around me and observed the guests. The men were in their forties, casually dressed in sweaters and slacks; the women wore expensive slack suit outfits, their faces made up with great care, their hair beautifully done. Their talk was animated with much arm waving. It could have been a party in any part of Canada.

The wine flowed. More bottles appeared. More toasts were given.

These people were not your run-of-the-mill Russians, and it was all the more apparent when someone produced a guitar and the singing began, with my guide obviously being the star turn. On my tape recorder I can still hear Andrei's authoritative skill on the strings and his strong voice dropping down to bass. I never knew if he was singing of deep love for a maiden far away, a song of battle, a lullaby to a child, or a lament, but the effect was pure Russian, straight out of their literature, moody, gay, soulful, brave, and very impressive. The guitar passed around the table and four of the men sang but none as well as Andrei.

I knew he was musical because I had heard him play the piano in a waiting room, and it was clear that he was a professional. I wondered, then, why this young man of twenty-nine was shepherding a foreign journalist around the country, living on 180 rubles a month and trying to support a wife and child in a tiny apartment when, to my mind, he had so much talent. I did ask him later and, as usual, he grunted. I was a foreigner. It was none of my business, the grunt implied. If the government – read bureaucracy – wanted him to play nursemaid to a visitor, then so be it. It was only from casual remarks he made later that I concluded his true love and real vocation was music. Later, I found out that his father, a hero of the war, was a professor at one of the Soviet Union's most prestigious musical academies.

The evening was deepening and more food was brought out, a huge bowl of chunks of meat in gravy that must have cost someone a fortune and hours of standing in various queues to get enough boiled potatoes, steaming beets, and several small plates of wild mushrooms. I now realized that, to city-dwelling Russians, these mushrooms – which to me tasted no better or worse than any others I had eaten – spoke to them of drizzling rain, the birch forest, the quiet trails, the long silences of the afternoon as they searched and picked; they represented freedom.

A huge cake was brought in and sliced, but before it was eaten, the birthday toasts to Boris began. Helena made a speech. A beautiful young woman who had slipped in late made another and Helena told me later she was Boris's girl-friend. One man, a professor, read a poem, standing on his rickety chair, emoting, flinging his hands about. Judging by the shouts of laughter, he was either praising Boris or making fun of him.

The party was taking on depth and vigour. I was enjoying myself. Perhaps it was the warmth. The beer, the food, good and plentiful. The red berries from Siberia, expensive, in short supply, had been gobbled up by the handful – as Helena told me, "They are supposed to make men and women . . . ah, how you are saying it in English, yes, it makes them lustful." Well, if it did, that was good, too.

Then Helena made another small speech, this one greeting me from a foreign land, and the nodding around the table told me that, yes, although they would not speak to me in English, I was welcome. Boris, too, rose to make a speech and I picked up the word "Barry" several times. God knows what he was saying but from the shouts and cheers and clapping I believe he treated me well.

Then he pressed a small object into my hand and I thought, "Christ, nothing to give him." I threw my arm around him, gave him a hug, and shouted, "Long live Boris!" It was the right thing to do.

When I sat down I sneaked a look at his gift. It had felt strange, a shape I could not identify. It was a tiny elephant, three inches high, grey in colour, made of soap. To my dying day I would have wondered about that gift if I had not asked Helena and she explained, "It is because he likes you." That, of course, told me nothing. Regretfully, I gave it to the chambermaid in the hotel in Leningrad the next day and although she thanked me and gave me her gold-toothed smile I did detect a look of puzzlement. A soap elephant?

After the toasts and the cake, Helena silenced them and explained that I would like to ask some questions and she would translate the answers. I said, "I would like to hear, to know, what you all think of *glasnost* and *perestroika*?"

Utter silence.

Then babble, all talking at once. It was obvious they were setting up an agenda in true bureaucratic style, deciding what they would say, or could say, or whether they would say anything at all. The back-and-forth flow lasted about three minutes and then one man, deep-chested, with a carefully trimmed beard, obviously impressed with his importance, rumbled in English:

"We are all friends, we are talking very openly, we all are very friendly, and that is *glasnost* to us."

Obviously no answer whatsoever, but typical Russian "bureaucratese."

"But what about *perestroika*?"

Helena came in fast and said, "Oh, we don't want to talk about that old stuff."

Old stuff? I had to remind myself that *perestroika* meant the reconstruction of the country. Its education, its politics, its industry, its economy, its international relations, things that would, if carried out, affect the lives of every Soviet citizen and perhaps change the course of world politics, and all I got was "that old stuff." A group of presumably some of the brightest and the best, certainly members of the elite, and not one challenged Helena's remark.

I've wondered about that reply because, as this is being written, *perestroika* is three years old and nothing that has come out of the Soviet Union, legally or through the back door, has indicated that anything has really changed. The question that should be asked is, "Is it possible for their system to change?" Or, more to the point, "Is *perestroika* merely a buzzword, as *glasnost* is?"

Then, a woman who was a doctor, beautiful but with a sad face, asked, "Barry, in the West they talk about the KGB. Are there any KGB agents among us?"

A great shout of laughter.

I shouted *"Nyet, nyet, nyet,"* and raised my glass of beer and clinked it with Boris's wine and somebody yelled, "Off to Siberia with you," and there was more laughter.

I was dying for a cigarette. The dacha was a no-smoking zone.

I edged my way out and into the night, which was blacker than 200 feet into a cave. I lit up. As if it was a Royal Performance in London and nobody leaves until the Queen does, the door opened and several others came out. It was drizzling ever so gently; matches flared and five cigarettes glowed in a circle as we stood, inhaling deeply.

First question: a woman asked, "How did you get here?"

I described the trip, the forged permit, being stopped by the highway police, and a man said, "You were fortunate, my friend. Foreigners are not allowed here." His English was good.

Going to the heart of the matter, I asked, "Why? There is nothing here. All I could see when we drove in were these dachas, these little houses. What is so mysterious about it? I've been in your homes, your apartments, and your factories, hospitals, schools; I've walked the streets in Moscow and Leningrad very late at night and nobody has stopped me, or told I couldn't do these things. Why here, in the forest, is it unlawful?"

Of course, I knew. Long ago, during some long-forgotten crisis, it was decreed that no foreigners would be allowed more than 30 kilometres outside the major cities and the Americans had retaliated and neither government had risked losing face by lifting the restriction, so only well-escorted foreigners could venture beyond those invisible boundaries. I told them so.

"Yes, we know," spoke another cigarette, "but let us not talk of this thing. This is a happy party."

I asked, "Why is it that you did not speak to me in the house? You all speak English fairly well. I'm a Canadian. We are a huge country, and only the Soviet Union is bigger. We have the same climate in many ways and I find the Russian people a lot like Canadians. But we have no army, no navy, no air force to harm you, and Soviet ships come into the city where I live to load lumber. We trade our wheat, and some of your farm machinery comes to us and some of your cars. Is it not possible to talk of many things?"

They debated this, probably electing the one who answered: "Friends do not talk of political things in this way."

"You do in your cafés, your homes, I know that, and I've been on your buses and other places and I know you can't be discussing the weather, not the way you get excited. At first I thought fighting would start, but then I found out everyone was just talking."

Another cigarette said, "They were probably arguing about how the director was or were they could find a bracelet for their daughter's birthday. Many things. Where there might be vodka for sale. Should we go to that store or this other one? Maybe even, what do you think of that girl who just walked by, what she would be like in bed?"

Everyone laughed and another said, "All these things would be political, too. That is the Russian way. Give a Russian boy a big meal and a litre of vodka and then he wants a girl. It is our way, you see."

For a few minutes more the talk ebbed and flowed, becoming more friendly and frank, and I asked again: "Here we are in the dark, so we don't know who we all are, and we talk like this, and you wouldn't say anything in the house. Why?"

A woman said, "Listen . . . do you hear that music?"

"Yes, Andrei is playing the guitar. What about it?"

"Well, he is in there, so he can't be out here in the dark. We do not know who he is, and that is why we can't talk with you. He is from Moscow and he works for Novosti, which is the department that . . . "

"People do not talk around men like him," said another voice.

I said, "Look, Andrei might not be too bright but I doubt very much if he is a spy, an informer, or whatever you call them. Of course he is not known to you, but neither am I."

Everyone laughed, and a man said, "When you asked about *glasnost*, *perestroika*, he was the one who told us not to say anything to you."

I made no comment, and we all finished our cigarettes in the darkness.

Inside, there was dancing and one young woman ran up to us, quite tipsy, and made rapid hand gestures to her mouth, saying "puff, puff, puff" and then rolling her eyes, grabbing her stomach and moaning as she fell to the floor. The point was clear: smoking was bad for us. Everyone applauded, someone handed me a can of my beer, and Helena motioned to me. "Come, now we will go and see Boris's picture wall," and she guided me into the crowded kitchen. Yes, there was a wall covered with photographs. Boris as an infant, as a schoolboy, a young student, several in the army showing young men clowning around in typical recruit fashion, at university, with assorted girls, with his parents, at banquets with glasses raised in toast, cross-country skiing, a party on the bank of a stream with bottles strewn around and a drunken look to everyone, a funeral scene, wedding shots. Nothing unusual. The picture story of a boy growing up and soon there perhaps would be one picture of a white-haired foreigner standing, holding aloft in triumph a small soap elephant with his arm around the beaming Boris.

Boris explained each picture and the guests tossed in wisecracks, I supposed, but nobody translated. From the hooting, the gusts of laughter, the blushes coming and going on Boris's round face, it was obvious that ribald comments were being made.

It was all good fun.

Then it was time to go, and I wondered where all these people were going to sleep. On the ride over to the dacha that belonged to Sergei's father I was frankly dubious that the car would survive. We hit potholes at high speed that actually bounced me off the roof and flung me against the side of the car but I was not surprised. I had learned by now that my guide was perhaps one of the worst drivers I had ever been with, which made him a typical Soviet driver. Andrei had explained their motor-vehicle testing and driver-training procedures, which seemed just as advanced as those in Canada, if not tougher. However, their driving was still atrocious. Their way of beating the system, I suppose.

With Sergei directing Andrei, go left, go right, turn here, we finally arrived and groped our way into another dacha. It was a small, two-storied building, and Sergei lit a fire and we drank cups of tea, and in a sly way that was typically Russian, Andrei said, "What were you and those others talking about? You were out there for a long time."

Sergei stepped in. "Let me show you your room."

It was a box about seven feet by five feet but enough, and he threw covers enough for a Siberian winter on the bed.

Andrei said, "We must go out." I asked where and he said out, just out. I told him I had hired that car from Intourist, the Enemy of All The Tourists, and if it was banged up, if I had to pay damages, I would go right up the line, to the top, to the Kremlin, to Mr. Gorbachev, and I would see that justice was done. Meaning his neck would be in the noose. I sat for fifteen minutes smoking, the waves of heat from the efficient airtight stove washing over me softly, and then I went to bed and drifted towards sleep.

Forty years ago, after the war, there were no roads into this area, and I wondered how people got the building materials in. This dacha had obviously begun as one room, then another was added, then the upstairs. The staircase was still only a crude ladder. How did they get the lumber in? Carry it board by board from the railway? How long did it take to scrounge nails and windows in a Russia still recovering from the Second World War, and if you believe your Soviet mentors, still recovering in 1987? Who came to build the chimney and who dug the well and how were the beds and tables brought in, and where did the money come to buy these things?

I could see it was all of the crudest construction, slapped together, floors uneven, junk furniture, no phone, none of the amenities that Canadians take for granted, but goddamn it all, it was their dacha. It was their own. Their apartments in the cities were owned by the state, the government. Their every action could be scrutinized. They were moved around like pawns on a chessboard that had squares they could not see and the other player was faceless. But this was their refuge. This was what it was all about to the affluent but average Russian: a place to call his own.

I opened the window and the cool September air, moist from the hours of drizzle, rushed in and I thought, "Here I am, where very, very few foreigners ever are allowed to go." But I felt at home.

It was still black as pitch, about five o'clock, when I heard noises, voices, the boys had come back. Was the car a shambles? I would find out later. I could hear a chunk of wood being put in the fire box and then silence. To hell with them all. Russians like to party. Let them. I just wondered where they got the stamina.

Next morning I checked the car at the bottom of the lane and there wasn't a mark on it. No wonder they had won their share of the war. It was more than luck. Andrei must have got drunk and Sergei had taken over.

I couldn't have cared less.

🕎 *"We Are Smarter Than Russians"*

"Yes, I am a Jew. The Russian word for it is *zhid*. They, and I mean the KGB, the world knows they are trying to exterminate us. I don't believe this. I am not sure what they want to do with us. They hate us, yes, they hate us. But isn't that the history of our people around the world? Oh yes, just look at your history; in your country, Canada, there is anti-Jewish feeling. In the United States of America. And isn't it ironic that even though the Americans hate us – money grubbers, that's what they call us over there – they have kept Israel alive all these years? With money. With support. Without the Americans Israel would never have been able to fight off the Arab armies. In France, now there is a place they hate Jews. Let's not even discuss Poland and Germany. You have heard of the Holocaust? Of course, it is old news now like last week's soccer game, Leningrad against the Dynamoes. But, as you can see, life goes on.

But we were talking about me as a Jew. My father, he was born Lazar Gorodetsky in a town west of Moscow. It was one of those towns the Nazis captured and then our army took it back and then the Nazis captured it again and when the war was over, there was nothing there. People living in old shacks.

Hardly a building was standing. It was in the path of the terrible fighting. When the war was over, the government said the town was worthless. Why build something out of ruins when everybody who was left or who came back, they could be moved into The Centre or to another city? So the little town is no more. My family, there is no more of us, and in those days it was possible to change the name and my father changed his name. So my name was changed, too. My sister. My young brother. My mother was killed in the fighting. We became a new family, I was just a child but we became Russians. Not Jews. My father knew that nothing would change for the Jewish nation in the Soviet nation. Yes, I said nation. Does that surprise you? I think my father was very wrong in doing this, pushing like this, but it was in his own mind he did it, so it doesn't matter. So, my friend, the name Lazar Gorodetsky does not exist except in some old records they will never find. Mine won't either. I was born with the first name of Lev. My sister Tanya. See, she has a different name, too. My father was a doctor at the front and was wounded. After the war with his new name he enrolled in the institute in Kiev and became an engineer. You see how clever we must be. I said Kiev. It really was another city. Even today there is deception.

Not many people know I speak very good English. It is good, isn't it? Yes, I thought so. Nobody knows I am a Jew. I am not ashamed of hiding under this Russian cloak. I do it for my family. My wife, she first asked me why I was circumcised. I said my father was a doctor, and he was, and he circumcised all the babies because he thought it was the hygienic way to do things. She accepted that. In the bathhouse a bully came up to me once and pointed to my cock and said, 'Zhid!' Some others gathered around and I said, 'Do I look like a Jew? Where is my brown eyes? Blue just like yours. Where is my curly hair? My nose, is it hooked like a Jew?' I told them about my father being a doctor and hygiene and they said, 'Okay, you are all right.' When I came out there was a man standing in the lobby, a man with a cane and white hair, and he stopped me and said, 'It is all right, I know. I was in the switch room when that fellow was talking to you. Keep your secret. I am the same as you.'

I could not deny him and I said how did he know. He said, 'I know. We can tell. Can't you tell from me?' I looked at him and thought, 'Ah, here is a very clever informer. They are very clever, these KGB.' But then somehow I knew and I trusted him and I said, 'Let me take you for a coffee.' We talked and smoked for a while and then I said, 'All right, I believe you.' We had not spoken a word about Jews or Israel. Just about everything. Getting acquainted. I said to him, 'I believe you. Now I believe you, but why are you not circumcised?' and he laughed and said, 'Because my father was smarter than your father was. He knew. Circumcision is not a big thing anyway. Natives in many foreign lands, in Africa, do it. It is not a Jewish thing at all. Therefore you could say it is meaningless. Why wear a badge if it is going to cause you trouble?'

I can tell you this. That wonderful little man became one of my best friends. He is dead now. The funeral service was in his apartment. A Jewish service, but without the body. Not good, but necessary. He gave me some of his books and I treasure them. Not much, but little books for children written in Hebrew which I keep carefully hidden. My grandchildren, five and seven, believe me, my friend, they have not seen them yet. They still do not know they are Jewish. *Zhids*. It is the blue eyes. Russians, they think only Russians have blue eyes. Silly of them. Stupid. They know nothing of the world. Only a few chosen few, a chosen group of the best. The rest go through the educational system and come out like talking dictionaries. They know all the words but they don't know what they mean. They can't apply the words.

But I am a Jew and in Russia, as you say, I keep my nose clean. That is another thing. Ha-ha. My nose. Dickens, his Fagin, his Jew, he had a nose like this, out and big and like this, you see. Shylock, Shakespeare's Jew, his nose, big and out like this, the long coat and the bony fingers and his terrible words. No, my nose, it is a Russian nose. Russians are proud of their faces. Look at the women. So many are so beautiful, and their men, the pictures of young soldiers on parade. Of course, they choose the best Russian faces for those special pictures for the magazines, but they are Russian faces. Not English, not German. Each face, good skin and blue eyes and brown hair. A strong look. You would call it a good look. They are proud to die for the Motherland, you would say. In bloody battle. There will be no more bloody battles for us. For the world. But my nose, my face, my hair, my children's faces, they are Russian and more like that because they are half Jewish. That does not make them less Jewish, their blood, you know. But we do not practise Judaism in our apartment. You know why, of course. I married a Moscow citizen. She does not know I am Jewish. Oh, how delight shows in my eye of the mind when I think of this.

There are tens and hundreds of thousands of informers, and yes, I will admit, some must be Jews. There has to be some. But first long ago in 1917 the secret police was the Cheka. Oh, the stories I have heard others tell of these villainous devils, these murderers without a face. But it is the Russian bureacrat's nature that if something gets a terrible name everyone is fearful of it . . . I should say even the ones who command these organizations are fearful the terrible claw of the bear might turn on them, then what do they do? The words 'Terrible Claw of the Bear' is the nickname for these organizations. The Cheka which was crude, it became the OGPU, long words I won't bother you with. Then it became the GUBG and then the NKVD and yes, I see you nodding your head, yes, everyone has heard of that. Stalin. Our beloved Stalin, the murderer of millions. Russians, Jews, Ukrainians, Uzbeks, what did it matter to him? He massacred just as many of his own people of Georgia and yet they still worship him. Georgians, they . . . well, it is hard to explain those Southern races. Then the MGB, which wasn't so bad, but then the KGB and they are the ones you read about in your small books on international spying. We get them here. Clever spies and beautiful women and this and that. What nonsense. They have smart men at the top but they recruit peasant boys to do their filthy crimes.

But informers. Like this. If they came to me and said, 'We want you to inform on the people in this apartment block,' I would say, 'I can't. There are 120 families in this block and I am away a lot on business, the Ukraine, Georgia, Armenia. I can't do it.' 'Oh yes, yes, you can. You won't be alone. There are others in this apartment block who work with us.' You see. I didn't know that. I am a responsible person to the state with a good Russian wife who works in the agricultural laboratory, two nice kids, a car, and I do things right. But if I refused, said no, no, that would be thought of that I am an enemy of the state. Not an enemy, no, not me. But uncooperative. So, uncooperative, I am not a good citizen. So they say, 'This man sometimes makes trips to France and England; he could be untrustworthy.' I have to think fast. If I were asked to inform, I would have to say yes. Like *da, da, da,* yes, I would be glad to. That is the first step.

I know how this works because everybody knows how. One day at my office I will get a phone call. 'Comrade, we have not had a report from you,' some voice will say. I will say, 'Nothing to report. Everything is quiet. Maybe that fellow Anatoly and his wife, they're making moonshine by the bucketful. They're selling it to taxi drivers, anyone who comes. They must be making a mountain of rubles.' The voice will say, 'Man, smarten up. We've known that for two years. Get something. Make reports.'

I can see you smiling. No, this is the truth. So what do I do? The widow in the next apartment? Hers is bigger and maybe someday she'll change with us. A widow of a veteran, all alone, and she has three rooms. We have two, my wife, me, our two children, two rooms, a kitchen, and a toilet. So nothing on her. My God, I forgot. The dentist down on the second floor. He's got a steady bunch of people in and out at night, like a brothel. He fixes teeth at night in his kitchen. Grey market, and he must be making a mountain of rubles, too. Curses, I say, he's just making a living at night and besides, if I informed on him and they kicked him out, where would we get our mouths fixed? What, wait five months for a clinic appointment? No.

But the report. I guess you make them up. Little things that everybody knows anyway. This one has had eight abortions and that's a scandal. This one works in an electric-bulb factory and steals and sells to us. So, no. Another one, he steals tires and sells them on the black market. The schoolteachers, three of them, they live together. Maybe they are lesbians. I don't know. But you see the madness of it, everybody spying, but nobody caring much if they are spied on and what is the difference?

It is a crazy system. It is enough to break your heart. To answer your question, yes, I think they know who I am. I do not think it is possible they would not know. No, I don't want to leave. Why? This is my home. We have always been here. I am Russian. I am a Jew but I am a Russian. I love Russia. I love our Motherland. I have travelled. My job. I am trusted. Yes, maybe I would like to go away, maybe for year, maybe two years, but always to come back home.

This is not a bad country. It has been bad for some ways, but it is our country. Jews can have a good life here. We are smarter than Russians are. We don't get the best of the jobs but we get the good ones because we can make things work. We are superior . . . ummmm, ho, yes, smarter than Russians because there is more harmony in our homes and we all teach our children to live with the world. Not all this family fighting.

We have waited a long time for our leader. I know he is respected in Western countries. He is not feared. That is why he is so valuable. I think this man Gorbachev is our only hope and in the time to come you will hear many other good things about him. He is a realist and he has . . . he knows our country must be made to work. You see, we have to be competitive. It is my strongest belief that this will be done. The world must wait, the United States of America must wait, and we in this country must wait. This man Gorbachev has many plans and he is smart. Yes, you are right. He is cunning, too. But you must understand, he has to be. This man Gorbachev is going to do great and wonderful things with this country. He needs time. Maybe years. Twenty years. He may not be alive then, but the start he is giving us with *glasnost* and *perestoika*, they will live on, after him and I are gone. This is our hope."

❦ *"Glasnost* Is Like the North Star"

"One of the dumb things Peter the Great did was say, 'On the Neva I will build a great city.' This was good thinking by Peter, you must understand, because the Neva is a wide river and he knew that Moscow was not the city to be what he called the open door to the rest of the world. The Neva went to the sea, to Holland and England and Germany and Poland, which was a wealthy country then. But this was a very bad place to build a city and a seaport. Too low and it had flood when the tide of the sea and the wind, they were confused with each other. This happened, and it still happens today.

You can see for yourself that we have great palaces, great houses of the rich. The Tsar and all the people around him, they had huge wealth but still Russia was very backward. That was what Peter the Great tried to overcome. Remarkable man. Over . . . well, maybe, seven feet tall and when he walked, ordinary men had to run to keep up with him.

He did some great things, this man, but he did a lot of many foolish things. He did not have perspective. He wanted Russia to be like other nations which he had visited. You see? He wanted things to be better for his people, progress, but his country was much so like it is today. I mean the size of it. Sometimes, they said, he would hold his head in his hands and say, 'Oh, my Lord, is there anything that can be done for this country?'

Peter the Great, as you called him, he knew something that he learned from the Holland people and the English. The Germans did not count in this because Germany was just a bunch of small states. But Peter, he knew, if a country was to be great, great like his name says, the Great Peter, he had to have ships for trade and a big navy. This is what the Holland people and the English people had. They were rich and strong. So then he built this seaport city and where we are standing now, where this café stands, this was all soggy is how you would say it. Yes, marshes. Mist [pronounced 'meest']. You are always crossing a bridge here because of our canals. He had to build canals. It is a sad thing to declare, I know you will agree, but thousands of people died in construction of this city. Somebody said 200,000 die. I think that is too much, but it is simple to see, to understand, many died of diseases from the wet ground. Many die of starvation because never was food in enough proportion to each man.

But there came this city and the people of Leningrad, they say, 'Ah, Moscow, it is only a regional city.' They are not fooling themselves. They know our city is greater because it has the soul of the Russian people. What is Moscow, I ask you? Big, yes, and there is where the work is done but Leningrad, how this city has suffered. But people come from other countries and say Leningrad is the place to visit. Moscow, bureaucrats and old buildings and nothing works.

That is a bit of history. Very little. We could sit and I could tell you what has happened in 300 years because my family has been in this city for 200 years. They have seen everything. My grandfather was here in 1917 and he saw the beginning of the revolution. He stood in that great square and said, and he told me this, 'Paul, I was not there that day but I went the next day and I heard of the fighting and what had happened outside the Winter Palace and I knew that there would never be another day.'

I could talk to you for hours about what has happened in this city in the Great Patriotic War. I can tell you things my mother told me. There was great starvation and the sound of the artillery guns all the time and people died of the cold. If you had one piece of bread on a plate in front of you, that is what the people had to eat for one whole day. That. That. In half a minute you could eat that. Then our guns and our brigades drove the Germans away and Leningrad was saved.

I am telling you that this place was named for Lenin just two days after he died. It was because we wanted to name our most beautiful city after our most beautiful and wonderful leader. We would always love his name and his mind and the great palaces. Even while the bombardment was on, people worked on them to restore them. In the museums, people slept in deep basements at night because they had no homes to go to.

I am a student. I am twenty-two and I am a son of Leningrad and I love Leningrad and even in the war when the German shells were falling, it was in the Russian soul to keep it beautiful, although it was a terrible place to live. There were not enough carts to take away the dead people. People had eaten the horses. They ate rats. A cat was a feast. Soon, I am told by my mother, there were no rats. No cats. No dogs. Even the rich wives of the intellectuals and the bureaucrats could not keep their poodles. People found out and would steal them.

Look at our palaces now. They are still being restored. This takes years and years, and people say, 'If you are a proletarian bunch of guys, why do you worship these riches and palaces and churches and cathedrals?' I am pleased to answer that question. It is because Russians love beauty and it is part of our heritage. We had a wonderful history with great people who are artisans and craftsmen and architects and builders, so why should not the people see the great days of the empire of the Tsars? Because they are all gone, that does not make their monuments and works less. No, I will tell you Russia has always been a great country.

Now you can see where this brings us to the great Lenin. He staged the revolution of the workers and the soldiers there in 1917 after working on his great plan for many years. He was in exile, you see. Lenin was partly Jewish, but that does not matter. It did though, because it made him a better thinker. He did this all alone. He did not have many advisors. Not great advisors.

I should say this because I am being honest: Lenin didn't know the serfs or the people on the farms or in the thousands of villages over this country. He was an intellectual. It really was not a revolt of soldiers and the workers. They did the revolution with their guns and their actions, but Lenin was an intellectual. So he did it for Russia, and I said the Russian people, but it did not really consider them at the start. That came later. It was not a big revolution at first. Some people died, some, but not many, but it was more like what we would call a revolution on paper. A revolution of important ideas.

Our Lenin believed in socialism. He believed in communism. But he was a wise and humane man and he said that socialism must come first. It must come first. You understand. This huge country like Russia could not be changed over in a few years. First we will give people freedom. To think. Not to fear. Then we will give them clothes and food and apartments and theatre. There was all this, but it was not for everybody. But we will start with socialism. We have the Communist Party and the leaders but we still do not have communism today.

I am going to tell you some secret I share with some people. I do not think we know what communism is. Communism this and communism that–what is it? Can you show me something and say, 'In my hand, this thing, this is communism'?

People do not talk of Lenin – Vladimir Ilyich Ulyanov – any more. Oh, I am wrong. They talk of him, but no more than we did when it was Brezhnev and Andropov and the rest of those puff fools, and I think in the days of Stalin. But we think of him because our parents and grandparents know he was the one who led us to our first victory.

We must first have democratization. An American told me last month that we didn't know what it meant. He was wrong. I can tell you what he was misinformed about. He had no education of the Soviet Union . . .

Ah, my friend, you have caught me. Yes, the Soviet Union. Not Russia. I am young but I think in the old way. Our Motherland, we will die for her, our Russia of our life and blood. Yes, you are right.

Beloved Vladimir, he knew that the bureaucracy was too big, so strong, and it must be crushed. He felt people's representatives would do this. He was wrong, we can see. He thought truth would come out and would always be before the people. He was wrong because there was Stalin, who was an evil man. Lenin knew Stalin was evil. He called him rude. He said he was bad guy to lead our country. Yes, he knew. But Stalin was strong and he won the Secretariat position. Premier Stalin, and he made many horrible mistakes but he controlled the army and the army controlled the deputies. What the people felt, most of the time it was worth no more than the dung of a horse in the street of some stupid village in the Ukraine.

Even now, after hundreds of years, we have to always keep learning that we must fight to know the truth. The greatest evil we have had for centuries is that the people have never seen the truth. Truth, oh truth, yes, but it is what the Tsars and Stalin called the truth. Now, we must know our truth. All the truth. That is, my friend, the first step and that is *glasnost*. The Politburo, the deputies, the bureaucracies must never keep this truth of our history from us. That is what the great man Gorbachev has told us, and his *glasnost* is not coming easy. There is parts of our people that say no, the truth, it is not good thing for us. All the people I know want *glasnost* and that is why I am telling you these things. Now our problems must be told.

Lenin knew about *perestroika*. It is a word familiar to all of us for a long time. Russian word. Old works, tear them down and build them so they will make goods cheaply and when the workers make these products, they will be in good conditions, no noise, no dust, no smoke, no uneven floors, and no old machinery. No drinking and no saying they are too sick to work the day after.

I know, we all know from 'Vreyma' at night [the 9 o'clock Soviet news hour] there is much hunger and poor in your countries. We see that every night, along with pictures of our great machines cutting wheat in the Ukraine to feed cattle which give us meat which we do not get to eat. But we know your country, the United States, English, Spanish, we know they have hard troubles, too, and people who are hungry. Everybody eats in our country but we do not eat like you do. You eat better and yet you have people who are homeless, no apartments, old clothes, awful looks in your eyes, drink. Drugs. We all know that, but if you have money you can eat and eat and eat meat, and all we get are sausages. My mother says that if Stalin was alive and a plant made sausage like that, something would happen to the manager or director or work boss which would be bad.

This is all my talk. But *glasnost* is more than just writing and talking about these things. But the more our people talk, the more the authorities will have to listen. Then more they will have to do to see things better. But it is long. *Glasnost* is really just a friendly wind. *Perestroika* means making the Soviet Union a modern country. If I have to use the word 'meat' again, I will. It is not a good country with the size our country is and our wonderful resources of coal and oil and minerals, and our huge farms so big they stretch far to each side from where you stand and it cannot, they all can't give us meat. Meat, you understand, is something I use to show you what is wrong. Meat means everything. It means new ways of life for our Motherland.

Perestroika will come. It has to, to fulfill the wishes and needs of the people. Yes, I know. I know it will take a long time. I may not live to see when this country is perfect. But it must come. We are too late now, if the clock says nine o'clock in the West and we are only at two o'clock. Four o'clock, maybe. We must fight. Everyone must. Students like myself. An iron-worker like my father. A secretary like my mother. An officer on a merchant ship like my brother. My sister who is married to an engineer in Georgia. All of us. We know now. There is a new and big star shining up in the sky every night, and that is *glasnost*. It is like the North Star, guiding our ship. The star of *glasnost* will lead us to *perestroika*, which is waiting over the horizon. You will see."

THREE

Tallinn: a Non-Russian City

✿

"The Old Town Is Our Pride" . . . *"Independence Is Not
a Dream"* . . . *Dinner with the Captain's Wife*

*One could easily fall in love with this old city on the Gulf
of Finland. And in the classy Hotel Viru the maid tells me,
"Over there, just across the water, Helsinki," and we look
out over the sparkling water and down at the once-bustling
port, now with only one deep-sea freighter.*

*Everything works – the television, the radio – the food is
better, the service is good. How can this be! This is the
Soviet Union. "But we are not Soviet!" a teacher in a café says.
"We are Estonian. They are the invader. Production in this
country is 40 per cent higher than in the Soviet Union." And
a student wearing a New York Yankees baseball cap tells me,
"There is no looking over the shoulder here. I spit when a
Russki goes by. Our freedom, it will come. We will be independent again."*

*The spirit of Estonia lives in the Old Town. It reminds me
of Old Quebec City with its narrow, winding streets and*

quaint buildings. I wander in the sunshine, people are friendly, eager to talk.

A new guide and I drive out into the country, going north to a fishing town. Holsteins graze in the deep green grass, a tractor ploughs out neat dark furrows. The driver waves, I wave back, Canadian farmboy style. The farmhouses are tidy and painted and the land looks prosperous, well tended. But after a visit to a herring cannery in the village Sergei tells me, "Sad. Old machinery. Old boats. That manager, his task is impossible. Production, Russian style." He laughs. "Oh, he is a good man but did you see his eyes? He is tired. He has to compete with the Norwegians." He laughs again.

Yes, sad. But back in Tallinn spirits are high. Western music – jazz, blues – plays; in the cafés there is laughter, the people dance.

❦ "The Old Town Is Our Pride"

"Tallinn is nothing much. You won't like it. The people there do not have the spirit," said a Russian who approached me for a Western (Rothman) cigarette in the terminal at the Leningrad airport. "You will find them unfriendly and they should not be trusted. Always whining, crying about something. You should not even go."

Tallinn is the Estonian capital, fewer than half a million people, but I immediately felt at home, a feeling that came with a rush when the Hotel Viru came in sight, tall and proud and noble. A contrast as different as fire and ice after the rathole of a hotel I had stayed in in Leningrad where the water was undrinkable, the food intolerable, and the service nonexistent.

Ah, but I was told later by my Estonian guide, the Viru was built by the Finns, and the Swedes had a part of the contract. The elevators worked and nothing in the lobby set it apart from a first-class hotel in Toronto. Smaller, perhaps, but it functioned.

My key was waiting, a smartly dressed young woman escorted me to the bank of elevators – the largest I was to see in the Soviet Union – and it was 5 P.M. The halls had been cleaned that day and the room was made up. She spoke perfect English and I asked if she was Estonian. Of course she was. It was not a stupid question because in order to "conquer" the stubborn Estonians, the Soviets had imported many tens of thousands of Russians to blend with the population and run the key industries.

"You have come from Leningrad. Welcome to Estonia. You will find that life is different here," she said. "Over here, and I will show you [she pointed out the window] the Gulf of Finland. The harbour. You can't see it but Helsinki is over there. The difference, you see. Finland is free. You may not like them but they are free. They drink too much, they do things we do not do . . ." She snapped her fingers twice, flicked her head, did a quick series of dance steps. "Let me say this. A great many Baltic people speak Finnish or at least they can understand it. That water out there, the sound waves it carries across the water, that is our view of the world. Back there [jerking her head in what she meant to be the Soviet Union] back there is just a bad dream which will not go away."

I told her I was meeting an Intourist guide in the café. "Do not bother with that man. Go to the Old Town. You can walk, it is not far and it is very old. Tallinn is famous for its Old Town. It is where the young people are. There are taverns and music and dancing and talk. Perhaps someone will talk to you. Yes, everyone will, when they know you are from Canada. There is a great dream of many young people like myself to get to Canada. Unfortunately . . ."

At the door she turned. "There is something you should know. I don't think you do. Canada is one of the many countries of the West which does not recognize the occupation of Estonia, Lithuania, and Latvia by the Soviet government in 1940. To them, I think, we are still a free state and you will see that we are not free. I wish you a good time and good luck and if you want a coffee and a cake before you go out, there is a café downstairs. A very lovely café, but it closes at six o'clock."

I asked when the dining room opened and she said an hour later. I said it didn't make sense to close the café at six and there would be nothing open until seven.

"I know. We run the hotel but the manager is Russian and he makes the rules. Now do you see what I mean? Nothing can make sense as long as they are here. I speak this way because Estonians don't care if there are listening devices in the rooms. Four hundred years my family can go back in history. We have seen it all, and more and more of it all. There is nothing can surprise us and nothing that can hurt us. One day they will be gone and we will have made them be gone. They don't know. They say, ah, they are just a little people . . . but there is the spirit.

"You came in by the plane from Leningrad? I thought so. Did you notice our straight roads and clean fields and the little farmhouses and the cattle and how well they were done, and . . . Well, did you?"

She was right. From about 8,000 feet up, flying low because of the scarcity of air traffic everywhere in the Soviet Union, I had noticed a difference, as though the border between Russia and Estonia was a white line painted across the land. The neatness, the orderliness, the compactness, and even, though not apparent, the sense that even the grazing cattle had a sense of purpose.

"We are very proud of our country. We are Estonians. There are Latvians. There are Lithuanians. We are Northern Europeans. The Russian administrators and factory managers who are sent here, they like it because we make them look good. We are industrious. Our fishing fleet catches more herring. Our farms produce more wheat and milk and other good things from our gardens and our factories produce more electronics and a thousands other things. People say, 'Ah, you are so good because you are more like the Germans.' Yes, we are. We admit that because things work here. I have been in the Soviet Union, the Russian part of it. I took two years in the hotel institute learning to do what I am doing now. Then I and my group came back and the deputy manager, who was a dear man, gone now, he said, 'All right, forget mostly what you have learned over there. Now we will teach you how to run a hotel.' So we did, and that is why you will have such a good time here. Welcome to the Hotel Viru.

"About our industry and industrial life. I will show you something." She moved back to the window. "There is the port. It has nineteen berths for big ships. How many do you see? You would think it would be full. How many ships can you see?

"Yes, you see one ship. My father told me that when we were independent long ago, before Hitler and Stalin made their deal and the Russians moved in [the Non-Aggression Pact of 1940, which set up the USSR for the invasion by Germany] and took us over and that was the end of us, he told me the port used to be full. It was a big harbour. Now it all goes to Sweden, Göteborg, other harbours. Our trade, the things we make, even the electricity we generate, it goes back there, to them, when we should be trading with the world.

"Now we trade with each other. Look at our stores when you walk about our city, this Tallinn. The shops are full of good things. You could go out right now and buy wonderful pastries and cakes. Our shoes and clothes, they are better. The Soviets say, 'Now, all but this much has to go to the Soviet Union people,' and we say it is not fair. Nothing is fair. Let us trade with the world like we used to and let our young people do what they will do. It is fine to have our own dances and culture and our wonderful writers and our festival, each city and town has its big festival, and even our box fighters, they are better than other parts of this big bad country.

"See our houses and apartment blocks in this city and, if you can, go to the farms and see the wonderful things we grow. We can do this and it is because we are Estonians and are proud of ourselves. In the war we were fierce fighters and lost many men when we fought the Germans and the Russians. Now, we fight to protect ourselves and what we have left. Write all this down. Ask any Estonian. All of them will give you enough for a book. We are proud of our writers, there are so many, and our poetry, oh, it makes the heart be so proud. But what good?

"Go out and spend some money and see the Old Town and think what this city was and how good it is still. Compare it. The Old Town is our pride. There is much to see there, and you will meet people who will talk to you.

"I must go. There is work for me to do. This is not our tourist season any more but there is always planning. You will find our dining room very good. Enjoy your stay. October is a lovely month in our country. The farmers have had a good harvest and they have money and they come into the city and they spend it."

She waved a hand at me and left. After inspecting my room, which was very comfortable, I took her advice and headed for the Old Town.

👋 *"Independence Is Not a Dream"*

In the Old Town, with its narrow streets and little shops, buildings had been renovated and modernized, but they retained an ancient flavour.

On a main street there was a cluster of young men in a rough queue and thinking it was a tavern I joined it. Minutes later a man and woman came and stood behind me and he asked if I was American. I pointed to my Maple Leaf pin on my lapel.

"This place is full, you know. You might have to wait for some time. It will be dark soon. Do you have an American dollar bill? I have a plan."

He took the bill, went to the head of the line, pushed the door open, and gave a loud fingers-in-the-mouth whistle. A minute later he came back and told us to follow him. It was simple enough. He had given the waiter the dollar bill and suddenly space was found for us.

Seated, we introduced ourselves. He was Karl. His wife was Lydia. They were Estonian. He taught in a high school and Lydia was an elementary schoolteacher. They were happy to talk to me, and happy when I paid for the first round of brown litre bottles of beer. He was thirty-three, she was twenty-nine. She was the perfect blonde; he was tall, blue-eyed, and lean of face. Both were well dressed. She was wearing a vivid red Western-style sweater with a yellow scarf and was perfectly made up. They both wore wedding rings and he saw me looking at the large ruby ring he was wearing on his right hand.

"My ring, it is from my grandfather. He gave it to me from his affection. It has been in our family for a long time. Two centuries. It came from someplace in Siberia. I suppose it was a mine where the first political prisoners were. I treasure it. This ruby is worth a great deal of money. In America, New York, a friend told me it would be worth many thousands of dollars. American money. Not these things [he riffled through the rubles on the table]. These are worthless. They buy goods and things, bread and beer, clothes and gasoline, but they can't buy what we need.

"The ruble is the laughing joke of the world. There was a program on the BBC World Service a while ago and we listened to it with great earnest. It said our ruble was worthless, and yet we charge you so much as tourists. You are being deceived. You tourists, you do not know. This beer is 80 kopeks. Figure it out, please, what it costs you to change your American Express 100-dollar cheque into rubles and what you get in rubles, and then what this beer costs you. It makes it very expensive. You are being deceived by the ministry. They just keep up the museums and the old churches and have the big buses and the Intourist hotels so you will give them your hard currency. They do not want you. You are just a money supply to them. If the Soviet Union did not have your money supply it would collapse in a heap on the floor beside you. The country is bankrupt, didn't you know that?

"When the waiter comes again, put down a 5-dollar American bill and I will speak to him. Then he will bring beer free all evening, or until you go. The 5-dollar bill, he will turn into a money trader for 20 rubles. That will be three days' wages for him. If he turns it in to a drug dealer he will get 40 rubles. The drug dealer does not care. He and his gang will make so much on drugs anyway, it does not matter to him. If the waiter is caught he will be punished. If the militia catch him with a drug dealer he would go to a camp for many years.

"The drug dealer? He would be questioned and tortured to give answers about his friends and then he would be shot. I mean, he could be shot. The authorities would know who he is and they might turn him against his friends. He would still be a drug dealer but when the time came, the police would arrest everybody."

"This is what they have done with my country," Lydia said. "The Russians. Anybody can buy anyone. Anything is for sale. Low price, high price – it does not matter."

The waiter came and Karl spoke to him. The man looked at me and nodded.

"Now we will have more beer and that will be good," Karl assured me. "It will not cost him anything. He will just bring it and . . . you see, it will not be marked as a sale. He may put some rubles in the money box from his pocket but he will still have a lot. His wife will be happy. He is a good man, but he is at fault in one way. I will tell you because I know him. He is Estonian. There is a fishing village north on the coast where there is a factory and his wife worked in the electronic plant and he was discharged. It had something to do with stealing some rope and tins of herring. It was not much, but he was unable to work there any more and they came to Tallinn. The big city. He is a small-town man.

"He went to the transit base of the bus company and got a job as a driver. They trained him and he liked it but there was this tragedy in his life. He was so ashamed of being caught that he began to drink. Bus drivers are not supposed to drink. They are like locomotive drivers and airplane pilots and other drivers and one day he had some vodka when he came to the terminal at three in the afternoon to take out his bus. This was the day another driver told him there would be no alcohol test, so he drank. That was so. There was no test. But in the cafeteria where he had tea, another driver smelled vodka and he reported him. When this man got to the terminal point of his route, they were waiting for him and they made him take the alcohol breath test and it showed he had been drinking. He was discharged again. This was very bad. He now had two marks of discharge on his record book and nobody would hire him. His wife was working but that was not enough to keep them alive with food and then they said this fellow is not very bad. They said, 'Another opportunity, then it is over for you. There is a bed in a jail waiting for you.'

"They gave him this job, and you think working in a tavern is not a good place for a man who is a drunk. We have lots of drunks. People drink not to be sociable, as we are doing, but to be drunk and forget the troubles of life. The boss of this place is smart. There are these pills. Every time he comes to work the boss gives him a pill, a small brown pill. Take it or go home, he is told. He takes it. If he has some beer or vodka he gets very sick. They watch him to see if he is getting sick in the toilet and then they will know. He doesn't. It will hurt him. The pill is very powerful.

"We have known his story for two years and he is a friend of ours now. He makes his 170 rubles at his job here and he makes much more sometimes. If there is a tourist, then he will get a gratuity. He steals from the management. He puts down four bottles of beer and he pays the money box for only two. He does that five times a night and the students here, they drink a lot of bottles and nobody catches him. The boss knows he does it. The other waiters do it. The boss does it himself. It is called cheating, as you understand, but everybody has to do it.

"When I whistled he knew my whistle and it was him that came to the door. The guard at the door, he will get 2 rubles for letting us in when there are others before us. It is the way we do it. Maybe the boss will say to this waiter, 'You owe me 8 rubles.' This fellow will not say why. He will give the boss 8 rubles and, you understand, that is the way the system works. The boss may say that to him three times a week."

Lydia said, "Estonians are not corrupt people. We are honest and our character is good. It is the way we do it. This is a good tavern and most of the students you see are the sons and daughters of Russian managers. It is okay to cheat them. They are not wanted here. No Estonian will cheat an Estonian . . ."

"Sometimes," Karl injected.

"Yes, sometimes." Lydia laughed. "But mostly we cheat the Soviet guys. It is the same in my school. I teach the little ones and we have meetings with the parents. This is a Russian woman I am talking to and I say, 'Little Josef, Mrs. Asanova – I am making up that name – little Josef is not doing well with his lessons. He is not attentive. He bothers the little girls. Pulls their ribbons. Spits at their feet. Mrs. Asanova, I am sorry but something must be done about your little boy. I may have to report that he is sent to another class.' Oh, the poor bitch turns white. She puts her hand to her eyes. 'This cannot be,' she says. 'He is so good at home. He helps with the dishes and is good with his sister. What is happening? Holy Mother, what is this hell I am facing?' I say, 'Mrs. Asanova, little Josef is only seven years. Maybe I can help him a little more. I could give him some special attention. I'm sure he is a good boy.' This is me laughing inside. This is a joke.

"Two days later, little Josef comes with a box of chocolates and all nicely in paper and he says it is for me. A present for you, dear teacher. A gift from my father. He says he hopes you will take it.

"When I come home and have made our dinner, I take out this box and I say to my husband, 'I want to guess what is in it.' He will say 20 rubles and some chocolates. I say no, maybe 30 rubles. Her husband is manager of the hydro station or he runs the printing office of the state. It will be 30. Then I open it and there are the chocolates and a letter, an envelope. In it, 50 rubles. I start throwing chocolates at my husband. The poor man can't catch them and eat them. His mouth is full and we are laughing.

"Little Josef, he starts doing very well, but not good enough. At our next meeting of parents, Mrs. What-did-I-call-her, she comes up and I see there is some fear in her face. 'Little Josef,' I tell her, 'he is improving. I think I can make him even better. I will try very hard. You have my promise and my cooperation.' I am saying send me some more chocolates and 50 rubles, you bitch from Moscow, or wherever you came from to make our lives miserable with your terrible ways. Two days later, she has bought the chocolates and Josef, he gives me the box. Yes, of course, 50 rubles in bills. Five new little reddish 10-ruble notes. I put them in my pocket. That is two months' rent plus our hydro-electricity, and thank you very much.

"My husband does the same thing. He can even do it more because his boys are fourteen and it is very important that they do well in their astronomy and physics which he teaches. Astronomy for the space programs and physics for the science institutes they must attend. The sons of a Russian boss, these boys cannot go and work after trade school. It is important that before they go into the military they get a year in a good institute. It means much to them in the army. It means the most when they get out and have the papers and . . ."

"It can only be done so much," Karl added. "These people stick together. They are not part of our society. They have their parties and the women, the biggest gossips in the world. If one said she had given money to Lydia and the other said she had, too, then there would be very serious trouble. You have to know. It is a dangerous game we play but it is done. Not with Estonian children, no. With only the Russian children. Students. Their fathers have lots of money. They have stolen it, too."

Lydia said "We have a great deal saved. Every last Sunday of the month we take a bus and go out to walk in the country. There is a place and we lie down on a blanket and have food and something to drink and while we are there, my husband digs this little hole by this tree. Very carefully. Other people walk, too. Then he pulls out this leather bag and it is our money. We do not put it in the bank. The records would show. Where do these poor teachers, how do they get this money? We did it in the bank the first time and they caught us and we said we were giving English lessons to Russian pupils. That is important to them. They have a great desire to learn English, but the teaching of it in the schools everywhere in the Soviet Union is very insufficient. That is why they have tutors. We said we were giving special lessons and that was why we had 500 rubles to put in our bank. They told us it was a crime, but it was not a crime. It was and it was not. Do you understand? After that, we said we would not give lessons any more. It all went into the brown bag in the woods. Even in winter we go and have a winter picnic although it is cold and my husband digs up the bag with his knife. That is when we drink vodka. It is warm. Sometimes we are quite drunk when we get home.

"But we were caught, is that not so? My husband will explain. I am like my mother; I talk too much."

Karl said, "Two weeks later the manager of the bank mailed a letter to me. We do not have a phone. Few families have a phone. There has to be necessity for it. The letter said we must come and see him and his boss, too. It was important. We went to his apartment and they were very nice. The bank manager is a cultured man and his boss is very important. The boss said he understood we taught English to children. Yes, that is true. Then he said 'You are then hired to teach my two children who are nine and eleven. Two boys.'

"How big a class can you teach?"

Lydia took over. "My husband was in a stiffle of a time. I mean sizzle. That means you are worried, does it not?"

I told her yes and that she spoke English very well. Karl, too.

"Thank you," he said. "So, that is how we are now teaching English at nights. He asked me and I could not refuse. There might be an investigation. They can watch you all the time and you do not even know it. We now have nine students and we have more money than we can use. It has to go to the bank. I am sure the manager is watching. Now we are trying to get a plan in our minds. We want to go to London. Our visas will take time, five or six months. We have always wanted to see London. We have listened to the bbc so much and there are English television films that come across the gulf from Helsinki in Finland. We will have a good time."

"We don't want to leave this country," Lydia said. "This is our home, poor Estonia. Sad, so sad. Latvia, our neighbours in

Lithuania, our friends, we are all in the same position. We wish the Russians would go home and leave us to our livelihood. We have prosperity here. There is much money. Everyone is happy but for the one thing, the big one which makes a dark hole in our hearts every time we think of it, and that is the Russian bear. He is growling now because of the freedom movement. The people are going to come out in the big square here and demand our independence."

I told them they were dreaming.

"What is this dreaming, I ask you?" she said, and I felt the sudden hostility. "It is not a dream. It will come. There will be something. Do you not read your Western newspapers? There is *perestroika* and *glasnost*. The Politburo will have to give us some independence. Already we run some of our affairs. We are a competent people. You know we are not Soviet. We are Western. Look at our factories; they are so efficient and they produce so much and we were a good and prosperous country before the Germans came. Before the Russians came. These times will come again. The Russians, they will go. In my heart I am sincere about this. I know. In Latvia, too, and in dear Lithuania, which has suffered so much. You will see. I promise you, if you come back in five years you will see that we will have independence. Like Finland has from the Soviet Union. They are not so free, but they are free to themselves and their affairs and it will be the same as us, for us, I mean. I promise you that on my heart."

The waiter came and I said no, no more. I had dinner to eat and it was after six and they said they must get to their apartment. They had four students to teach and they would buy some sausages in buns at a kiosk down the street.

"We didn't ask you about Canada," Lydia said. "We know all about it. There are many Estonians in Canada and we get letters and our friends do, too. That is partly why we speak English well. We write to them in English. Toronto, Winnipeg, Vancouver, we know of these cities. I hope we can visit them someday. To ride in a big secondhand used car you can buy for 2,000 dollars with a radio and windows that go up and down, and drive for 400 miles in one day and get gasoline anywhere you want. Just pay the money and go on, that is a dream. To own a big farm of a hundred hectares on the river bank near Winnipeg and have cows and horses and pigs, beside a river, that is a dream. It will not be ours because we do not want to leave our wonderful country and the gulf and our sailboat and our two dogs. They could not come with us. But Canada is a wonderful country. It sounds like a dream . . ."

"For some," I said as we parted. "For some, but not for everyone."

❧ Dinner with the Captain's Wife

To be in a such a fine hotel, after the horrors of Leningrad's hostelry, was sheer joy. The bathroom was in good working order, the bed was the narrow Russian type, but soft, and there was a writing desk and an easy chair. All in all, the room was comfortable, even easy.

My Russian guide had wandered off and I was sitting in the coffee shop with an Estonian guide, Leonid, from the Novosti Press Agency. The beautiful waitresses had provided their usual fast, efficient service, and now we watched a succession of smashing young women parade through, dressed in the highest Western fashion. I didn't want to ask who they were, since they didn't fit the picture of young women I had built up in Moscow and Leningrad. But I cautiously asked about two beauties sitting across from us. What did they do?

"Oh, I know one of them," Leonid said. "She's a secretary for one of the ministries. The other girl is, too, I guess."

Leonid was an entertaining fellow who started off by saying, "Now I will tell you all about me," and began with his childhood during "the Great Patriotic War." Things had been very tough under the occupation by the Germans, and apparently not much better when the Soviet armies, aided by Estonian troops and guerrillas, retook the country in 1944. He went to Russia then, as an evacuee with his mother and sister. "So now I am Estonian, this is my mother country, but after all those years in Moscow, now I am Russian. The people here don't know what to make of me. I am both. I survive in both," and indeed he did. There were few people I met whom I liked as much, and very few whom I enjoyed as much because he had a thousand stories of his travels through India and other Asian countries, always as an athletic instructor, a coach in boxing and other sports. A good-will sort of fellow.

"In Bangladesh, I had nothing to do. They had no sports equipment. They had nothing. I am a middleweight boxer and look at my nose. I have taken a few hits on it. I was training their boxing team and there was nobody big enough to fight their heavyweight champion. I said I would, to give him practice. Maybe he could pick up a few things from me. In the third round I knocked him out. I didn't mean to. I just hit him and he was out. Then they had soccer. I'd kick a ball around with them and I was the best player on the team.

"I could have stayed there forever. I didn't stay in a hotel like they wanted me to. I'm an independent guy. I'm Estonian. I got a little bungalow. Money? I had lots of it. A little bungalow, such flowers you never did see, all around it, and two servants. That was a good life. I'd go to this club where it was all Americans and English people, people from all over the world, and we used to drink, drink, talk, talk a lot and that's how my English got so good. Listen to me. Pretty good, eh?"

A light-hearted fellow, a good companion, with spirit and a sense of humour and once he called over to the two girls, and they laughed. When I asked what he had said, he said, "Oh, nothing. Just a little joke in Estonian. It is kind of hard to translate."

Okay, I understood.

In America we'd probably have called him a hustler. But a good one, a good fellow. I'd say he had the Estonian spirit, just as the Intourist woman who showed me to my room had the spirit. Best said, it would be called the entrepreneurial spirit. Both were friendly, both knowledgeable. Non-Russian.

On reflection, to make a contrast between them and Russians, Ukrainians, Georgians, and Armenians was easy. The Estonians were Westernized, or Europeanized, and the fact television came beaming in from Helsinki, just over the horizon on the Gulf of Finland, probably had much to do with it. Also, on my transistor I picked up Finnish radio, heavy on the Artie Shaw and Guy Lombardo and the Beatle songs, such a sharp contrast to the heavy and hard and impassioned voices that fill the airwaves of the rest of the country. I never knew what these Soviet commentators were saying, but it all sounded so dramatic and imminent, as if the latest success story of a collective farm at Volgograd would turn their lives around forever.

"So now it is time to go," Leonid said, and I noticed he timed it with the departure of the two secretaries. Nothing wrong with that. He was just being gallant if he offered them a ride home in my rental car. "I will see you tomorrow morning at nine. Okay? The dining room is there. I hope you have a good meal."

He had promised to take me back to the Novosti building, the pre-war American consulate fitted out with offices and a library, tiny dining room, swimming pool four times larger than a bathtub, and sauna. We would have a sauna. Had he forgotten? Or had I misunderstood?

At seven-fifteen I presented myself at the desk in the large dining room, as tastefully decorated as the lobby, and a waiter, after consulting with his conscience, decided I looked legitimate and led me to a table for two. I didn't expect service immediately. After all, I had just spent three days each in Moscow and Leningrad. Waiters there have this aversion to serving people. I asked for a beer and it came in ten minutes, along with the menu. Ah yes, this was a Russian menu. Twelve meat dishes, and four of them pencilled in with prices. Of the four, two were available, and one was the dreaded shashlik, the shish kebab of outdoor barbecuing in the West.

I counted the tables. There were thirty-eight. On the far side a party of six were having a birthday party. Down at the end, another couple sat. Not exactly the high tourist season. Another ten minutes went by, then twenty and then a woman appeared at the door. Ah! This was something else again. A waiter—why do they always wear short-sleeved shirts and black vests, and why are their arms always very hairy?—led her down the long room, straight to the little corner of Estonia they had decreed I would occupy in splended isolation. Ah, she was a foreigner. She was getting the same treatment. Closer, closer, and then he sat her at my table. Thirty-five other tables unoccupied, so he sat us together.

She was about thirty-five, well dressed, expertly made up, and we smiled and she ordered a drink, a hefty Scotch, or perhaps it was some kind of juice. Anyway, a biggie. I smiled and said, "Do you speak English?" No, she shook her head. Perhaps

French? No. She said, "Deutsch?" No. Well, here we were, the two of us, and she spoke no English, I spoke no Russian, and a long meal was ahead of us. I longed for Loquacious Leonid who would have had us falling off our seats with his funny tales of faraway lands.

Look! You just cannot sit across a small table for an hour with a person you've never seen before. Smiles do wear out.

I called the waiter. I told him who I was and asked him to translate and thus provide a basis for some miming and hand talk. No, this fellow said he spoke English so badly he didn't feel he could do that, although he told me of his inadequacy in good English.

He spoke to her and she smiled. Okay, now she knew I was a Canadian. Not an American tourist from Kansas City or an English bank clerk from Birmingham or a heavy-machinery salesman from Lyon.

I took out some paper and she began to giggle. I caught on right away. Always fearful I would run out of note paper, I had shoved a handful of toilet paper in my pocket when I was in the washroom at the Leningrad airport. It was the same bond and strength and size as my notebook paper. I smiled at her and made a helpless gesture. She nodded and said, "Da, da, da."

First I made a crude drawing of Canada, marked "Kanada" on it, and marked in Vancouver Island, put a drawing of a house on it, and pointed to myself. Ah yes, I lived on an island. Then I drew the shape of a book, took my pen and made signs of writing, pointed at myself. I was a writer of books. She got that. A stick woman, my wife. Stick drawings of a boy and a girl, and wrote the numbers "33" and "30" underneath them, pointed to them, to me, and voilà! I had two children.

Damn it all! I had left my photographs upstairs, which would have solved a lot.

The waiter seated an older couple at the table in front of us, handed them a menu, waited until they had ordered, and walked away. I said, "Goddamn that waiter," and pointed to our empty tablecloth, our menus, and him. She turned, barked out a command, and he scurried over. Okay, I'll try a salad, the hamburger with the fried eggs on top, ice cream, tea – never coffee because it comes in thimblespoons and is very expensive – and another beer. She ordered and tapped her glass. Another

Scotch? Who cares? Art is long, and life is short. We didn't have much time and now it was her turn to do the drawing.

She communicated. She was a housewife. Well, that was easy. Two children, eight and ten, a boy and a girl. She had been visiting her mother in Odessa and a brother in nearby Moldavia. Tomorrow morning she would fly to Leningrad and spend two days. Then she would fly north to Murmansk, the great Soviet port and super-hush-hush naval base. Ah, so her husband was a naval officer. I drew a picture of a man in a uniform, with medals, to confirm my interpretation. Every officer, even without combat service, seemed to have an array of medals. They don't make jackets large enough for their medals, which they wear as ribbons, six or seven rows deep.

Suddenly, she said, "My husband is a captain of a ship in Murmansk."

In perfect English. Her husband was a captain of a ship in Murmansk.

That was it! I mean, that was it! Try as I could, I could get no more English out of her. That was all she spoke, and when you read that the Soviet schoolchild speaks English, that English is their second or third language, depending on whether they elect English or German, do not believe it. They study it in school, as many as four hours a week for years, but they won't speak English. They can but they are so self-conscious of making an error that they will not. Or perhaps there was another reason? But I was convinced that this handsome and expensively dressed woman could not speak any more than "My husband is a captain of a ship in Murmansk."

I drew a picture of a modern freighter, long, a low deck, a large wheelhouse at the stern with a funnel, and on the bridge I drew in a figure of a woman and pointed to it and then to her. Did she travel with her husband? On many Soviet deep-sea ships the captain's wife is allowed to travel with him. She took the paper and drew a much smaller ship and under it she drew a fish. Ah, he was a skipper of a fishing boat.

Our meals came. Mine, the large hamburger with the two eggs and the usual salad of tomatoes and cucumbers. A good meal, by Soviet standards, and they do not skimp on the butter and bread, that heavy dark bread on which, if all else fails, one can exist. She had a large piece of meat with vegetables – perhaps they called it a steak – but it was hard going for her. No doubt of that. She held up her fork and giggled. She had pushed so hard with the fork to anchor the meat to cut it that the pressure bent the fork.

She snapped out an order and our waiter came hustling over. Her rapid-fire conversation let him know things were not to her liking, and he took the plate and ran to the kitchen. Within three minutes was back with an order of hamburger and two fried eggs. No nonsense about this lady. Right behind was the head waiter with two dishes, small pickles and the pickled cranberries that are so delicious and painstakingly picked on the taiga and which Siberians love so much. In English he said, "For you and the lady. Thank you. Thank you." Free. On the house. The first and last time. This woman was in control.

She didn't warrant special attention. She wasn't the wife of some important official who would cause trouble for the hotel staff. No, they just did not want her to demand the complaint book and write in it that the service and the meat had been lousy. These books are important. There is no faking them. When a catering official shows up, he asks for the book. Heads don't roll because nobody is ever fired – after all, everyone is a civil servant – but there might be some shouting and arm waving, or just one of those long and deadly looks. Beware, comrade, beware.

She spooned out two spoonfuls of cranberries for me, and she ate the rest the way we eat peanuts.

When the waiter came with the ice cream there was another exchange, not sharp this time. What was it? About me, obviously. He wanted my Canada pin but apparently was too polite to ask. A Russian waiter too polite to ask? Ah no. But an Estonian waiter, yes. Finally he said, "The button?" She pointed to me, to the Maple Leaf pin and to him. What the hell. I had lots more. I unscrewed it and gave it to him. Another one for his kid's collection. He thanked me, and that was that.

But it wasn't. He came back carrying a half-litre of vodka. Making a bow, he handed it to me and then took it back, up-ended our wine glasses, and poured. I touched mine to hers, bottoms up, and he refilled, with about five drops in another glass for himself. We all touched glasses, bottoms up.

It was time for her to go, goodbye, goodbye, and we shook hands and she left a 5-ruble note on the table. I followed a few minutes later and left the same amount.

On the way out, I counted the guests. The old couple who arrived after I did were now in one of those deep discussions with the waiter that seem to go on forever. The birthday party was dying down. There were only two other couples dining and it was eight-thirty. Hardly a big night for the profit-and-loss sheet.

The next morning I asked Leonid why the waiter would sit a stranger at my table when thirty-five other tables were empty. It didn't make sense. I had enjoyed myself, despite the language barrier – anyone who appeared friendly or sympathetic or had a twinkle in the eye was a welcome relief.

"Now, my friend, we should think that over," answered Leonid. "First I would say that maybe you looked lonely and wanted company. But maybe that is too simple, too Russian. Remember, I am Estonian. So I will think of something else to please your curiosity. Okay, I think this. Each waiter has a territory, I think you would call it, so many tables. Oh, okay, a station. That is a funny word for it, but okay. Not a train station. An eating place and he is responsible for that. He has to set the tables and serve them and then clean them and set them again for the next day. Am I right? Is this the way it is done in your country? I think that is so. Then the reason the waiter sat the lady at your table was this. He sat the lady with you because he would have only one table to set again. If he had put the lady at another table he would have had to set two tables. He was just saving work for himself. That is a good explanation, I think."

Well, a bit unusual, yes, but yes, I admitted it made sense.

Did the captain's wife get to Murmansk? I'm sure she did.

FOUR

Kiev: the Heart of the Ukraine

❧

*Better Than a Soccer Game . . . "How I Learned to Speak
English" . . . Clean-Up at Chernobyl . . . Yuri, a Streetwise Kid
. . . Tea for Two . . . How Petya Got Rich . . . The Old
Babushkas . . . "Grain Is Gold" . . . Then There Was Olga*

The broad boulevards of this city are inviting. Birds are twit-
tering in the trees, broad-shouldered men and beautiful
women with a sense of style smile in friendly greeting. I
watch an exuberant sidewalk mime show. In a hot-milk bar,
at a table for two, a man flicks my Maple Leaf lapel pin:
"Waka. My aunt from Waka, Alberta, she sends 50-dollars
from Canada every month. That's maybe 200 our rubles. I
live well, me and my family. Maybe better than Gorbachev."
He grins widely. "Butcher, he knows me, cashes money, 3
rubles to dollar, maybe more. Gives me good meat, fine pork."
The butcher can sell that 50-dollar bill to a drug dealer for
perhaps 400 rubles. Illegal, yes, but everybody is happy, making a little, or a lot, on the side.

A streetwise kid tells me his father is on an icebreaker in
the Arctic and gets fresh lettuce and radishes in the winter.
A young woman tells me how her brother got rich bringing
in cars from the United States. I pass a legless veteran of the

Afghanistan war and throw my change into his tin pan. I talk to a group of students. We speak of Gorbachev and I say, "Don't waste him. He's your only hope." Do they understand what I mean? Even though he is Ukrainian, Gorbachev is still mysterious to them, and probably irrelevant.

Out in the countryside the wheat harvest is in. "Grain is gold," my companion tells me. The dark rich earth stratches before me endlessly. I have a good feeling. Is it because of my prairie background and its Ukrainian communities?

✿ Better Than a Soccer Game

"I was studying at the University of Kiev in 1981 and there was to be this soccer game. It was the university team against an army team in the huge stadium in the middle of Kiev. You know the one. It can have 100,000 people and everybody was excited.

There were about 30,000 people there, and they said that 16,000 of the spectators were from the Red Army, the officer cadets. Young soldiers being trained to be officers. They were sitting in big blocs and they were in their uniforms; the students and the other people sat in another section. It was a good game and I forget who won but it doesn't matter.

But all around the stadium there is parking and every space was taken up by these big Red Army trucks. You'd call them troop carriers. A driver and five people could sit in the cab and then there were seats for the people in the back. Every one of these trucks was new. After the game and before the soldiers were marched out, the people walked up and down, just looking. They just had never seen so many new trucks. All the trucks in Kiev were like what our gravel trucks are, and all old. Ten or fifteen years old. These trucks, they looked as if they had just come from the factory. The people of Kiev had never seen so many new vehicles in their lives. It was a sight you wouldn't see.

One thing is: where did all these trucks come from? The answer is from the army camps, but not only around Kiev but from camps maybe 200 kilometres away. They had used all that time and gasoline to take those cadets to watch their cadet soccer team. The people marvelled at them. Then they were chased away when the cadets marched to their trucks. They loaded them up and went.

The people talked about those new trucks for days. How there were no good trucks in Kiev or on the farms. It was something to see. Better than the game."

₩ *"How I Learned to Speak English"*

The café was quite crowded and I had never seen him before. He brought his mug of tea and a bagel-like bun to my table and stretched out his hand and said, "My name is Vladimir. You can call me Vlad. How are you?"

Fine, I said, and he countered with that simplicity I found so often, "And you like Kiev? A wonderful city. It is the finest city in our country." I could agree with him, having only seen Moscow and Leningrad and Tallinn in Estonia. I told him it was a city a person could live in. Moscow was too big, Moscow was not for me.

"All those people. Millions. Where do they come from? Where do they go and what do they do and when they go back to the underground and the buses, where do they go? I don't know. I have been to that city three times. I would not want to go back there. Too big. No wonder they drink so much. A dirty city. Cold in winter, cold in the people's hearts, and they think they are much better. Look at our statue out there of the Silver Lady. That is terrible. Terrible taste. That is not Kiev. That should be in Moscow where there is no taste. I say that because I was born in a little village out there, over there, not far from where we are today, and all I want is Kiev and a little house to live in when I retire and grow vegetables and have a cow, three pigs, and many chickens.

I went to higher education and I am a teacher. It is impossible. I can teach them nothing about their country. They all want to be doctors and scientists and army officers and . . .

nobody wants to do what is good for our country. They are unruly. Rude. Parents don't know their own children. Even a sheep knows her twin lambs. The parents, they see their children at breakfast and at dinner and then it is work for them, all day, and dinner and TV at night.

Our children, they can't be taught. I think not. You understand? Is it the same in your country? We don't have enough books and the children steal them and go to another school and sell them to children there. A school where the parents have better jobs. It is an education, but what good does it do them, or our Ukraine? Even history. They do not learn. I teach geography but that is only one of my things I do. I teach soccer and we have had a form in to the Committee For Equipment for the children, to make them better players so they can win prizes. They say, 'No. You had some of these things last year.' We put in another form and we explain that we only got half of what we had seeked for and it was no good. Why can't they make soccer balls? The Japanese do. We should buy from them. Or from Hungary. They make good soccer balls. Good shoes.

Many months later the leader replies to us. 'Comrades, you must learn we have to make sacrifices.' We are making sacrifices a long time ago. I was a boy when Great Patriotic War was being won. I lost two uncles on the front. But that was forty years ago. No, all the money must go into making apartments for the people. I would take you to my apartment if I could. I would tell you a lot of things. I could fill your notebooks with things. But I won't. Somebody would say, 'That Vlad. There he is. Doesn't he know it is illegal to bring a foreigner to his apartment? He's a teacher. He should know better.' They are suspicious. All these people.

In our district, where we live, the apartment building, they ask, 'That Vlad, he knows so much English. He is up to something.' I speak good English because I studied it hard, from the first year, all the time. Books. There was an old Jewish man in our apartment with all these books. He came back after the Germans left and everything was terrible, and he went into the place behind his apartment where he had put them into a hole in boxes and he dug them up. He had run away when the Germans were coming. He went to the East with others. The ones who stayed, they were killed. Babi Yar. You've heard of that place? It is the terrible memory in Kiev. All the Jews

in Kiev were taken there and shot to pieces by the Germans
and that was too bad for them.

They were English books. Written in your language. When
he died he gave them to me. I was not old enough to know
what this fine gift meant to me, but I do now. I read all of
them and I have them. There were 217 of them, and that is
how I learned to speak English like this. Ask me any word. I
know what it means.

Now, Mr. Canadian, tell me about your city. Is it as beautiful
as Kiev?"

✿ Clean-Up at Chernobyl

"Would you like to visit Chernobyl?"

That question surprised me. Trying to change a prearranged
schedule with Intourist is like pulling teeth from a bucking
bronco, and visiting the site of the world's worst nuclear plant
disaster would have thrown mine totally out of whack.

I asked, "Why would I want to visit there? Isn't it all cleaned
up, scrubbed down, repainted, and back to normal, as far as it
can be?"

The Soviet official said, simply, "Oh, we thought every
Western journalist would want to visit there. So much has
been written about it."

I answered, "Of course, a great deal has been written about
it, a lot seen on television. After the fact," meaning it had
been cleaned up and I implied it was now a propaganda show-
place of Soviet efficiency. "Besides, it was pretty much of a
one-month news affair. Many other things have happened in
the world since then of considerable importance, you see.
Sure, the word 'Chernobyl' will always mean 'nuclear disaster,' but it is just a memory now. These things happen. It was
human error, wasn't it?"

"Yes," he said, "and the men responsible will be punished,"
and I corrected him. "Have been punished, is that not so?"
remembering the publicized trials, and he said, "Oh yes, yes."

"The people who will suffer are your people anyway. It's your crop lands that may be contaminated for years. Your sheep and cows that were affected," I added.

End of conversation. But if I had said yes, it would have meant I would have had to hire an Intourist car at enormous expense, so no thanks. And I knew that anyone who was led forward to be interviewed would say, "Yes, we did have our trouble here. But everything is fine now. No problems. Look around you. See?"

Later, my guide told me that he was kicking himself for not having volunteered to be a clean-up worker at Chernobyl. Some of his friends had gone and they had made 1,600 rubles a month for four months–an eye-blinking sum when one considers that commanders of the Soviet's largest airliners make 1,000 a month, said to be the highest civilian wage in the country–whereas my guide made 180 a month.

"Yes, that is what they made. They were volunteers and there was no danger, they told me, and they were dressed right for the job, and they were fed and lived free and the work was monotonous, not dangerous." In his voice was the regret of one who had missed the opportunity of a lifetime–6,400 rubles for four months' work was enough to pay off his debts and buy the good things of life.

"My wife and kid," he said. "You see, it is because . . . " His sentence trailed off and we spoke no more of Chernobyl.

☙ Yuri, a Streetwise Kid

As I left the Hotel Rus a lad of fourteen, one of the many who approach you when you are not accompanied by a Russian guide, came up to me. He wanted to practise his English.

He said his name was Yuri. His features were Mongolian, I thought, but no, he said, "I was born in Kiev and I live with my mother and my sister in a small apartment." His sister was training to be a nurse: "Her wage, that will be so small. She should try to be a doctor." Well, why doesn't she? Yuri said the principal of her school decided she would be a nurse. So that was that.

His mother? "She works in an office, from eight until sometimes as late as six o'clock. It is a long way by bus to our apartment, so I am waiting for her to finish." He'd go shopping with her although, "Gone will be all the good things. Just some old sausage left, I think."

His English was not bad, but as we walked and talked, it deteriorated and soon he was almost silent and at one point he put on a Walkman set of headphones. I asked, "What are you listening to?" Nothing, he said. He had no batteries. I said, "Look, I've got my camera. It takes AA batteries. Let's try them." No, mine wouldn't work, he insisted and he wouldn't even try them. "This takes our batteries, don't you know. Can't you see that?" Then why didn't he buy some batteries? He'd been trying, for weeks, but there were none for sale.

Did he like school? No. Why? "The teachers are stupid. The school is old. It is cold. The other students keep me out of their games because I am different." Was he different? His skin, couldn't I see it was different? He came from the North. His English was picking up now as he became agitated. His father's mother was a Northerner and he had her skin, the darkness. So, what I had mistaken for Mongolian was actually that of a Northern person, an Inuit-type.

What did he want to do? That was simple. His voice became animated. "I want to be like my father." His father was a crew member on an ice-breaker in the Arctic. A big, big ship. He had been there for three years, not coming home at all. He even spent his annual month's holiday on the ship and, amazingly, he would spend two more years on it. They grew their own vegetables, radish and lettuce and carrots on the ship. There was a swimming pool. It was, and here he had difficulty, but finally he said, "It could be a village that floats on the water." Waaaa-tor.

"When his work is finish, he will come home and he will have so much money, this much," and he stretched out his arms, "and we will build a house on the farm my mother was lived on. Where she was born as a baby. A house and my father will not have to work again, just get a car and drive people around and make money."

"So you want to go work on this big ship and make a lot of money like your father. Then you'll come back, and drive a taxi, too. Is that it?"

"First I will have to finish my education. For a long time yet, but he says that when I am ready he can help me get the job. Five years away, if they still let it that way. You don't spend any money. You will have 20,000 rubles. Like my father. But you don't have to work any more. No factory."

I thought, into the ice-breaker service at perhaps eighteen, if the army doesn't pick him off. Wouldn't lonely arctic service be considered combat pay? Out at twenty-three and set for life. Capitalism never offered it so attractively.

We were passing a hot milk-and-bun stand-up bar and I steered him in and he said, "A café there. We could have Pepsi."

Ah, the all-Russian national drink!

While we stood at a table against the wall I handed him a 20-kopek piece and said, "Go out and give this to that man sitting out there."

The begger was a veteran, still wearing his greatcoat, and both legs had been shot off. He had his army cap turned up on the sidewalk and there were fewer than a dozen coins in it.

"Not want to. He is beggar."

"Go on, he is a soldier."

"No, people will see me. Won't be good."

A young man who was at the table when we arrived but who had ignored us, reading his newspaper, suddenly spoke from behind it in a very commanding voice. No mistaking it.

The boy grabbed the coin and when he came back they spoke to each other. I asked, "What did he say?"

The man put down his newspaper and said, "My name is Nick. I could take you to the police if I wanted to, because you are speaking to this boy about the war. They would have a few words to say to you. It is not a good thing to talk about something like that here. . . . Yes, my English is perfect."

"You think it is. I know it isn't, but it is not bad. What did you tell the kid?"

"I told him to put the money in the man's hat. I told him that I would ask the soldier when I left if the kid had given him the money. I won't have to now. He would not have come back if he hadn't."

I said we were not talking about the war. "I only told him to give the money to the soldier."

"I see you are from Canada. The badge. Why do you wear that? I never see Americans wearing those badges."

"Very simple. It shows that we are not Americans. Did you get that? Not – n-o-t – not Americans. Canadians are not Americans."

He folded up his paper and said, "It would be interesting to talk to you, but I must go," and he shook hands, a firm and strong grip. "Toodle-do," and he smiled.

"Not very Russian," I said and he replied, "I am Ukrainian. We are not Russians. Soviets, that is true, but not Russians. Like you Canadians, you are not Americans," and he was gone, firing a quick *brrrrrrr* of words at the boy.

"Okay, Yuri, what did he say?"

"Nothing. He just said, 'Stick with this guy. He is not a cockroach like some. Ask for his button.' All he said."

He walked me back to my hotel and I took out my wallet and gave him an American dollar. "Do you know what this is?" Yes. I told him it was for showing me around, talking to me. He grinned, shoving it in his pocket.

"What will you do with it?"

"Four rubles," he said, "I will sell it to get 4 rubles."

Streetwise, this kid.

I wished him well and he gave me a double-handed handshake, both hands on my one, something no other Soviet had done to me.

"Remember Yuri," he said. "I am named after our bravest cosmonaut. He was smart man and I be smart. Thank you for little feast. I was very hungry. My mother will thank you, too, when I tell her. I will go and get 4 rubles for it now, and we will have something very good for dinner soon with it." He turned to go.

"Study hard in your school and don't care what the other children say."

"I will remember that very hard. You are a good man."

As we parted, I gave Yuri my button and, quick as a flash, his hand went into the breast pocket of his jacket and he came up with one of his own, twice as big, garish, a medal of some type. "No, I don't want it," and handed it back. But he said, "Yes, yes, it is for you. You are now my friend," so I took it. I still have it.

Tea for Two

"Do – would you bother if I sat with you? I am glad you speak English. Yes, you are a Canadian. I knew you were something like that. I can tell by your clothes. I would like to buy you something. Is it coffee you want? No, tea? Oh, I am sorry, they don't make good tea in this café, but I will get it for you.

Here is your tea and some sugar. I am drinking it, too. We will both use my spoon to stir our tea. They only had one spoon left and so we have to use it together. That is favourable, isn't it? Is 'favourable' the right word? You can see my English is not the best but I know 'favourable' means good. I like coffee but it is getting too expensive.

Now we will talk. There is nobody here. Oh, those girls in the corner. They are nothing. I know what they are talking about. Boys, or I mean young men, or where to buy lipstick or who has had an abortion. That is like the world today is here, lots of abortions. We can't have so many peoples and they must work to buy those lipsticks and clothes. Those girls, they are dressed very favourably, would you not say? Soon they will get married and then life of them will be very hard. It is not a good life for a young lady in Kiev, but it is better than other towns in the Ukraine and that is why they come to this fine city.

It is a beautiful city, don't you think so? I was born here and all my life except when I was in The Centre. That is Moscow. I would want to take my training here but they say, no, Lyubov, that is my name, what is yours? Barry? I have not heard that English name before. What does it mean? Just Barry.

I am a doctor. The hospital is not far from here. There is a place there where we eat but I don't like it. The food is always the same cook. Our committee had a meeting and we went to the director and he wouldn't see us. That is when we saw his assistant and he is a good man but he is not a Party man and he said, 'Why do you people come to me? Don't you understand? The cook is a relative of the director, a cousin. She gives him the best meat and things like that.' One of our doctors, he spoke and he said, 'There is a new way of doing things now. That is not favourable. Don't you know that because you should know that. It is in the General Secretary's new rules. These things cannot be done any longer. We are protesting the bad food and you are telling us the boss is getting the good food for him and his family and his friends.' This other man, who is not a strong man, he said, 'You should know better, my friend. This is Kiev and, besides, these rules don't apply here. Maybe in a few years. I want you to go back to work and don't bother the boss about these things. He will not listen to you and it could be hard for you. Do you want to be sent to a nice and new hospital in Chita or Krasnoyarsk, where they have no equipment?'

Chita, I know, is in Siberia near Baikal and Krasnoyarsk, I know that is far away, too. He can do that to you. He will just say he wants you transferred and you will have to move and then you would be far away from your family. We are quieting our thoughts on this food after that. This is why I come over here and have something. It saves me money, too, and I can walk in the streets and pay less money and see people. There is a beggar from some war or accident with no legs and I give him money sometimes. Oh, 20 kopeks, 10. If it is less than 10, a 5 kopeks, he will sometimes curse me, but I laugh and say, 'Those killers in the hills, you should be happy. They could have cut out your heart and roasted it and eaten it.' The people in the hills in Afghanistan, they do that to our boys. I have been told. That is an awful thing. It will be over soon. We will win. I know that is the truth. But war is a terrible thing.

You ask what kind of a doctor am me? I mean, what am I? That is a good question and well put to me. I am what they call in English an internist. Yes, you are right. You point to your stomach. Good. I am a doctor of the insides, the belly. That is your word, is it not so? I don't think we use that for people although animals have bellies. I make them better if I can, but our hospital, it is not the best one and this makes it harder. We cannot get the drugs we need. The medical books we get from

France and Sweden, they describe drugs and methods we do not do, although maybe we will someday. This is not a hospital for Party members and officers of the army. It is for workers, factory people, and people who do not have the favourable cards to get them in to good hospitals. This is what you must understand. There are hospitals for them and then there is the good hospital.

You should not make any mistakes here. In our hospital we do the very best ... very, that means more than the best, is that not true? Yes, thank you. Thank you very much. See, I used 'very' again saying more than thank you. I am learning my English on you. If I say something bad you must tell me. This is the way to learn. That is true, wouldn't you say? I am telling you these things because you understand. You have that kind of feel in your face. I can understand that. I think it is very much right to speak English.

Thank you for telling me I speak English. So you see, I have told you what I do and what I am doing here in this café. Now would you please tell me what you do and what you are doing in our lovely city?

... Ah, a writer. We have many famous writers in the Ukraine and in the country. They are widely looked ... I mean, they are read a lot and it is very hard to get their books. The newspaper says the book of a poet, just anyone who is a good poet and who speaks of the land we all love so much as possible. It is a great land, and it is a sad land. There has been so much trouble. Tears, tears, tears, I could never tell anyone how many tears we have cried for this country. It would be hard for you to believe. But it is our country. Our Motherland. We see movies and they are about the Great Patriotic War and we see those Nazi people marching to war, to kill Russian and Ukrainian boys and girls. I can tell they are singing songs about hate. Our soldiers, when they are marching to face the enemy, they are singing love songs to their country. This country. All the republics. I will not tell you that we would like to be our own country [a long pause], but for the Ukraine it is too late. We are the USR in your alphabet and it is too late. We suffered badly in the war. It was the Nazis who killed many, many of us and then our own armies fighting towards Berlin they killed so many of us. Have you been to Babi Yar? That is where the Nazis killed, they will tell you, about 1,000 times 100 Jews. They took them to this place and killed them with machine guns and buried them. People take flowers every day and put them on the monument. It is a very sad place. Little flowers and little notes in Yiddish saying, I think, 'God rest your soul.' Things like that. People tell me these things.

This is a time for more tea and maybe they will have washed the spoons and we will have a cookie. I have time. Would you like that?

Now, you asked me what I make in money. It is 240 rubles a month and sometimes there is a bonus. I have about 260 rubles. That is not enough. I have a husband who is a welder in the auto works and he makes more money. Alexei, he has about 280 but we have a boy who is fourteen and it is hard for us to . . . Ah, 'make ends meet!' Is that the way you say it in Canada? I would remember that. It is good. Make ends meet.

I wish I was like my friend. Her name is Irina. She is Russian, a Russian woman, and she works in the hospital. She is just a nurse but we talk. She lets me know things about her. She is what I think you would call a slick. She is smart. You tell me if this means slick. Irina and her boy-friend have more rubles than my family does. It is a secret but I can trust you. You have a good face. Oh yes, I can tell. I do not sit down and drink tea with a foreigner and talk about things like Babi Yar and how the director is stealing the workers' food. We will not see each other again. That is true.

I have an uncle who is a big doctor in Los Angeles in California and he came over to Kiev three years ago. It was a show of important doctors. The uncle and my father were brothers but the uncle was taken to America by an old uncle a long, long time ago. Maybe fifty years ago. He became most important doctor and the picture of the house he showed me . . . let me describe it. It had eight bedrooms and six bathrooms. You can see the ocean. It has grass growing and he has a big boat. Nobody has a doctor in this country who knows he has a boat, don't you think. A boat like this one. It is white and it is long. This long. He asks me if I would like to visit him and his wife but I say no, that is not possible. He said no, it is possible. He says he can make it happen. I say no, please don't try. It, this thing of visiting him, it would be bad for me. I would be questioned by them. I would get a letter saying I must come to the headquarters and they would ask me why this man was asking me to go to America.

This happened when he visited our apartment and he said, 'Do you live here?' I said it was our home and he said I was a doctor and I should have a big house. He saw some rugs we have on the walls and he said, 'Where can I get one of those?' He would want it, he said. I told my uncle it was when we went to holidays in Azerbaijan and in the market, that is where we bought two. He thought it was something very pretty and I said I would try and get him one, but he would have to come and get it. I could not mail it. That is not possible.

Then my uncle said, 'I am going to send you some money.' It was not for the rug, he said, but to help us as he thought we were poor. We are not poor. I told him we were happy. He said you can't be happy if there is no money and you have to live like this. My husband does not understand this English and when I told him he said my uncle was being aggressive. Is that the word? No, I guess it would be your word 'rude.' He wasn't. He was a kind man who wanted to help us.

He went away and in two months a letter came for me. It was just a letter saying thank you and in it, now, I will tell you this. There was in it an American money bill of 50 dollars. I could not believe it and I put it away in a book for a month or two weeks, and one day I told my best friend, this Irina who is a nurse, I told her what had happened. She said, 'My boy-friend will give you 200 rubles for it.' I said, "No, that is the under-ground,' and she said nobody would ever know. I did not tell my husband but I thought, and then I said, 'Yes, I will do it.' Everybody wants to get the best thing for herself and, oh, I don't care. I couldn't spend it. They would ask me, 'Why did you get all this money from an American?' That would be bad. So I gave it to my friend and next day she gave me 200 rubles.

I thought, 'I can't do this. My heart will fail me if something happens to Irina for what she has done.' Then I said to her next week that I would give her 20 rubles for helping me. I am telling you the truth. She laughed and said, 'Ha-ha, my boy-friend already has given me 25 rubles.' Then she told me that her boy-friend had sold the bill for 500 rubles. He had made a profit on me of 300 rubles and I asked her how that could be. This was not possible. She said, 'Oh, you little foolish woman. You don't know what is happening and you work in a hospital with me and you're a doctor. My boy-friend sold the American money to the drug peddler and he got 10 rubles to each dollar. That's the way it works. You can get 10 from them because they will buy drugs and make much, much more money. The 50-dollar bill is the size they like. You are fortunate your uncle sent you it that size.' I am telling you about the way she said it and I was shocked. I was also scared. Very scared. And then she said nothing could happen. How could anybody know? I thought about that and I said to myself that night, yes, how could anybody know? I had 200 rubles and I took them from my hiding place and I spent them.

I think it was three months later when my uncle wrote me another letter. He thanked me for my letter and did not mention me coming to America but in tissue paper, like toilet paper you can buy in the hard- currency store in the tourist hotels, he had put another 50 dollars. I just jumped around the room in happiness. I wasn't afraid any more because nothing had happened to me and the next day I told Irina. She said you see, and I gave her the money and I told her I wanted 250 rubles. You know what I'm going to say? She said, 'That will be done but I want 20 rubles this time,' and I said, "That is all right. Why should your boy-friend who I don't think is a good man any more, this man should not get so much." She said I was right and I said, 'All right, if he is not a good man for you, why are you with him all the time?' She didn't tell me but I got 250 rubles and gave Irina 20 and then it happened again, and twice more and then I got afraid. Something funny happened in our apartment building. I heard that the boss of it who is a sneak was asking our neighbours how I could have so much money and, you know, he is an . . . well, we have a word for it. Not a spy.

Yes, that's the word. He was an informer.

So to keep my husband and me from getting hurt I wrote my uncle and said we loved him but he would have to stop sending, I called them little gifts. He is a smart man. Look, if you go to Los Angeles and see the house he lives in, you will know. I couldn't explain but I mailed the letter to his son who is my cousin and he lives in a place called San Diego something and I addressed it to him, but he would know the letter was for his father. So he would send it to him. I didn't say it in such words, but I told him that sending these little gifts was dangerous. I didn't tell him about the informer man. I couldn't. And then that is how it all happened. It was good to get such a lot of money but there was not the faith I had before that it was a secret. People, when they start suspicious here they talk and talk and other people say things and soon, it could have been a bad thing for us.

I'm sorry, Barry, but do you understand I must go now? I have been talking all the time. It was good to talk with you. I don't know about you. Do you have children? I hope you have a nice travels in our great country. I must get to my post now. It is five minutes to walk and I must be there, so I have to go. Give my kind words to all the doctors in your country. It must be a nice place to live. Goodbye. Goodbye."

ɯ *How Petya Got Rich*

"My brother Petya–Peter–our family calls him the Little Bear because he has much hair on his body, he was an engineer on one of our big ships that carry cereals from the American harbour of New Orleans to our country. It would go to Odessa and other harbours with grain which we would use to feed our cattle and use for other things.

One time his ship was in this American port, two of his friends told him that if he had American dollars they could buy an American car. This was about ten years ago and my brother told them, 'We have three more days to load, so let us go and see this place where they sell these cars.' So they did go and what they saw was important to them. They could not believe what they saw, he told me. There were many, many American cars of all colours and shapes and sizes and because Petya speaks English quite well, he talked to the seller. The man said this car was costing 700 dollars in American dollars and this one was 800 dollars and, you see, these were the prices with the paper on the front and they were so cheap. They were good cars. 'Drive one around and I'll come with you,' and my brother did and he said to himself, 'If I could get this car to Odessa I could sell it for 5,000 rubles,' because they were such beautiful cars. Then they had to leave as their ship was loaded with wheat, but he did not forget and he thought a great deal and he went to his commander, you call him the captain, and he asked if he could . . . if he could buy one of these American motors, he could carry it back on the ship. The captain said, 'Yes, but it must be right. There must be the real documents,' and Petya said, 'Well, I will see what can be done about this.'

Now how does an engineer who gets 300 rubles a month, how does he get American dollars? That is an important question. He had about 9,000 rubles in his bank and he thought, this is what he thought. This is what he did. He had visited a family of one of the Americans from New Orleans who was an official who came on the ship. Yes, a pilot. He guides the ship. When they asked him to visit their home he was most happy and friendly and when he got there he gave this man's wife a bracelet made of amber. We have lots of amber. It comes from the Baltic and people make it into bracelets and this kind of ornament for ladies. It cost him maybe 30 rubles and the wife was so happy she wanted to buy more. But that was all Petya had. Just that little thing as a present. She said, 'If you bring me more I will buy them from you.' That is what came about them. This deal of business.

"This is what my brother did. He took a lot of money out of the bank and he went and he bought all these amber things, the most beautiful he could find, and when his vessel went to New Orleans again he went to visit the lady and her husband. Here, he said, and he opened his parcel and the lady was happy. She said, 'What is this one for sale, and this one?' And my brother thought, this one? It had cost him 40 rubles and he said, 'I can sell you this for 100 dollars,' and the lady was happy. The next day she invited some friends and said, 'Look at these things. Amber, how beautiful. Would you like to buy them?' They bought and that was how Petya made 2,000 dollars. He said there were only maybe six or seven ladies and they bought a lot of things and the lady who was his friend, she said, 'You leave the rest for me and I will sell them for you and when you come back you will have a lot of American money.' Do you see what I am saying?

The next day my brother went to this place where they sold the cars and he saw the same man and he said, 'This one, can I drive it around?' Yes, the man said, and he did and he bought it for 700 dollars. It was what people call a Chevrolet and it was built in 1972, so it was called old and he got the documents and then he bought another automobile. It was a Dodge car and it cost 700 dollars and the men from the automobile place drove them to the ship. The captain, he said, 'Petya, I said one car. You have two. Take one back.' My brother said that the red car was his and the blue one was for his brother. 'Okay,' the captain said. 'You're the one who will hang for it,' and after the grain was loaded in the bins of the ship they put the two cars on the deck.

'Now,' thought my brother, 'what will I do?' He had lots of time on that long voyage as our great ships, you must know, are very democratic and they have good working times and schedules and Yuri is a good mechanic. He polished the cars and covered them when there was bad weather and he worked on the motors and cleaned them. He said they were wonderful.

The captain told him he wanted the cars gone and when they docked at the harbour in Odessa my brother went to the man on the winch and gave him 10 rubles and said, 'Let's go, my friend.' Over the side and down and my brother drove the car to a big warehouse and then he did the same with the other. Nobody knew. It was night, early in the morning.

He went to the bureau and he bribed the clerk, maybe 20 rubles, and he got the licence for both cars and paid the insurance, and then he went to our home and asked my father to talk to people at the ministry office, to say did anyone want to buy an American car? My father was quick: how much? My brother said that his cars were much better than anything they could buy new in the city of Odessa and he would sell each one for 4,000 rubles. That was a very, very good price for a car.

When my father came home for dinner that night there were four men with him and he said, 'These guys want to buy our cars.' 'Four,' Petya said. 'I only have two and, you see, they have the documents. But when I sell them I am not to be taken to be responsible. Just say you bought them from Petya.' One man said 4,500 rubles, which is an amazing amount of money, but he was a foreman and his wife had a little business selling cakes for weddings and parties. And so the other man, he said 4,500, too. This was something nobody had dreamed of. Petya was now rich. He had earned a great amount of money and he said to the two other men, 'I will be back in seven weeks. Two more cars. They will be 4,500 each.'

He did it again. He bought as much amber as he could, only these bracelets and pins and these neck pieces and they fitted into a small bundle, and he did the same thing again. Do you know what I am saying? He gave his captain another 200 rubles and the man on the winch 20 or 30 rubles and the clerk at the bureau for the licence, he paid him and the American lady had sold all the beautiful things he had given her to sell.

He bought two more cars and he sold them. He asked, 'Has there been any trouble?' I was there. The man who bought the first car wanted another as he had sold his for a good profit and he said yes, but friendly trouble. Militiamen on traffic would stop him and look at the car and get in it, and sometimes he would drive them a little ways and they would say they wished they could buy a car like this one. I am his sister. I was so proud of him. Only twenty-four years old and big men from my father's ministry were asking him to do this for them. I told him charge these fat things more and he said he would buy them better cars. He said he would buy two Oldsmobiles. Do you know that automobile kind?

The next time he came home it was with three of these cars and my mother, oh my mother, she was afraid. She said, 'Petya, you must stop this. People are going to gossip about you. It could be serious. Maybe they are watching you right now.' He said it was legal and he paid his taxes and got his documents and he paid the necessary amounts of money . . . these things we say is *blat*. Kind of wrong but everyone does it. Give me help, I will give you help.

Then my brother got very, very smart. Anya who is his girlfriend and is now his wife, she told him, 'Listen, my lover,' she told me she said, 'do it once more. Bring home three cars and I will arrange for them to be sold to people in my ministry, the top guys, far away. In another city.' Maybe Kiev, and Yuri said yes, to Kiev. What did he do? I'll tell you, he sold them here in Kiev and for a lot more money. Odessa is a small city, not much big, but Kiev has all the big guys.

And then Anya was getting scared and she came to me and said, 'Petya must stop this. I am afraid for him and I don't like my lover being away all the time. Tell him to stop. Besides, I have had three abortions because I do not want to have our children and bring them up myself and I have to work and who

would look after the babies? I want to do that myself.' I told
her she was right and I went to my brother and I told him our
mother wanted him to stop and Anya did and he said he would.
One more trip, he said. One more.

You know what that stupid one did? He brought back two
more, a big Oldsmobile, a 1979 one. Yi! What a beauty. *Da, da,
da.* And a little car, a sportie, he called it. Red and little. Very,
very fast and he sold it to a rich man who made his money in
bad things. He was from Georgia, where all the thieves live.

When the man drove away in this sportie, that was the day
my brother quit his job. He went down to the bosses and said,
'No more for me. I'm getting married. Get another engineer.'
He came home and that night we had a drinking party of it
with cakes, too, and the Scotch whiskey he always brought
home, and there were toasts and then my cousin Andrei got up
and said, 'To the richest man in Odessa District!' Everybody
raised glasses and smiled and my mother said, 'If the militia
comes, what good is money?' And my brother said, 'To grease
them. They like money, too.'

Now he is here in Kiev and lives with his wife and children
and the ocean and the ships are far, far away, and you know
what I mean. I am saying, my brother was smart. The next
time some bureaucratic guy might have got jealous and said
he would get him and that would have been bad. The Ukrainian people, we are a good bunch of guys. Everybody likes us.
But with these Russians in here in big jobs, you have to be
careful.

So now, it would please me to tell you what my brother does.
He has a nice apartment, three rooms, two kids. Just enough.
And he drives a taxi. He has all the money he ever will need
and he likes to talk to people. Maybe he is in the money
exchange for tourists, but I don't know. He has a good life
driving a taxi and he is his own boss. And thank you for listening. My brother is the story of the big success of our family and
we . . . my mother is the one who is the most proud of him.
The way we of this country think, that is the best. Her son did
not have to go to war and now he is a man of peace and has his
taxi and is the owner of many, many thousands of rubles and
he is very happy.

Some guy doesn't know him and asks, 'You, guy, where you
get all this money?' And my brother says, 'One day a little bird

flies down on my shoulder and tells me how I can get lucky.'
Then he laughs. Nobody is like my brother."

❧ The Old Babushkas

Why are the street sweepers old women? And why are there
so many sweeping the streets of the major cities when the
people are so conscious of littering? Is there a fine for littering?
Yes, but has anyone been fined? My guide did not know.

I remember one old woman with the standard broom, a pole
with a bundle of sticks tied to the end, sweeping in rush-hour
pedestrian traffic, making strong strokes, not caring if she
bashed people's ankles. Pedestrians saw the broom slashing at
them and made a nimble skip. I was standing beside a building
as she advanced, head down, giving it her best shot. Would I
be swatted? Of course. Her next swipe came right at me and
I jumped, she grinned, showing a mouthful of gold teeth, and,
for good measure, took another swipe and another. A game
she was playing? Her protest against the system personified
by these well-dressed shoppers and office workers while she,
such a hard worker, was reduced to sweeping streets for a living? Was she one of the city of Kiev's pariahs? Reduced to such
menial work, for pitiful pay? I asked my guide.

"No, she probably has a little apartment somewhere, with
a husband, and they have pensions and they live well enough.
She probably wants to do it, else she wouldn't be doing it.
She's probably worked hard all her life and she doesn't know
what to do with her time. It is hard for old people to retire.
Our women, they can retire at fifty-five, but who wants to
retire then? Yes, someday they must retire, but there are
always ways. They like to beat the system, and you see it here.
You see, she might only work a few hours. For a few more
rubles a week, she might have to start working at seven in
the morning, but when she is finished she can sit in a canteen
for a couple of hours and talk with other old women. This is
part of her day.

Maybe she goes shopping. She will know where things are for sale. She has heard of a store where there is meat. Maybe fish. A bagful of candies. Toys, little wooden things which somebody carves and sells and makes a little more. A store where they are selling a new book or a new supply of spoons have come. She can stand in queue and get these goodies. She may know where vodka is being sold, and she'll buy a bottle and make five or six rubles when she sells it again. If her neighbour wants meat, she can sell it to her for a bit more. She can buy two kilos of mandarins or grapes for 8 rubles. She'll take those. People come home at night to her street, she'll ask them if they want to buy. Of course they want to buy.

Everybody has money, but if they work, how can they get to the stores where things are for sale? You must think about these things. But here is this old babushka and what she buys for 70 kopeks she sells for a ruble. I'm not saying all of them do it. No, no, no. Some of them do it and they make a good thing of this kind of business. You see, they are smart and clever, these old women. They have lived through a lot and they have had hard times. They do these things and nobody can say no to them. It is their business what they do with their money. They earned it. That old woman who tried three or four times to hit you with her broom. Now, take her.

She gets 120 rubles for her pension. I think that is it. She has had a hard life and the Soviet people owe it to her. She produced sons who may be dying in the war. She has her problems. Then she may get 60 rubles for sweeping. This is the socialist way, I think, of saying, 'Babushka, 120 rubles in pension is not enough, but if you want to work for more, you can sweep.' Now she has 180 rubles and that is a very good wage and look, she is out with all the people. If she is like I told you, she can make more. Maybe 100 rubles more, if she can find good meat and things and can sell them. And her husband, the old man. He sits in front of the television and watches the foolish things or he reads a book and people like you say, 'Oh, that poor old woman, sweeping streets.' Go, my friend, and ask her. She is laughing. I know that. She doesn't care about our new *glasnost* and *perestroika*.

There is nothing new to her about that. She has heard it before. She doesn't care about cost accounting and how business will change and what factory is behind on its quota and what factory is ahead and everybody is getting a bonus. Our Gorbachev doesn't mean anything to her, not that old woman. She got her gold teeth, like you say she had, long before he came along. She knows of the days of Stalin, and if you ask about him, she'll just spit and say, 'I know all about that. He was a bad one.'

But do you know what else that old babushka with the broom will say? Please believe. I am sure of it. She will say, 'We could do with the kind of him again.'"

☙ *"Grain Is Gold"*

"There is in us a great yearning to survive, and that is why I decided when I was a young man that I would become an expert in agriculture. It was not a decision I made without much thought. My mother wanted me to be a doctor and my father thought to be an engineering scientist and discovering new products, that would bring great honour to our family.

These were very hard times for my mother and family. It was in 1948 and our country was in a terrible position. People were starving and there was a great deal of discontent and people did not know what to do. There were nine in our family and my mother had been, well, she had been in a mental hospital because of great grief. I was the youngest. I was nineteen then and we had been moved when it was the time when the Germans came and we went to a safe village far to the east of Moscow. There were my three sisters, and five boys.

My brother Ilya was in the front lines when the Nazi Germans rushed across the frontier and his unit was killed. Another brother was a lieutenant in a tank battalion and he was killed in the defence of Stalingrad, which was a long battle and made the Germans know they could not defeat Russia because they could not get to the oilfields of the Caucasus. The next brother to die was Semyon and he was killed in the defence of Estonia when this was in 1944. Every time my mother got the news her heart sank lower and lower and my father was working in the arms factory for twelve hours a day and he could not comfort her. My other brother had a shrunken arm and he could not serve in our military force and he worked in a clothing factory making uniforms for our soldiers. This is what my sisters did, too; they were older than I was. Then there came a time when my mother could not work and the authorities said she should stay home and feed us. They also gave us six other workers to feed in our house and they slept in a shed. The authorities gave us food for my mother to cook and my mother was cooking and doing the washing for thirteen people and this was harder work than being in a factory.

No, there were twelve people because I was usually away. I was thirteen and this was in 1942 and boys of my grade in school had to work for farms to grow food to feed the people and the soldiers, and it was then that I became in love with the land. Then it became my dream to become an agricultural engineer and at the state farm where I worked, the director was a kind man and he told me all he could. He could see I was developing to be a farming engineer and he gave me his books to read and would talk to us boys for many hours.

I will go over all those years when I was a student and then I went to another institute and many places they sent me. To the state and collective farms and I was to tell them how they could produce better and more scientific crops.

It was a happy time for my team of seven assistants, and for the first few years I was an assistant . . . grounds, I mean soils and then the plants, and I spent the wintertime in germination laboratory, and then I became the top of the assistants and then the head man on the team. There were all these times, great preparations to send teams to America and Canada and Argentina and we were taught English language ways. It was very pleasing as they gave us good instructions in the winters in pleasant places where it was not cold and I soon was able to speak English quite good, but although I practised my English a great amount, I never was selected to go to America. They said I did not belong to the party. Yes, I did not, but that was an excuse. They were not sending anyone.

We were living in a hard and severe land. There were food shortages and everything was rationed. My brother, he lived with us in a two-bedroom apartment in Moscow . . . an old building and cold, and with our riches of coal and the great promises of more and more and nobody would starve or be cold any more, it was a very cold time. On a birthday, a feast would be vodka and beets and onions and sausages and bread and more vodka, always lots of vodka, and my friends would get drunk and we would ask, 'What is wrong?' That was a feast in Moscow or Leningrad or any big city. Sausages. Sometimes none.

Many long years ago, and I am coming up in five years to my retirement and I ask myself, what have I and my colleagues done? Why is it like this? Why do we think that the weather is not a part of the great plan of ours? And, of course, when we fall short on our projects, we are blamed. The railways are not blamed. The departments who fix the road, how can we get our trucks over those roads and to the central silos and storage and the holes in the road are so bad that the trucks break down. This truck pulls that truck and both are full of potatoes or cabbages and then both are broken down. There is great leakage of wheat in the combines. Now, I will tell you this. There is up to one-fifth leakage in harvesting grain, and if we could build these machines which would not lose the grain, we would not have shortages.

The whole system is wrong. It must be fixed. It has been wrong for forty years and it is wrong for the next thirty years if we don't do something. A new system. Directed from the district. Not from Moscow, not from some far away. The sadness of it all. The years we have lost. The stupidity of the system. We know it is bad. The world knows it is bad. Nothing is ever done.

Yes, life goes on in the fields and on the big farms now. The seasons and the soil and the rain and the sun and everyone hopes and looks at the sky every morning. Will it be good? But in The System now, there is not much hope. If the peasant digs in the soil and the plant comes up and there is a tiny harvest, he should get more than he does for that labour and love. This is what farming is about. Now, there is nothing but there is a lot of cheating and underground market. Let it be in the open. Free and legal. Make it justice for all. Changes have to come and they should come step by step. The worker and his wife, they should know that their labour is worth more than the neighbour's labour if this fellow is drunk or sick all the time. Socialism is the true spirit but it is not enough on the farms. More must be done.

The farmer says, 'Who is my superior? Where is my boss? Has he seen how well I worked this season? Did he see how I saved the collective thousands of rubles by doing this a different way? Was I not the best mechanic of all the mechanics?' He can only look towards Moscow where his boss is. His boss does not know him. His boss knows what a tractor looks like, but can he run it? No, he does not have to, but it might be better if he could. He would feel for them. How can this boss so far way in Moscow make the decisions that affect the peasant man's life and also the farm and dozens of others, and that means the nation itself? That is why so many bad decisions are made and carried out, and the directors of the farm and the workers, they know the plans will not work. You can't glue wood with paint.

There is only one truth for us: 'The people must be fed.'

Our farmers, they love their land. The soil, it has always been rich and deep, the black soil of the Ukraine. In the spring the seeds were planted by the women, this way, that way, the hand throwing the seeds. Later it was the sickle, the harvest of the grain. Not that I remember. My mother does. The big machines came later. Before that it was horses.

Grain is gold. The grain of gold. Wheat, it should be our saviour like Christ in this country, the Ukraine. We can't be efficient because they won't give us the machines and the fertilizer. They say, we have twelve huge factories making fertilizer. Then where is the fertilizer? Nobody says the factory didn't make the quota because there was no foreign exchange to buy the ingredients from Turkey. Maybe there is only four factories. Nobody knows anything. Ever since I was a little boy, forty-four years ago, nobody tells us anything.

They say the bureaucrats, they will be gone. Nine million of them. 'Do not make fun of this idea,' my wife says. 'It will happen.' It will happen when the Volga runs backward. When the Black Sea turns red. When Odessa becomes a city in the sky. The big man says, 'Discharge nine million bureaucrats.' The thirty million bureaucrats laugh and smile and say, 'Yes, but who will we fire?' So, it will not come to be. Men don't fire themselves. That is the first law of government.

Grain is the golden plant and socialism killed it. The Ukraine, we have our great factories and our industry, but that is not the true Ukraine. The people are of the soil. They know what happened to them. There will be writing in the journals soon about it. The Russian rule. The foot of steel and iron on their necks. The Baltic countries. Watch. The fingers of freedom are coming out of their hiding places and reaching for the necks of the Socialists, and I mean the Russians.

Communism is not the answer for our terrible problems. Socialism is not, because that is what they say we have. It doesn't work. Every man wants to come home to eat in his own house on ten or two hectares of his land and he wants to eat pork he got from his own pig, potatoes from his land, and beer from his own barley. They took it all away from us and now it must be given back to us. The people are going to demand it.

Our friend Gorbachev knows this. He is Ukrainian. Born right off to the west of us here. A good man. Clever. He knows this. We put our hope in him, but the peoples cannot wait too long. They know they cannot have all of their dreams now, but they want them soon. They will not be frustrated much longer. They have been told lies too long, and these lies were always told to us by the Russians. It is very sad.

There is so much to do. My grandfather lived when the revolution came. My brothers were killed in the war. I have my dreams that it will be good for my daughter and my son. For me, how much longer have I got to live? Fifteen years, if we don't die of puffiness, all bread and no meat and vegetables. They say, how can you starve on a farm? You can't. But you can starve of starvation of the good things for the soul, that is true, and we are starving.

It all must change. I don't know how, but it must."

❧ Then There Was Olga

Then there was Olga. Comic relief, I suppose, but to the Ukrainians dining in the Hotel Rus she must have been something from another planet.

I had been told to make a reservation in the dining room, which I did for seven o'clock through the Intourist bureau in the lobby. When I arrived, the maître d' scanned his reservation list, which had about four names on it, hesitated, gave the almost empty room a look, and then, reluctantly, picked up a menu and guided me to a table. The time was 7:05 P.M.

I looked around the room, bored, and counted the tables and besides my lonely self, there was a party of about sixteen people behind me. There were white flowers on their table and the celebration was roaring along. A family affair, I judged, because they ranged from grandmother to children.

At 7:20 – one learns to tick off the minutes and hours in the Soviet Union, especially when in restaurants – one of the celebrants at the next table brought over a brimming goblet of wine. This was more like it. I saluted the party and smiled thanks. I would dearly have liked to be invited to their table. Travel is lonely.

Then I counted the waiters. There were nine of them, standing at their stations with napkins folded over their arms, but none seemed to be mine.

The maître d' had disappeared, and groups of people were piling up at the reservation desk. Finally he reappeared, probably counting on the growing frustration of the two dozen waiting people for his own gain. He would ask a name, scan his sheets, still as empty as ever, and purse his lips, tap his forehead with a pencil, probably thinking, "There doesn't look like any tip coming from this pair," and, reluctantly, it seemed, he would lead them to a table. That broke the deadlock. Perhaps it wouldn't have happened in Moscow but it did in Kiev because Ukrainians are not Russians. The dam burst and everybody headed for tables. Pell-mell.

Now it was 7:40 and a waitress appeared. I do not know what happened to the cluster of waiters who had been hovering. I pointed to a meat dish, a salad, and ice cream and coffee and flipped to the back of the huge menu and ordered a beer. Ukrainian beer is very good, if you can find a place that sells it.

Just as the beer arrived, so did a gaggle of German geese, tourists all matched in age, size, weight, dress, haircuts, and hairdos. They were ushered to a long table at the back where they would be virtually out of sight, but not out of mind. Every time I saw German tourists on a tour, I could never understand why they were treated so deferentially. The last of the big-time tourist spenders? The scourges of Russia five decades earlier . . .

The band arrived. I want to tell you about Russian dining-room bands. They are hired by the state, and therefore there is very little incentive to play well, and they don't. But they play loud and their sound equipment comes from Yamaha in Japan which makes the highest-quality electronic sound equipment, at electrifying prices, which the state pays. It seems a truism that the diner must be blasted off his chair, across the room, and out the door. Soviet bands play rock, hard rock, metal rock, so loud that it is impossible to carry on a conversation and, indeed, to tell whether they are even playing written music.

I doubt if one of these bands would survive in Britain or North America, but they did have a singer, a tall, beautiful girl with mannerisms so haughty one felt almost intimidated. The effect was spoiled, however, by the fact she had a piece of paper in her hand and was reading the lyrics and belting them out. Even so, I could not tell whether she sang Russian, French, German, or English.

But the remarkable thing was that the diners danced to this blasting and ear-piercing sound, and it was the way they danced that intrigued me. Some did the waltz. Others went for the foxtrot. This is 1940s and 1920s stuff. Some, I swear, were jitterbugging, and you have to be at least sixty to remember that. Some jived. Others just danced the way the kids do today. Women danced with women. Three girls would dance in a triangle, or two women and a man. Some danced by themselves, and they were the best, performing amazingly intricate steps, defying the laws of gravity with their sweeping and dipping. No man danced with another man, but partners exchanged with each other, and all the while the music shook the chandeliers.

And then Olga arrived – with a rush! Suddenly she and her partner were sitting at my table. Fine, and she spoke English.

Heavy accent and all, but English, and she snapped out an order in Ukrainian to a passing waitress – I was still waiting – and in five minutes there were three bottles of champagne and four dishes of ice cream on the table.

Only then did she ask if I minded their sitting with me, and I said no, of course not. Anyone who spoke English was a friend of mine. She introduced me to Stanley. Short for Stanislaus? He was an engineer. Now here's where the situation gets a little weird. She and Stan, twenty-five years ago, had been very good friends.

"No, not lovers," she emphasized. "You know, just drink and fuck."

Okay, and she was hazy on this but she had gone to Australia (pronounced "Euztrawlye") and then wound up in Los Angeles, where she had started a massage parlour. Now she owned several and was doing very, very well. Everybody who was anybody came to her massage parlours, she said, and rubbed her thumb and forefinger – money. She was loud and rude and brassy and overdressed and fattish and crude, but very likeable. Perhaps one might say, very Los Angelese.

Then the uproar of blasting sound began again, and she yanked the silent man to his feet and onto the tiny floor, and this woman could dance! Like a kid of seventeen who had done a lot of practising. The swarming floor had never seen anybody like Olga. Her wild and high-flying antics forced the other dancers to the sides where they formed a ring around the pair. In her tight black leather skirt and silk blouse with its overflowing bosom, Olga was a sight to behold. Stan, for that matter, got into the swing of it quickly and was a good partner. Not half as good as Olga, but he wasn't letting the Kiev side down either. When they came back she was huffing and puffing and she downed a glass of champagne. Bottoms up. So did Stan. They finished off bottle number one.

She said, "Ah, that was good. And it is so good to be back home, to see my mother and my sister. I live in this hotel; for two weeks I have been here. I see them every day. When I come, I bring them two big suitcases just full, full, full of linens and underwear and all the nice things I can think of. It costs me a lot but I think they live so poorly. But they don't need them. They have a warm and nice little apartment and they have lots of money. My mother has two pensions, you see. My father was an officer, killed by those Germans. My sister is a manager in a big store. So I say, 'Okay, if you don't want these things, what will you do with them?' They tell me they will sell everything to their friends and people, for lots of money. I give them lots of American dollars anyway, so now they are richer than ever."

The second dish of ice cream was gone and half the other bottle, and the music began hammering and away they went, and she's the Whirling Dervish of the Hotel Rus that night. Suddenly, the band broke into a Ukrainian folk-song. Snap, the heaving mass of dancers formed themselves, as if from long practice, into circles and revolved and sang. A very moving sight. Dancing and singing to a time long past, a past with no Soviet domination, no Soviet ways. Just the old ways. I was very touched by it.

My dinner had arrived, a salad of tomatoes and cucumbers as always, and a hamburger patty with a fried egg on top – my usual meaty eggs benedict – french-fried potatoes, beans. After what I had eaten in other restaurants, it all seemed quite North American.

By now Olga was crying. "Oh, I do not want to go home. I want to stay here. This is my home. Where I was born. I could stay here forever. Why can't I stay?"

I said something to the effect that she wouldn't last a month here living in the Soviet state, and after another swig of champagne – now into the third bottle – she admitted it was so.

"No, you are right. I have my business, all my shops. I have to look after them. All of them. What would I do? What can I do? You must tell me."

I said that would be impossible; I didn't even know her. I even doubted that she was telling me the truth.

Then she said, "And my plane leaves tomorrow morning and then I will be in L.A. tomorrow night and all this, my lover, my mother, they will all be gone. Behind. I will be there and they will be here. I don't want to go."

I could have asked her why she was living it up, dancing and drinking, the night before she was to leave her mother and sister, but I did not. I did say, "And who is Stanley?"

More sobbing, and she said, "He is my old friend. Twenty-five years ago when I had to leave my country" (ah-ha! I had suspected as much) "he and I were lovers. Drink and fuck, but he was a damn good man. I am in Kiev for two weeks and on the street I see him today. This afternoon. We recognize each other right away. He is the same, just look at him and look at me. I am not the pretty girl I was then. That's what my life in the States has done for me. So we spend the afternoon together, and he is as good a man as ever. Oh yes, I remember! And now he has to go soon. That is why the champagne. He has to be home to his wife and daughter by eleven o'clock. That is the last I will see of him, ever."

I took a good hard look at this man. Maybe fifty-five, stolid, strong of face, wearing a suit, the usual brown shirt and rust tie, the typical Soviet bureaucratic type, the nameless face one sees on a hundred streets, and yet this man had aroused this plump–dare I say fat–woman to heights of passion and despair.

Suddenly a rush of young couples flooded onto the dance floor. I had wondered why there was such a jam on the tiny floor when so few people were dining. Now all was explained. When the music began, about two dozen couples waiting in the lobby hurried past two waiters barricading the entrance and each man handed a bill to a waiter. Probably a ruble. The waiter's hands were stuffed with bills and the maître d' stood by.

These well-dressed couples didn't want to sit and eat and drink, but if they had they could have danced for nothing. They preferred to pay a ruble for ten minutes of dancing and then clear out. At a ruble a roundelay, it probably was cheaper. But the way the band was blasting through the routines, probably four an hour, three hours of dancing would be 12 rubles, very expensive.

I wondered how the division of the spoils went. The maître d' would take the largest cut because he had the most to lose. The waiters would share and so would the band. Maybe 15 rubles extra per worker per night. When the daily wage was probably about 6 rubles, that wasn't to be sneezed at.

The crash of metallic sound broke through my calculations, and there was the silent one being dragged to the floor. I thought, "He's not going to be much good in the two hours they have left to them," but there she was, jiving, jitterbugging, rock-'n'-rolling, making everyone else on the crowded floor look like statues, jiggling, bouncing, flying, exploding.

And now I sensed that the crowd was resentful of her. Who is this strange creature – obviously American and perhaps Jewish–which she was. But she was oblivious to it all, dancing the last few hours away with her lover of long ago who appeared to have the emotions of a fish, although underneath I sensed he was just as she said: "a damn good man."

When she came back she said, "And before I go, I will slip some American 10-dollar bills into his pocket. He will never know until I have gone. He will know what to do with them. I brought lots of money and now I want to spend it on him. But I don't want to leave him." Again the sobbing. I thought, "Does he think this woman is as crazy as I think she is?" Probably so. He seemed like a man caught up in a situation far beyond his control.

I had finished my meal and my litre of beer, and I felt it was time to leave these lovers alone and I reached over and shook his hand, patted her arm. At that moment the four musicians let forth with a gargantua of sound and she didn't even acknowledge my goodbye, for there she was, grabbing the bewildered engineer by the hand, and as I walked out the door, there she was, bosom bouncing, legs flashing, wilder than ever, dancing to her own tune, dancing the night away.

FIVE

Back in The Centre

❀

"That Old Woman Had Money"... "Call Me Rutha"... Dead
Somewhere in Afghanistan

I am back in The Centre before starting another leg of my
journey. Once more I explore the city, riding a few stops on
the subway, then getting out and walking in different neigh-
bourhoods. The apartment blocks I pass are old, before the
Second World War. Maybe older, who knows? I pass long
queues of people – old women mostly – patiently waiting to
buy the greasy sausages they'll cook for supper that night.

I find a market. It's thronged with people out shopping for
the fresh vegetables that farm folk bring in from the country
on weekends. Women paw through racks of clothing; vendors
hawk their wares – flowers, ice cream, bright scarves. No one
pays any attention to me, although I am told they are very
aware of the stranger in their midst. But in a nearby café a
woman sits down at my table and starts a lively conversation
with me. I ask her why she decided to join me. "You have the
right kind of face" is her answer.

Back in the hotel lobby, a teacher asks if I have any books to sell. No! Too bad. On the street outside a student has just asked me to send him English textbooks: "They are necessary to my future," he explains. Everyone wants to buy English-language books! I could have made a fortune by bringing paperback novels and Western fashion magazines with me.

No matter, they'll practise their English on me anyway. I buy the coffee, they buy the cakes, and we talk.

✿ "That Old Woman Had Money"

"I must tell you now that I have seen your face I trust you. It was very hard, you understand, when my husband said he had met you and he would bring you for a little supper. Jann is that kind of man. He is Estonian, but you must understand, he was brought here as a baby after the war, but asking a foreigner to his home, that is Jann. He is still an Estonian, he says, and he wants to know so much about the world.

When he gets back from visiting a friend [he had gone to borrow a bottle of vodka], he will ask you many questions. But now we will have tea and I will show you our new apartment. This new district, I think it only has about 10,000 people, but someday, when the underground subway comes, then more of the district will be built up and there will be 200,000 people. I like to think it would be a city itself with shops and stores and everything that goes with a city. Now, it is an hour and a half for me to get into the downtown parts of Moscow to do shopping.

In this part of our new district we have a laundry and the women do our sheets and blankets and that costs us one ruble a month. It is four days to get it done, so we must have another group of bedclothes, so when I am downtown in The Centre I always look for these things because I will be able to sell them to my neighbours. I do the same for pots and pans and dishes. They cannot get away because they must work. Every neighbour I know works but I have this hand with the arthritis, so I am a one-handed worker and there are no jobs. I can make money going and buying for neighbours. I know where the shops are. I can get meat. Sausage, yes. Fruit, these things come from other regions, and vegetables, my cousin has a little garden and we buy them from her. She has two dachas. She grows them there.

Yes, I was a teacher. I was for seven years and then I had my first baby. Then I had another baby, he was a boy. Alexei. The girl is Kirini and she was named after my husband's old aunt who lived with us. This old woman was always angry with me. She thought I was too young and gay but she was an old woman. Old women still think of old ways. My husband Jann said we would name the first girl after her and then we would see. That old woman had money. She had jewels and many other things and she would give one to my husband and say to sell it. It would be a ring, you see, or a bracelet and my husband would take it to his director at the works plant where they made machinery for ships. The director was rich and he would give my husband 500 rubles.

This old woman, the aunt, she died and we took her body back to the little village in her home country, Estonia, and she was buried there. We had a priest of her faith and two policemen stood at the gates and watched us. I thought this is very, very unusual. The militia at a funeral. Who was this woman? She was a nobody, just an old woman, but her husband had been in the Estonian war and he was dead, but he had battled against the Soviet Union and the militia. My husband said they wanted to know who was at the funeral. There was nobody, only nine people. She had no friends. Just a few neighbours from her district, the Old Town, came. My husband went and told them she was dead and they came for the respect they could give to her soul.

It was about six months later, and this was nine years ago, and my husband got a letter saying he must come to Tallinn. He phoned the man who wrote the letter in the state office and the man said, 'Come, we have good news for you.' My husband got the travel documents and he went and the man said to go to this warehouse and there would be some business for him. My husband took the bus and when he got there they

said, 'Where is your truck? We have your aunt's possessions.'
This was a surprise. There were boxes, big wooded boxes of
things which had belonged to my aunt and I must explain.

You see, my husband had come to Moscow when he was a
baby, a little boy of three. Good people had taken him in.
When he found he had an aunt, that was when he brought her
to live in our flat. It was very crowded and she was a nasty
woman and she never said she had possessions in Estonia.
Never once. Just the rings and jewels and bracelets and beautiful amber things. These were sold because we had to buy
things on the underground market.

Now here were all these things. Beautiful furniture from
days of a long time ago and chairs and sofas and, you know
these words, they are strange to me. Yes, antiques. From a
hundred years ago. He could not bring them with him and he
didn't know what to do. What was he to do? Poor man. Just
a bookkeeper and no wits for these kinds of problem. The manager of the warehouse said he would sell them for him and he
phoned some Soviet officials who were in charge of that warehouse. Next afternoon they came, colonels and more important than that. We will give you this much for that, this
wonderful table. You can see how it goes. An ignorant man
and afraid and then the bureaucrats left. They would come
tomorrow. The manager told him, 'Let me think about this.
If you give me this table, the one the colonel wanted, I will
phone a friend and he will come tonight and look at the possessions.' The man came and they drank vodka and had some
good sausages and bread and pickles and then the man looked
at what there was. He walked around, my husband said, and
his heart was shaking inside and the man said, 'We will give
you 30,000 rubles and my friend gets the table for free and you
go, and come back in the morning and the money will be ready
to take home with you.' This is a true story I am telling you.
This is the story that changed our lives.

And so it happened. My husband took the money and came
back and I fell down. I didn't, but I nearly did. I said, 'What
can we do with this?' He said we would do what we wanted
with it and he showed me the paper. It was a sale. It was honest. It was a legal document. I said 30,000 is good, more than
we can ever hope to save, and what will that man get for it
when he sells it to the officers? This is where the greed entered

my heart and I was afraid. My husband told me that when the manager of the building drove him to the airport he told him the money would come to 60,000 in selling these wonderful old things of furniture.

So that is how we got this flat. We bought it and nobody said, 'Where did you get 11,000 rubles?' We would have said our old aunt died. It is ours. She made our lives miserable and spoiled the children and we earned this money. Nobody asked. The flat was 9,000 but we paid another 2,000 to the boss and we went to the head of the apartment line. Bless this aunt, you will say. I say no. We earned it looking after her miserable needs. That old woman, she was a curse to us. And so that is the story ended.

It is a happiness story. It should be in a children's picture book that if you do things that are good for somebody who does not even care, then you will be rewarded. We were rewarded because my husband was the only relative left. The others were killed by the Germans when they took them away and drowned them in those two big ships. A very bad story. 'Come, fellow, you come, and your wife, come, and the two children, sorry, fellow, but orders are orders. Your ship to your new home is waiting.' They sank the two ships and everyone drowned. That was the Germans for you and today in Estonia they love the Germans more than the Russians. They say, 'One day we will get our independence and then the Germans will help us.'

Jann escaped because of this other family that took him and now they are dead. We would have given them something from our reward, but they were dead. Some of those books, in the shelf, my husband made that shelf with wood he found by the railway track on a picnic in the country. We brought it home and some of those books, they were the ones they brought from Estonia in the war. Running, the war was every-where around them, and that family brought books. We hon-our those books. Dickens, Thackeray. Seton, the animal writer.

After, my husband said you will not have to work any more and we will have more children. My poor husband. Everyone knows but him. I said yes, he was my husband . . . But when I knew I was with a baby, I would have abortion. I had four of them and he didn't know. Many husbands don't know, but

I did not want more children. The two I loved, they were
enough. Many of my friends have abortions. The twentieth
week, that is the latest. I have mine always about the four-
teenth week when there is nothing in there but a little sack
of something. In the morning, all clean, good nurses and doctors, and then you lie down for two hours and they give you
a needle of something and four pills and you take them with
some juice, even potato juice which is good with sugar, and
in the morning you tell your husband you are sick and stay
in bed. In the afternoon you get up and cook a big meal and
welcome your husband home. This is the way I do it. Some
wine and laughing and talking about the children and when
we will buy a dacha . . . Never.

Oh, the abortion. No, there is nothing to it. Some women
cry. Some say, 'I should not have done it.' I say to them, 'It is
better to give plenty of love and good things to two than have
six children and you starve in the winter when you can't even
buy potatoes and herring.' This is the way our leaders want
it. There are too many people in our country now. We cannot
feed them all. Nobody starves but they can't be fed. It is a very
large problem. I do not want to talk about it.

I feel very sorry when I have abortion, but I have not had
one for many years now. I am too old. But it makes me feel
sad. Those poor babies. But even for us before we got the
money for the things and furniture in Estonia, it was very hard
for us to raise two children. They need so much. We get much
from the state, our government, but it is still very difficult.

Our government is generous. A mother gets a year if she
wants to be off work when the baby comes. This is at nearly
the same pay as she would get in the department or the factory. There is always the problem of too many children and
no good place to live. This is why there are abortions, so many.
So many. Two is fine. A boy and a girl. Every Russian father
wants one boy. When the boy is born there is a great party, a
big one. People rejoice. Oh, Jann, you have a son. Let us drink
some more that he will become an important man. These are
big parties.

In the regions and the industrial cities far away it is different. Five children, six, all in one small apartment. Sometimes
the mother goes crazy. The father, he drinks. There are no
places for the children. This is one of our problems. We have

so many. Our government does a good job, clinics, doctors, kind nurses who come to the apartment, but it is very hard. My heart is for those poor women.

The young girls, too. They are not told about this in school. The instruction is not good. They go out in the streets to get out of the little apartment and things happen to them out there. We have always been a passionate people. Very passionate. We want to show our love. Then there is a baby and the girl is only fourteen. I have seen it. Sixteen, seventeen, what does a girl do with a baby when she is sixteen? What is it like in your country? My daughter, if she came to Jann and me, but no, she would come to me, and she said she was pregnant I would take her to the clinic. Sixteen. So sad.

Perestroika, you know the word. On 'Vreyma' every night they talk about it. It is not such a thing for us. I don't understand it. I think *perestroika* is about machines and factories and more meat in the stores and medicine and soap and film for my husband's camera. Tires, too. Our friends have cars and they are old and they want tires. Then *perestroika* will bring them automobile tires.

There are all these stories in the newspaper. There are no good things in the stores. Yes, there are not. There are shortages. But if you go every day, just over there behind the administration building, that is the store and if you go there you can find things. You keep trying. Or to the market on Sunday when the farmers come with their trucks. Whole pigs, and they cut the pieces right off. The man with the axe, hit, hit, and it is a perfect piece. You ask and he does it. Four kilograms and he asks you why you want so much. 'You are too pretty a lady to have eight children for four kilograms.' I say, 'Your prices are too high, you farm robber, so I will sell two of these four kilograms to my neighbours and then your pig meat won't cost me so much.' This is true. I like to talk this way to the farm men and their women. They have . . . very funny people, like, 'Hey, pretty lady, come over here and buy this melon, buy this bunch of flowers,' or 'Pretty lady, this jacket is just your size. Your husband will want to have you right away.' That is the way they talk, they yell these things. Ice cream, everybody has ice cream. That is not our word. It is yours. Our ices are the best in the world. Do you think so? Like our beautiful girls. Thank you. Clothes are too expensive. I do not know how these girls can buy them. They are only secretaries and assistants in shops. Oh, I do know. They have ways. Maybe a rich boy-friend, not the boy they will marry but another.

I am talking so much and where is my husband? He wanted to talk to you. He is a great friend of your Mr. Churchill. I know, yes, he is dead but he honours him. We have a picture of him. He has been delayed. Maybe he could not find his friend to get the vodka. Just a tiny drink for me and you and my husband can drink the rest. A litre is not so much, but you shouldn't drive. Our people go to jail for drinking. The militia are very strong against drinking. We have jokes about it. An accident, we see it and we say, 'Two drunken Bulgarians.'

My husband, he loves his home in Estonia. We have gone there. There is a lot of land and only a few people and they are different. They like my husband but I do not think they like me. They see him and they ask him if he is of their people and he says yes. His blond hair, I think. He wants to go there but not for always. Long visits. He says Estonia is the most educated of all the republics. Then Lithuania and then Latvia. He knows all these things. He works for one of the departments in the ministry of culture and he gets the books.

My husband says if there is trouble coming it will be in Estonia. This is what he hears at his job. There will be trouble. These Baltic people, they were their own countries for many years and then they were seized by the Soviet Union. That was in 1940. It was for protection of the Soviet Union boundaries. In the Great Patriotic War. My Jann says this is not so. It was a trick. Trickery? Hitler, the Nazis and Stalin, they took away the hope of these small countries. My husband will tell you all about it."

Alas, the husband did not come home and did not phone and she said something must have happened to him. We ate cherry tarts and part of a cake and I left. I phoned the next morning and she said he had arrived half an hour later, with a litre of vodka he'd borrowed from a friend, and was sorry he had missed me. There was no explanation why he took so long.

❦ *"Call Me Rutha"*

In Moscow, Sundays are as sluggish and dull as any Canadian city in the early 1950s and I'd spend those days riding the underground – 5 kopeks, about eleven cents Canadian. Even on Sundays the subways are jammed, and I would continually wonder, "Who are these people? Where do they come from? Where are they going? What do they do when they get there?"

I would take a train four stops – stations outside the main core are far apart – and then get off and it would be the same scene. Aged buildings, apartments everywhere, the occasional park, and I often wondered why I never saw a bunch of kids kicking around a soccer ball. Playing a game of tag. Just doing something. Anything. But no, the parks were used by strollers, families, lovers, teenagers with that looking-for-trouble nonchalance, and the policemen everywhere.

I got off at a major intersection and found a public market, with hundreds of Muscovites arriving, walking around, leaving. This was the Soviet economy at work. No state regulations. No officialdom except those prowling policemen eating their chocolate-covered ice cream bars and watching teen-age girls pawing through the long racks of clothing – jeans and blouses and sweaters.

Jeans. Yes, there are plenty of them. It became a world joke that the Soviets could not manufacture jeans and a tourist with an extra pair of jeans could sell them for astronomical sums, as much as 700 rubles for a pair of authentic Calvin Klein American jeans. How would any Russian afford a pair when the average adult wage is perhaps 200 rubles a month? So the Soviet government decided to "retool" factories, and now they make jeans. Tens of thousands a day. No jean shortages, no world laughing.

Some transplanted Georgians or Armenians had mutton chunks grilling over a barbecue but there were few takers: the Muscovite bred and born distrusts these people. In a long shed there were sides of beef hanging, whole carcasses, gutted pigs and sheep, piles of offal in trays for sale. Blood-stained butchers in their smocks could take a leg of lamb or a misshapen chunk of meat and, with one sure swing, whack off a piece exactly to the customer's order. Tables were filled with apples, small and wizened and ugly, which at first I suspected were culls. Then, I visited collective farms and saw these apples growing by the millions, so it appears that pruning and long-term cultivation are virtually an unknown art. However, here in the market they were being picked over, squeezed, commented on, and plopped into net bags for weighing. These apples in Canada would have been fed to the hogs.

In another section of the market were tables piled high with engine parts, headlights, door handles, transmission cases, steering wheels, knobs, buttons, belts, old spark-plugs, carbs, even front and back seats. Trade was brisk. These had been taken from wrecks and, I was told later, "dealers" buy them, drive to a town 200 kilometres away, and sell them for three and four times more than the price they paid.

There were no windshield wipers for sale. If there had been, everyone would have known they were stolen property. That autumn there was a nation-wide shortage of wipers and every driver removed them and locked them away when he parked. I asked why there was a shortage. Didn't every auto come off the assembly line with a set? Yes. Then why steal them if every car has them? "They are easy to steal and if there are enough stolen, then there will be a shortage soon. Isn't that so, don't you think?"

I said, "Then anyone who buys them will know he is buying stolen goods. Not so? In that case won't the police be on the alert for people selling windshield wipers?"

"Yes," was the reply, "but that's the way the system works. One has to have windshield wipers because it rains a lot sometimes."

The logic of that thinking escaped me. I gave up.

I was sitting on the rim of a cracked and defunct fountain when a Lada taxi rolled up, hopped over the narrow curb, and drove virtually into the centre of the throng. The front door opened and a very large woman got out. The two back doors opened and three very large women emerged. They could have been sisters, but all Russian women look like sisters. Perhaps that is unkind but it is the hair style, pulled back in a bun, the heavy wrinkled faces with the determination that nothing will stand in their way. A carry-over, I suppose from the war when many were tank commanders, soldiers in the artillery, bomber pilots. They do have a military quality. Their clothes are black, severe, not so much as one flash of colour. They have thick, strong legs and heavy black shoes. Remember, these women were all over sixty-five at least.

One approached and said, accusingly, "You are from America?"

With a sense almost of joy that I could talk to someone, I said, "Canada. Your arctic neighbour. You buy our wheat. We come and spend our money."

"Why are you in this marketplace for Moscow people? Is there something you want to understand about us? You won't find it here. Go to our museums. There are many in our city. There are many in this country of ours. Go to the Hermitage up there in Leningrad. You will see many important things. About our history."

I wondered where she had learned to speak English. It wasn't bad, but her belligerence was scary.

"In our war, you know the one, I was a clerk in the Soviet Embassy in London, England. I was a typist and then I was a clerk. I know Canadians. I know about all the Americans."

"Was it a good time for you?"

"That time was a very good time. I still hold to my fondest memories of that time and someday I would like to go back to it. It is sad that Mr. Churchill is dead but he was old those days. I used to see him. He drank too much but I think he was just tired. My memories of him are very happy."

What was her name? She thought a moment. "Well, you strange man, come with me. We can talk and I buy things. My name? Call me Rutha, the name they gave me when I went to England. None had our own names.

"I have come to this market with my sister and two friends and I am going to buy flowers. My husband is an invalid. Sunday when I come I buy flowers. Not in the colder times when bandits and whores from Georgia bring them, sell them for three rubles – that is for one flower. They make a fortune and spend it on good things from our stores and nobody can do a thing about them. Bandits. Cossacks. All of them. There is trouble ahead. What is that machine?"

I held up my tape recorder. No uproar. It didn't faze her, but she asked me to play back her voice and I rewound it a few seconds, punched "Play" and she heard her description of the Cossack Georgians.

"That is worthwhile little engine, valuable I would think," but she expressed no curiosity as to why I was taping her. They never did. Perhaps they just expected foreigners to be curious. She did not ask my name. Curiosity never kills their cat.

After she bought her huge carnations, wrapped in the green paper she had brought, she led me back to the decrepit fountain, settled herself, dug into her purse, and handed me a ruble note. "I will make our hospitality buying you ice cream. One for you and one for this tired old woman. My friends will be along and we must hurry. But before we go, I must buy some meat. Some of our sausage. You can't buy it in our stores and you can here. You get the ice creams and I will get the sausage. Just over there."

Then we talked. She lived in an apartment. An old one, she emphasized. From other days, she said. Meaning what? Before Lenin, she said. She was sixty-seven, she had her pension and her husband had his, plus his war disability pension. She sought for the word "amputation" and sliced at her arm. Ah, he had lost an arm. Yes, chopped off. Where? She smiled and said, "At Kursk, the great battle of our Great Patriotic War. You have heard of it?" Oh yes, a great tank battle, the place where the Germans realized they would never conquer Russia. She smiled broadly. Her teeth were gold. Yes, her husband Boris had been a young tankerman. "It has been a terrible battle; he is the great hero in our family. He got medals for saving his comrades, but so long ago. Now it is too bad. The grandchildren do not want to hear his stories. It is always the way. The young people, I don't know what is going to happen to them."

"Then you are talking about *perestroika*?"

"No, no, no. I am talking about life. This thing we have, this *perestroika*, we don't talk about it. Why should it bother old people? We not care. It is the young people who care. They should not care too much. They will not listen to the old people. Things, they are the same and they always will be. Some things different, some kinds same. I not worry. I will be dead in the cemetery. They want to live like the Americans and the English, they cannot be blamed. Young people, they are too young to know how things are in this country. I was born, my mother and father lived in a little town in the Ukraine. Then I came to Moscow and I was young and I went to the institute and

studied English. For special reasons, they told us. I learned
English and I was flown on an English bomber to England one
day in the war. Because I could do better there. You
understand?"

"I understand. Everybody had to do his duty. But your English
is good. Do you meet many people you can speak to?"

"Of course, and can't you understand? I don't talk much to
people like you, but I have my books of Dickens and Jack London and Mr. Mowat and Mr. Greene and, you know. I find
someone I can talk to. Those old women in the apartment
house, they say, 'Why do you do it? It could get you trouble.' I
have not been in trouble. Nobody bothers old woman. Maybe
thirty years ago I was younger, I could have been when we had
the cult of Stalin. You have heard of that?"

I said yes, it was well known, and she said, "You see, I knew
you would be a smart young man."

I said I was sixty-one, not much younger than she was, and
she laughed. "Yes, I can see. You are not young, but you are a
lot younger than me. You have lived in Canada. That is different. You have not lived in this city and seen what we have seen
and, okay, I will tell you. Canada is an easy place to grow. Here
it is hard, it has always been hard. Not easy for children. They
should have the nice things we old ones worked for. All the
time they are going into the *blat* [the black market] and doing
things and I say, 'No, no, no, you must not.' All they say is,
'Old times is far away and we should get all these things.' Your
magazines, they pay 20 rubles to get West German lady magazines. Where are these clothes for us? I say, 'You plant a seed
of corn. Wait, then it grows. Then.' They say, 'We can't wait.
We are tired of waiting.' It is bad. It tells my heart something
is wrong."

"What about *perestroika*?"

She smiled. "Ah, that. That is like a little bit of sun. But it
won't happen. Not when I am here. Our leader, he has the
ideas," and she tapped her head. "The big plans. Every day in
the newspaper, more ideas of his ideas. He is only one man and
can do nothing. We need a strong man. Gorbachev, why are
there so many bad jokes about him now? Because the people
know, he is ideas, plans, but same old way. We need another
Stalin. A strong man. Very strong. Like he was. A good man,

an intellectual person like our Gorbachev, he can say this idea is good, do as I tell you, work hard and everything will be good again."

"You said 'again'?"

"I mean, good like it should have been again. Not like it was. Like the great man Lenin promised. All those ideas. I am not an intellectual. I do not wear nice bracelets and work in big office and think, but he was a man. Lenin, our gracious saviour, he destroyed those Romanovs. He gave us ideas and we said with a mighty large voice, 'Yes!' Do you hear me? A mighty voice. No more torture, no more of anything that is bad. Then others. Stalin. He was good in the war, just like Mr. Churchill. But he killed people. He said everybody was his enemy. Mr. Canada, how could any man be crazy so much as that man? I ask you that sincerely and with great spirit. How? That peasant with the fat face, Khrushchev, but a good man. Brezhnev. Now, we have a new one. Maybe he can do something. I don't think so. His ideas are good but they won't work until there is steel again in his ideas. We need a man like Stalin to put these new ideas into good.

"We need *perestroika*. Even me, this old lady, I can see that. Look at the blankets I bought just three months ago. All wore out, teared, not worth 3 rubles. I paid 27, nearly, well, one-third of my pension. It is good I still read my English books, I can't say these things any other way. Give us back a Stalin to make Gorbachev, this man's plans, to make it work. A strong man. A good man. A Russian. A man with the heart of Russia in him. Big. Like a mighty statue. Let the rain and the wind fall on this statue, his head, and it will still be the same. This man Gorbachev, he is tall and strong, but we need a bigger man. Take the plans and agenda of our new leader Gorbachev and make things grow. Like the corn seed that becomes a tall one. Until then, nothing. Look at me, my friend. Listen. I say, give us a man like Lenin, his ideas and hopes for us, and a man like Gorbachev, what he is, and then put in the steel of Stalin. Then it will make our country be working again. Not just what now it is.

"This is the most wonderful, great, big, oh, how do I say it, big and wonderful country in the world. I am Ukrainian and in London I was still Ukrainian, my heart and soul, and oh, those poets of my country. But now I am Russian. My feel is Russian.

It is of the earth. How you call it, the dirt. The dirt is filled with our blood for a thousand years. Our tears. Our blood.

"Now I must go. My friends, they are getting our taxi. That white one. Why do they paint them white? Black does not get dirty. White gets dirty. It is not right, to have foreigners who are visitors think our taxis are dirty. Silly old cows they are. On the way home they will talk. 'What were you saying to that American?' The driver, he will be drunk. We gave him a small bottle of vodka to make to stay and not go away while we did our buying here. It is home brew we make in our bedroom. A little bottle. He will talk, too. It is an hour from here, he will be drunk and yell and say, 'I saw you talking to that man. What did he say? Was he a . . . ' sorry, he will use a dirty name on you. I refuse to say it. I like you. I like Americans and Canadians and people from France and Italy. I like the world.

"Goodbye, goodbye. Now, don't go back and say this old woman, Rutha as I was when I was in London, is, you know," and she tapped her head. Crazy.

Then she left, hustling off with her flowers and her Polish sausage. I thought, well, the taxi driver will ask what I talked about, but all I heard was old Rutha talking. I liked her. Merry eyes. A mouth half full of gold teeth. A left hand that slapped my knee repeatedly until it felt numb. Old clothes, but clean. A proudness about her. A dignity. A dwelling within her of a spirit that was admirable. A tough old bird.

❧ Dead Somewhere in Afghanistan

"My country can't win that war. My brother told me so. He was there, and he said every night those natives, they shoot down on them, bombs and bullets, and they knew where our boys were. People would go out of the city and tell somebody else and he would tell somebody and the Afghanis, they would know where the trucks and supplies were hidden for that one night. Boom! The bang, a bomb exploding.

My brother, he is twenty-five and a sergeant, not an officer. He would not go back there again. He wasn't hurt but many, many of his comrades were. A lot dead. They would not go on patrol at night. They say we have lost so many soldiers and pilots that we will never know how many were killed. Bombs and bullets. In the night. When the sun comes up, he said they would look and there would be nothing. Hills and mountains. They knew, of course, the enemy he was up there.

The hills are brown. The rocks are brown. These fighters, these killers, brown clothes and, you see this, too, they have brown faces. They know each other. They are brothers and cousins and friends and they have these guns, what do you call them? American rockets.

So, our soldiers and pilots and others, they can see nothing. There is all brown things out there hidden. Caves? They hide in caves in the light and when it is dark, my brother says they come right in close. They have a few captured and they get their bodies back. The guerrilla people throw the body, the bodies, on the road and our soldiers find them in the light. They have no penis. They have no hands. The stomachs are cut open and he says, this is what he says, their insides are wrapped around their neck. You know. These things inside you. Yes, intestines, that is the word. They do awful things. No eyes. No nose.

I should not be talking to you. There are police around. A policeman might come in here for coffee and he'd ask why. Just tell him, I will translate, that we are talking the hockey. Tell him you were telling me about hockey in your country. Don't say any war. No, nothing like that. You see what I mean? You cannot write about my country unless you know it. They will tell you that. So we were not talking about my country. It was your country and hockey players we were talking about. Anybody can be an informer. That is the word, is it so? Informer? My best friend could be.

My brother Eduard, I know he is a brave man. But when he comes to our home he has been on the border with his men for a year and he says, 'Pytor, here is rubles. Go get me drink.' I go to the woman on the floor down, you see. In another apartment. I say I want a litre of vodka. She says no. She don't have it. Everybody knows she makes it herself, in that tiny kitchen. I say, 'Give it to me, old woman.' I say it is for my brother who comes back from the war. Oh yah, oh yah, and she laughs and brings me a bottle in the hall and I give her some money. 'No, no, no, no,' pushing it away. She says she don't take money from soldiers. She is from Kiev, she says, and she knows about war. She says, this old woman, awfully old but pretty smart, she says she is glad the war is over for my brother. 'From me to him, for his bravery.'

Eduard, this brother, he pours me a drink, one for him, one for the lady who makes it, because she follows me. Then he drinks the rest himself. He is not drunk, not that we can see. It was the second bottle from the old woman that made him drunk. He is telling me all this and crying, yelling. Hiding his eyes like this, with his arm, like bombs are coming. The old lady says, 'Where are your medals?' and so he yells at her, 'You old cow, that is not a war for medals. I won't wear them. Let the officers wear them. Then they would be called medals for clever hiding because what they did was hide. The boys like me, they were the ones who should get them. Now I don't believe in medals. Pieces of tin. Like that old fart Brezhnev, him and his medals. He got us in this war. We call it our Vietnam.'

[Several times while in the Soviet Union I heard people refer to Afghanistan as "our Vietnam."]

This is when my brother takes up the litre and he looks at it, and he is still all right, drunk, but okay. Just loud. Waving his arms, like this, you see. Then he takes that bottle and drinks it all down and the woman, she says, 'He is finished.' I said what was this she meant. She said, 'He will die. It will kill him.' My brother said, he said this, 'I died out there with my friends. Pray for your God, old woman, for our Motherland in this fucking mess. Don't pray for me. I will be all right.'

Then he turned away and said to me, 'When Mama comes home, tell her not to wake me. I will see her in the morning before she goes to work. This day has been long enough for me already.'

Next morning, well, I am worried all night and I sleep on the floor by his bed and I hear him breathing, you know, like this. Hard. Hard. Is this the right word? Oooooaaaaaggggh. Like that. But he gets up in the morning and he is having a hard time and he says, 'Give me a little glass of vinegar,' and I do and he says he'll be better then. Then Mama says she is not going to work that day. No, she is not going. I know why. She will stay and see that Eduard would not drink vodka no more. Like he did.

That morning it is nice and we walk, a long way. Eduard, Mama, and me and then we eat. He is with plenty of money, you must understand, so we eat. Then we go to a park and we walk on the grass and then he is fine. He eats maybe ten ice creams. He says he used to dream of good Russian ice cream, and we talk. No, he is not going back to the war. He is finished with that part of his life. Now it will be easier and I am sixteen now, you see, but fifteen years old then and he says I will not have to go to the war. They don't take the kids. That is why the war is so bad. It is the good soldiers like my brother who get killed. He says the war will end in two years. That will be in 1988, next year.

We know that. Everybody knows that. We talk about it in our school. Not with the teacher around. Some boys say they would go to work in the North if they had to go. They wouldn't fight. Some will go to university because of their parents. We know our leaders made a terrible mistake because real soldiers cannot fight shadows. Shadows with American guns and rockets. So we will be like the Americans. Say, 'Look, you whole world, this war is over. All done. There is no more war.' Then we will go and there will be no more poor mothers taking primroses to the cemetery and putting them on the memorial because she has no grave for her son. He is dead somewhere in Afghanistan. Blown up. No more war. Peace, maybe, but I don't know. I will learn more about it when I get to be older and that is the time I will tell you about this part of the world business. I will write you. Goodbye. Thank you for letting me do my English with you. It is important to me. It will give me a good job."

I gave him my card, but he never wrote. I didn't expect him to.

SIX

Tbilisi: a Georgian Experience

Three Drunken Georgians ... Not One Bikini in Sight ... "In Georgia, We Are Different" ... Russian Bears and Georgian Tigers

A Georgian at dinner says to me, "If trouble comes for Gorbachev, this is where it will be." (A year and a half later, the newscasts were full of stories of riots, young marchers being beaten, killed by poison gas. My dinner companion was all too right.)

But this evening he is full of wine and song. This strong, dark Georgian, proud of his heritage, is the leader at the table, raising his glass, making toasts, recalling the history of his people in the rugged Causasus Mountains.

My guide and I drive to Gori – a perilous trip avoiding the wild Georgian drivers – to visit Stalin's birthplace. The park containing his simple peasant home and an echoing museum is deserted. The only other visitors are East Germans making a routine stop on their tour. No images of Stalin are visible in the Soviet Union, but they say that pictures of him can be found in homes – carefully put away when anyone arrives at the door. His name is still mentioned, usually in reference to

the terrible times past. But the old people say he had to do the
things he did. "We need a strong man like him."

Back in Tbilisi, I see a factory where the young Stalin
worked when he was a revolutionary, and I swear they are
still using the same tools. But no one seems to care. They drink
their wine and cognac—no vodka here—and tell how the Geor-
gian tigers will defeat the Russian bears.

❦ Three Drunken Georgians

In Georgia, I was told, there is a cult of Stalinism that
embraces all the people and his name is revered and so, on a
warm and sunny day my Russian guide Andrei and I decided
to visit Gori, the place of Stalin's birth.

Gori is thirty-five miles from the capital of Tbilisi, along a
two-lane winding road through bleak and browned hills. The
traffic was fierce, every driver trying to jockey for better position, gaining a dozen feet, half a second of time, at the risk
of life and limb and fender, driving over the centre line into
oncoming traffic or swerving off on the crumbling shoulders
to make a few yards. There is absolutely no rhyme or reason
to this kind of senseless driving but it is done everywhere and,
remarkably, the drivers – and a car is a Soviet's most prized
possession – rarely seem to have even minor accidents.

A passenger needs nerves of steel. White-knuckled all the
way, I said, "Maybe it is because you all took chess lessons
when you were young, in school, and there is a certain reverse
logic which connects chess to driving habits."

It was a sarcastic comment and my guide said, "We don't all
take chess in school, and I don't know what you are talking
about."

We detoured to one of the old capitals of Georgia as a short
stop-over, strolled through the centuries-old unused church
where wedding parties arrived to lay flowers on an altar, and I
remarked, "The brides don't look all that happy."

Andrei replied, "Georgian brides never look happy."

If a five-word reply could contain a deep meaning as to the role of the Georgian wife, that one did. However, it was the first time my Russian guide had been in Georgia, so I thought it was a statement that must have a meaning a foreigner could not understand philosophically: the Russian dislike of all Georgians.

There was a restaurant and the square in front of the church was thronged with people – not foreigners, just Georgians – and I suggested a "bite to eat." Now there is an expression, along with a thousand others we use every day, that brings a strange look to their faces. Why a bite to eat? Why not a whole meal? Or a tart and a coffee? Why a bite?

"The restaurant is closed."

"But why? This looks like one of their busiest days. A Sunday. All these cars, these people. They'd make a lot of money."

"Maybe they've run out of food."

"How could they? They'd at least have bread and jam and tea, coffee, something to drink."

"Maybe they just took the day off to go somewhere. Let's go."

I said, "Well, I'm thirsty. There's a Pepsi-Cola machine. C'mon, I'll buy."

"It's closed, too. Can't you see? There is nobody around it. If it worked it would be busy," and he was right. A Pepsi-Cola machine is, anywhere, as busy as a Tabac stand or an ice cream stand, and so away we went.

In Gori we parked in a small square and my guide went off to find where the Stalin monument and museum was, this tribute to the man these Georgians revered. The man who had controlled mighty armies for decades, through a terrible war that ravaged their country. The man whose slightest whim had brought death or exile in Siberia to millions of innocents and whose totalitarian rule over his country was catastrophic, a disaster from which it may never recover. Josef Stalin, Man of Steel. Uncle Joe to us during the war, a man then looked upon with affection but, in truth, one of the world's genuine human monsters.

Down a long tree-shaded street, and finally we saw a red tour bus nosed into a small parking lot, and we walked through stone gates and into a long rectangular park, its grass uncut for weeks and newspapers blowing about. Down a cracked cement walk we went to a pillared structure that encased Stalin's home, the crude cottage he was born in to peasant parents, a tiny cottage sparsely furnished and without even an attendant to explain its contents.

Farther on was a large building, the museum, two-storied, with a large entrance hall and quiet as a tomb. Where are all the visitors making their pilgrimage to the man they revere? In another huge room on the second floor, the same. A museum without people.

Pictures of the young Stalin, the military Stalin, the revolutionary Stalin, and the political Stalin. Picture after picture after picture, plaques on the walls, inscriptions from world leaders of every stripe and from Soviets, too, praising him, his works, his leadership. My guide put on his political hat for one brief moment and said, "You will see there are no praises from Lenin. He did not want Stalin as his heir to the Motherland, as he recognized him for what he was."

The guide could have gone further, describing him as a dictator who crippled the already weak Soviet economic and agricultural system, virtually destroyed the pre-war military by decimating the officer caste, thus leaving the country unprepared for the German onslaught of 1941, and at his death left this federation of republics the socio-economic wreck it still is struggling to rebuild.

But in another huge, high-domed, and marbled room half the size of a ballroom, ah, here were some people. Drably dressed, clustered around a guide, a motley crew of East Germans off the red tour bus were being lectured about this man, this Stalin whose great wisdom and military genius allowed the Nazis to sweep over the borders to ravage, rape, and pillage the country. How ironic. The only tourists in Gori were the Germans!

Bored, I wandered downstairs as a group of youngsters, seven or eight years old, were led in by a guide and her droning chant began. Soviet kids. Who was this man? Why all this fuss? I could imagine the guide saying, "Here is the man who succeeded our great leader Lenin and these plaques and mementoes and gifts are from the great men of the world praising him." Did Churchill ever praise him? Yes, of course, for political wartime reasons. Might not the children ask, "Who was Winston Churchill? Who was President Franklin Delano Roosevelt?" They knew about the Great Patriotic War, the Soviet name for the Second World War. But did they know that the Soviet Union only defended its own territory and won it back, at terrible cost, while the rest of the world, Great Britain, Canada, Australia, New Zealand, South Africa, India, and finally the United States, fought the Germans and Japanese in every corner of the world? Did they know about the Allied convoys on the Murmansk Run that supplied the Soviet war machine at murderous cost? Only in 1987 did Gorbachev gratuitously recognize their vital and valiant role by awarding medals to surviving Allied merchant seamen. Or about the Northwest Staging Route through Canada and Alaska that supplied their nation with guns and ammunition and bombers and fighters to strengthen their will to push back the Nazis? Did these children know these things? No, and they never will.

Have they ever wondered why Stalingrad's name was changed to Volgograd? And how do their history teachers explain the magnificent defence of the city and the defeat of 350,000 Germans around a city that got a name switch when Stalin was de-Stalinized? Do they call it the Battle of Volgograd? Now, there is a question.

There was Lenin and then there was the dull and unimaginative Brezhnev—and I have heard Russians speak his name with contempt—but who was in between? Why, Nikita Khrushchev, of course, who first denounced Stalin, who first introduced his own version of *glasnost*, who first tried to introduce *perestroika*, but he is history. Just a leader, not a great leader, and when he died his death was announced six days later in three lines on an inside page of *Pravda* saying 'Comrade Khrushchev died in hospital . . . " et cetera. Three lines, so they say.

It was with a sense of wonder that I left this ghostly marble place, the only Stalin memorial in this nation of 285,000,000. But where were his Georgian worshippers?

Another red busload of East Germans pulled up as we were leaving. Had they come to gloat? Were they doing penance? Or was it just another stop on their thirteen-day scheduled tour? Something they'd paid for? I could have told them they would be disappointed. Nothing in that grim place, nor the words of their guide, would tell them of the Stalin years.

There are no busts, statues, pictures, plaques, of Stalin anywhere except in this quiet, small city in a hot, arid valley, but I was told that in many homes his picture hangs on the wall, a small plaster or bronze bust sits on a table, to be removed when visitors come or even if there is a knock on the door, even a messenger bringing a parcel.

In Gori we had an incredibly bad meal in a huge and ornate and empty hotel, the impressive ballroom-like restaurant containing only a bored manager in shirt-sleeves reading a paper and two Georgians arguing over bottles of wine. I settled for a plate of jellied beef – 80 percent jelly – and two bottles of lemonade, which is green and delicious. My guide had a plate of shashlik, the only meat available on a list of twelve meat dishes. Was it good? He replied, "Old sheep." Shashlik is always tough mutton, even in Gori, the place where the troubles of the world today really began.

The guidebook said that a million tourists a year visit the Stalin museum. On a wonderful day in early October there were about sixty. Two buses, Germans, and schoolchildren, two teen-age girls, a Canadian visitor, and his guide.

The drive back was uneventful, just the roaring, swerving, heaving mass of autos and trucks. My guide pointed out the ruins of a monastery high on a crag and said, "Built by the monks. In wars they would shelter the people up there. Georgia has been fought over many times. It is a land of sadness."

A large black sedan roared past us towards oncoming traffic and I said, "Three drunken Georgians." Andrei smiled.

Fifteen minutes later, their car was off the road, smashed, and amazingly, a traffic policeman was questioning the three swaying men and a helicopter was lifting off.

"Patrol," my guide said. "Their small crash saved them from a coffin."

"What will happen?" I asked.

"They will try and bribe the policeman, but they will be taken away. A car will come for them. Jail. Maybe a long time. It will be good for them."

"Three drunken Georgians."

He said, "Sunday. Too much wine. Georgians. They will be sorry now." He looked at me and smiled.

In the audit of life, Georgians and Russians are on opposite sides of the ledger.

❦ Not One Bikini in Sight

One afternoon I was chatting with a group of tourists from Saskatchewan who had just visited a collective farm in the Ukraine. One of them said, "And we didn't see one cow, one tractor, one chicken, one pig, one worker. Looking around I had difficulty believing it was a farm."

He added, "During that entire day, including about five hours driving around through the countryside, I saw only one person who appeared to be actually engaged in agricultural work. That was a young woman with a rake, who was all alone in a large field, and dressed, oddly enough, in a bikini."

A day later, I had my own odd experience while passing orchards in southern Georgia. The trees were so heavy with ripened apples that they were literally raining down, judging by the numbers of the ground. It was impossible to tell the size of any individual orchard, but here was a very bountiful harvest that should have been picked many days before. Yet there was not a soul in sight except the goat and turkey herders along the road.

Something was amiss in organizing the work force here, because right in the midst of this parade of orchards there was a hay field, perhaps fifty acres, and in it, at my guess, were about forty men and women turning over the mounds of hay so they would dry properly. In Canada, one machine and one man could have done the job of those forty workers, while those workers could have been harvesting those apples, which bring such high prices in the distant cities.

And I didn't see one girl in one bikini in one field with one rake.

❦ "In Georgia, We Are Different"

The destination was the Museum of Georgian Folk Architecture and Life, a vast tract on the sunbaked hillside overlooking the teeming and traffic-jammed city of Tbilisi, a city unique among others I had visited because it had vitality. Its volatile citizens had a zest for life, so different from Moscow and Leningrad, where the never-ending and slow-moving crowds all had the same pace, the same clothes, the same grim faces. There was no joy in their hearts.

We took a taxi, my guide and a well-dressed young secretary from the Novosti Press Agency office who spoke Georgian, and as we entered the park, climbing upward on a broad asphalt road, I questioned the taxi driver.

He was fifty-one, a Georgian, and he was content with his life. For years he had been a long-distance truck driver, long hours and poor accommodation, an exhausting life. Eight years ago he had gotten this taxi job and now he was happy. He lived in a two-bedroom apartment with his wife and his youngest daughter. His older daughter had married and he had three grandchildren. His wife did not work, highly unusual; she stayed home to look after the child of nine. She had been a sound engineer in a television studio. She was happy, too.

His salary was 200 rubles a month and he was his own boss. He liked that. The harder he worked, the more he made because he operated under the quota plan. These plans operate for a factory of 5,000 workers as well as for a single taxi driver, based on the quota system. Some bureaucrat in Moscow estimated how much a taxi driver in an eight-hour shift in the far-off city of Tbilisi should earn, and a percentage went to the state. If he exceeded his guaranteed 200-ruble salary quota, he received half of the extra earnings. This driver, during the winter months, said his bonus was about 100 rubles more, and as he also earned a bonus of one-thirteenth of his regular salary, his earnings in a good month would be 315 rubles.

Considering that a woman construction labourer was getting perhaps 150 rubles a month, a journalist about 200, a doctor in a hospital about 220, an equipment operator with the high-risk job of boring out subways about 400, a taxi driver in Georgia did very well indeed.

He could use his own car and make more money, but why? To answer his own question he pointed to the windshield, which was badly shattered in two places. What happened? A couple of drunks had got in his car—yes, he could have refused them, but he hadn't—and the one in the front began cursing his pal in the back, then smashed his fist into the windshield.

How long ago was that? About four months ago.Why hadn't the government fixed it? Oh, he said, there is a shortage of windshields.

What could he have done? He replied that he could have driven them to a hospital where they would have been put away for the night. A cold shower, a sleep, another cold shower, and then released with a 15-ruble fine. Fifteen rubles! Yes, a very hefty fine. But he didn't make a 'citizen's arrest'? No, they weren't bad guys. Just drunk. But now he was very careful about picking up more than one drunk at a time.

I brought up the question of automatic transmissions. No taxis I had seen had them. My guide said, "Our car works cannot do these things effectively. It is a very difficult thing to do. The big government cars have them but not our citizen's car. It is a question of buying a patent."

As I had before – and I knew I antagonized my guide when I did so – I said that even the boxy, tough Lada imported into Canada was fitted with automatic transmission. Mind you, it cost about 700 dollars extra, but Canadians paid willingly. Again my guide told me, "Our cars cannot be fitted with these devices. They do not work here."

Meanwhile, the Georgian secretary in the front seat had been translating our conversation for the driver and she asked, "He wants to know what is this transmission thing you are talking about. He does not know of it."

At the park I tried to tip him, but he said no. He had enough money. Two rubles. Enough.

As we walked away, my guide said, "He has no ambition. All he wants to do is drive that taxi. He said after being a truck driver, his dream was to drive a taxi."

I replied, "Then he has found his dream," and could have added, "And besides, he's making almost twice as much as you are."

There was no activity in the park, the foreign tourists having long gone, but there were two men building a platform, a stage, using rough-cut heavy lumber. They had started the project only two days before and it was well advanced, considering that construction of a building in cities could exceed its projected completion date of three years by four or five years. But this was only a stage. It is one of the wonders of the Soviet Union to visit a building site where even the cranes used in construction are rusting, as though the project had disappeared from the government's files and the skeleton will sit there forever. The first task of *perestroika's* masters should be to finish all the uncompleted buildings in the country.

But there was activity here, a steady pounding of nails, as we walked up the curving road.

We talked to the boss of the two-man gang, a bronzed and open-faced fellow of thirty-three with brawny arms. He obviously had a good feeling about himself. His name was Bodri Obolla and what was his dog's name, a grizzled bitch sprawled on some planks, tongue lolling? My guide said she was called Often and I thought, what a crazy name.

Then a woman's voice came from behind us, and she said, in perfect English, "Not Often. Her name is Orphan. She has no parents and she is old. She is fourteen."

The woman, Larisa, was the guide for foreigners in the park and from then on the interview went smoothly. She had seen us, and followed.

Bodri had been a carpenter for many years, but work around his village 230 kilometres away in Eastern Georgia was not plentiful. Four years earlier he had left his parents on their eleven-acre farm – very large by Soviet standards for a family – and come to Tbilisi. He found steady work, worked hard, and by my calculations he must have had a fortune in the bank. He earned 150 rubles a month but he stayed in a hostel for men – there are also hostels for married couples – and paid 1.5 rubles a month. In Canadian terms, that would be $3.30. There were three beds to a room, he said, but often he had the room to himself since the hostels were rarely full. There were cooking facilities but he often ate at the hostel canteen or at the buffet. He liked the hostel, there was a degree of privacy and it was clean.

However, making money was not Bodri's aim. His reason for moving to the city was to find himself a wife. A fine and robust chap like this should have found a wife long before.

"It is because he does not have an apartment," Larisa translated. "If he had an apartment he could have a wife tomorrow. Georgian girls are happy to be married, but he cannot offer her anything. No girl would want to live in a married people's hostel. He says he has his name in for an apartment, but it might be five years before he can get one. But he would have to be married." Catch-22.

The common refrain I heard throughout the country is the shortage of decent living quarters. It's a major cause of the alarmingly high divorce rate, and judging by the letters to the editor in Soviet newspapers, there is no end in sight, no relief, no hope unless *perestroika* policies launch a building program the like of which the world has never seen before.

"He says he is doing this job out of the love in his heart for Georgia," said the guide. "It is his Georgian pride. Our folk dancers will dance on this stage he is making and the tourists from around the world will stand behind that fence made of grape stems and watch them. That will make him very proud. When this is finished he will go back to the city to work, but he will be here for some time yet. There are many projects to do up here and he says he likes the fresh air and sunshine."

Larisa said, "At night he looks after his dogs and his animals," and explained that he had three dogs farther up the slopes, along with three calves, which he had purchased from his parents and which he grazed on the slopes. "When they are ready for market he will sell them to a butcher."

"This is an ambitious man."

She translated my words and Bodri replied that yes, he was. Having heard tales of Georgians, I asked if the sale of the cattle would go through the black market. She said, "Probably. I would think so."

However, he'd go back to his parents' farm to work as the crops became ripe, as did his two brothers and the three daughters and their spouses, making, he said, a total of thirteen hands helping with the harvest. They received produce for pay which they brought to the city and sold. He had a few regular customers and he made good money that way.

Through Larisa I learned that Bodri's parents also come to the city, hauling large quantities of vegetables and fruits by bus to the main market in the city. The buses are especially built for country folk, as half of the interior is blocked off for produce. They stay at a hotel for 2 rubles a night and sell their pears, apples, fruits, nuts, meat, at very high prices, three times as much as the official price in the state stores where the queues are long and the tempers edgy. Georgians buy at the market to avoid the queues, but also because the produce is fresh.

"In a day, maybe two, they will sell all their goods and go back on the bus," translated my guide.

"With a lot of money?"

"Yes, a great deal of money, and they will have had a good time and talked a lot and learned all the news, and they do this maybe twice a month. Georgians are like the Armenians. They know how to make money. Look at him. He buys three little calves, brings them to the city, and grows them up and he will sell them and make a lot of money."

I asked Bodri what his future was, and he skipped the part about a city wife, but he did say, "I'm a village boy, not a city boy."

He was anxious to get back to his sawing and pounding and Larisa took me by the arm and said, "May I show you some of our heritage? It is old Georgian, from east and west, many centuries old. This national park is being built with these old places which have been brought from all regions of Georiga."

East Georgia is a mountainous land, the green grass of spring withered brown by mid-July, a land of castles built by monks who gave refuge to the villagers and peasants when, since time forever, gangs and bands and armies of marauders on ponies had swept through. A guidebook said forty invasions, not counting minor raids. I felt that the people who lived in these dugout houses, cut into the sides of hills and camouflaged with planted bushes and small trees, may have had the right idea: The Turkish marauder says, "Nothing across that valley but a bunch of bushes," and his companion says, "Yeah, let's move on."

"Come inside our museum," which had artifacts from houses in one of Georgia's five eastern regions. "It was put here, just the things from the old days, in 1976. It has been a heritage in Georgia to preserve our old things, the way people lived. We did not get started until a few years ago, so we have much to do."

"Good for tourism, isn't it?" and she laughed. I liked her. First, it was pleasant to be talking to a person who was not suspicious, dour, rude, or indifferent. She genuinely enjoyed her job, a rarity indeed, and I complimented her on her English.

"Oh, it was difficult at first. I had graduated from the Institute of Foreign Languages. English and German. We all thought we knew how to speak English and German. We did, sure, but we didn't. We spoke English perfectly but first when I came to work here I found that I did not know English or German the way it was spoken by the visitors. It is your special words and phrases, your slang.

"That is what is important to learn and how to say it at the right place. You have to feel slang. It is important that you get it right, but it must come in its natural place. When Americans first came here I thought, I know English but I don't understand what they are saying to each other. But then I began to understand and so many say that I am like an American. At first it was hard for me to say 'sure' or 'that's for sure,' and things like that."

"That's for damn sure," I replied.

"Sure," and laughed.

Larisa added, "I could have been a teacher. But what's an English teacher in Georgia? Nothing at all. You teach the children and they don't care. All they learn is passive English. They talk like they are reading from a book. That is no good. Then they graduate and in half a year they have forgotten it. There is no satisfaction, so I decided to come to work in this beautiful park. There are the pine trees and the birds, the work is going on with these houses and buildings, and I can tell hundreds and hundreds of tourists about our Georgian heritage. It's the life for me."

We had been walking around a large one-room house, with its dirt floors and its walls faced with logs, and I said, "You know, when the Slavic settlers came to Western Canada, where I was born, a lot of them built houses like this. Right in the side of a sloping bank, dirt floor like this, the fireplace like that one with the pot hanging over the fire. But there was one difference. Despite what you might have read, there were no wars with the Indians. Their wars were with nature and cold weather and locusts and drought."

"Yes, I know," she said. "I have read your literature."

Simply said, but it amazed me; in my three weeks of roaming she was the first nonpolitical Soviet who had any inkling of what Canada was, who the people were, or – and this is only a slight exaggeration – where Canada was. They knew, but it was a vague wave of the hand to the west. "Over there."

I told her this and she said, "That is the fault of the educators. The children have general geography. They really learn nothing. They memorize, they repeat what the teacher says. They go home and study, study, study, and yet they know nothing of anything. What can you expect?

"Mathematics, chemistry, physics, oh yes, but nothing of the humanities. I think it will change soon. There is some talk now. But in Georgia we are different. We teach our true history and customs and our great traditions and our great men. Our poets. In the rest of the country, the republics are doing this, too. It is our way of keeping our heritage and our identity."

"But in Moscow they don't understand this, do they?"

"It is hard for them to understand. They are Russians, you see, but I think you will see changes soon."

I said, "To think that maybe ten or twelve people could live in this room. All together and sleeping everywhere. This was really cave living. But there's one difference. In Canada the settlers didn't have those holes to shoot guns at the Indians," and I pointed to holes in the wall about seven feet high up.

Larisa laughed and said, "Not holes for shooting. If invaders came, the people ran into the woods. Those are dowry holes. When a girl was born, her father would dig a hole into the earth and put in a pot. Then every time she received a piece of jewellery or a gold coin as a gift, she would put it in her dowry pot. No matter how poor the family was and how much they needed the money, the father would never take his daughter's dowry money for her wedding. You see, seven girls must have lived in this house. There are seven pots."

We went outside and she said, "And now I will introduce you to a wonderful old man. His name is Alexander and he is seventy-one and he is a volunteer. When he is feeling good he comes up here and sits in his chair and when the schoolchildren and students come, and visitors, he tells them about Georgian culture."

As I write I am looking at his picture, with his arm around Larisa. His is a kindly face, a wise face and one that is at peace with his world. He wears a knitted wood skullcap, a buttoned-up red and white checked shirt and a blue suit.

We talked. The translation was smooth, such a sweet change from the guttural grunts of interpreting I was used to.

Alexander came out of the war and studied and devoted his life to the literature of Georgia, a teacher all his life. Then, with his pensions, his apartment, well off, he decided he could add more to his life's work and became a volunteer at the park.

He had received a large apartment when he returned – wounded three times – from the war. He went to the special stores for veterans where they could shop for goods not available to the ordinary citizen. As part of his veteran's privileges he could travel anywhere, by plane, bus, train, at no cost or at reduced fares, and he had three pensions, war service, state, and regular pension.

I asked about the war, which, incidentally, Larisa called the Second World War. She was admitting that nations other than the Soviet Union had played a role in the vast global struggle. Alexander said he had started in Finland, that winter war of naked and cruel aggression against a tiny neighbour. Its consequences today still have a grave effect on how Finland conducts its affairs with its mighty Soviet neighbour. He later went to officer's school, fought almost to Berlin, and after the third wound was sent home. His war was over. Then the war was over.

"This may be difficult to translate to him, but tell him I was in 'the poor bloody infantry,' too."

He guffawed, and she giggled and said, "He says they had the same kind of expression in our army."

We finally left him, this gallant old warrior-teacher-historian-philosopher, and Larisa resumed her thesis on what was wrong with teaching in Soviet schools, zeroing in on English. She was convinced every student should speak English as it was the language of "the whole wide world." She said, "If I were teaching now, I would teach them from Robert Ludlum's books. I get them from American tourists who carry them. I know he is not considered a great writer in your country . . ." and I broke in, saying, "If a million people buy his books, does it matter? He is an entertaining novelist."

"Yes, famous, popular, maybe not a great writer, but he writes the way people talk and that is important."

We had to say goodbye, a reluctant one on my part, and perhaps hers, but my guide was anxious to get down to the city. He was hungry. He was always hungry. As we walked down the mile-long hill – there was no phone to call for a taxi – we heard shouts, yells. The racket became more violent as we approached and I said, "There is a fight going on over there in those trees. Looks like there'll be a murder soon."

"No, no. You are wrong. Just tree cutters. They must be deciding what trees to cut down. Nothing wrong," my guide said. "Just acting like Georgians."

"What's wrong with being a Georgian?" I asked.

"Georgians, they're just Georgians," he said with contempt.

I remembered he had said once, "I am just a good Russian boy."

❧ Russian Bears and Georgian Tigers

"Our poets are the best in the world. Ah, how they describe our mountains and our valleys and the little villages and the old women whose husbands make pottery and they sell it in the big market in the centre of Tbilisi. This is a wonderful city. An opera and academies and the universities and the river, it flows along, and there are trees and soon you are in the country and the mountains and then there is no pollution. This is a new word for us, this pollution. It is an American word, I think, and the authorities say there will be no more pollution because they will keep it away.

The people are friendly, and they are happiest of all people in the Soviet Union. We are a republic and we would like to be a state. Our own country. That is not to be. It is very old, and we have had the Christian religion for 1,400 years. This is not something they can take away from us. The old men and women keep it alive and when they are dead, the younger ones like me, and I am forty-seven years old, we will carry on our religion. On feast nights and our national holiday we go to church. Militiamen stand at the door looking cold and hard but we laugh at them. We pass by the statue of Lenin and give him this [the finger] and when we pass a statue of one of our great poets or writers, oh, we have so many, we do this [the salute] and go on our way.

If we go to the park where our artists are showing their pictures, we say, 'Why do you just paint mountains with snow on them and reindeer and lakes? Why do you not paint the scenes of Georgia?' They say they will not get the government grants or be allowed to travel. I know one man who is a wonderful painter and he told me he may sell only one painting in two weeks. That is being there on all day Sunday. He says, 'Come to my apartment and I will show you paintings of our mountains and our villages and our old people, the wonderful old women with many lines in their faces and those very kind eyes and their gold teeth.' Their money is in their teeth, you know. When they die, their relatives will take out those teeth and they will have the gold. Our gypsies do it, too. All gold.

We are also great singers. I know many of our old songs and the young people, they buy guitars. People make them. We are very good with making things of wood. Loving, they put such care into them and a good guitar will cost a young artist who sings six or seven months of salary.

Our women are beautiful and there are many fine actresses. They have, how you call it, fire. Yes, they have fire. We have many fine actors, men, who have great audiences when they are in the theatre. If you hear these people on the stage doing the legends of our people, you would understand.

Georgia is pure. I mean, there is not much other blood in our veins. This is the way we want it. These fair-haired Russians come as administrators, the bosses, as though a Georgian cannot be a boss, and they want to marry our Georgian girls. Ah yes, some do. The girls see the way it is. They will marry and move away and their hearts are always in their homeland and the mountains. They go to Moscow and they ask where the mountains are and people say, there are the hills, the Lenin Hills, and these people laugh. No mountains, no grapes on the high hills, no sheep up there and the shepherds and the old monasteries of the old priests built up against the sky. They want to come home but they can't. Just a few. We try and keep the blood in our veins pure.

In Georgia, an old building is 400 years old and it has what you call dignity. They have a process of being respectful. There are trees on the streets and the river is clean. The Moscow River, aaaaah! Not a river. It has its banks of cement and it has no soul. Our rivers are clear and cold and run out of the mountains and I can go and fish in them and catch fish and bring it to any house that is near and that will be my gift. They will cook it and we will have a feast and drink wine and sing and laugh and there will be a party. This is people you don't even know.

In Moscow, the subway. We have one in Tbilisi, a small one. In Moscow, people ride on it and do not look at each other. That is not the Georgian way. People should smile. In Moscow, everybody reads or looks sad and tired and old men spit on the floor which is an offence. People like to break the law there because it is their way of showing they hate the government. Their clothes are tired and grey and there is no fresh air. Dirty air. Moscow should be called the city of dirty air. When I get off the aircraft in Georgia I open up my mouth and breathe the good air and poeple say there is a lot of pollution. Some people even wear masks of cotton. I say, 'You have never been to Moscow. This is clean air.'

They say if a Georgian has a rough voice, it is because he smokes 40-kopek cigarettes. Very strong. But I think it is because we are always talking and our throats are worn out. We laugh a lot, we drink our good wine, and we sing and everybody makes poetry out of even little things. There are our mountains. You look at them and think it is the most wonderful country.

No, we will never be free. I don't think we could be. All the apparatus is in The Centre and there are too many Russians in our public now. There are Russian army bases, and there is a big air force base with terrible planes at them. There can be no freedom. We do not have the chance at all. Neither does any of the republics. Some, they want to. I know it will not be. Perhaps the Baltic countries. They are different. They were conquered in 1940 and the rest of the world still does not call them republics of Russia. Someday they will have their chance. Maybe this *perestroika* business will help them, but I do not think so. Something else will happen.

But Georgia, Armenia, our neighbour, just over the mountains, now they are like us although we have been enemies. Azerbaijan, maybe. They are Muslims. We are Christians. They do not mind dying, I think. We do. So we will always be the way we are.

This country, you must understand, has been in existence for more than a thousand years. There is nothing like it in the world. The Romans fought for it and the Moslems and the Persians and, yes, the Russians and others. The Turks, they were bad enemies. They would conquer and the Georgian people would gather again, in the high valleys where the vandals and their savage dogs would not come, and they would grow stronger and attack, and that part of the country would be ours again. But then about 180 years ago they thought, 'Why should we always be at war?' Even with the Armenians which was a smaller country and very corrupt with men who lived like animals. That is when we decided to join with the Russians who were going to conquer us. It was so big. That was the end –but not the end of Georgia. It is strong again.

We have learned to go along. The Russians are here, and they come to our vacation areas, the thousands, and Georgians take their money. We are not thieves. We are just smarter than they are. The Russians are the bears, many, many of them, but we are the tigers, not many, but fast and smart. There was a tiger killed not many miles from our capital only maybe fifty years ago. Today, that last tiger, his spirit lives in the Georgian people.''

SEVEN

Yerevan: a Southern Exposure

The Way Blat Works ... A Capitalist Under His Hat ... Only in Armenia ... The Right Woman Came Along

Yerevan, 190 kilometres south of Tbilisi over the mountains, is a city of one million. The day I arrive, Armenia is celebrating its national day and red, white, and blue ribbons flutter above the speakers' platform in Lenin Square. This is the only city where I ever see Gorbachev's portrait. Ten feet high. Gorbachev has ruled out cultism and banned display of his picture. My guide mutters, "These crazy Armenians. The guy who put that up could get shot. There's bad blood ... religion ..."

We head out into the country. Along the way I spy two men herding thirty turkeys on the roadside grass and, farther on, three men guarding the family fortune of fifty skinny sheep. But on a collective farm things are different. This one works. I am invited to lunch with a tractor mechanic – high in the job hierarchy – and every one of the men says "no, no, no," when I pull up a chair so that the wife can join us. It's all-male dining in this southern republic.

Their traditional yogurt laced with the purest of honey is wonderful. Again, the local wine and cognac are served to wash down the hearty Armenian meal.

The farmer asks me what his house would be worth in Canada. I say 160,000 dollars for the house, the land, the fruit trees. He is surprised and pleased.

On the way back to Yerevan, I ask my guide if the visit had been a set-up. "No, it wasn't. I'm surprised myself."

This is a country I could visit for a long time.

❧ The Way Blat Works

A small café in Armenia's capital, Yerevan. A gloomy place with old women sipping tea from glasses, grey cloth shopping bags piled at their feet, a cafeteria-style place, and when I received my glass the perky young counter girl waved away my money.

At the only table not full I sat across from a woman of about fifty, dark as all Armenians are with the Mediterranean or Persian blood, and I was prepared for the see-through treatment. It is amazing how two people can sit three feet apart, eyeball to eyeball, and one can make the other feel invisible. It happens everywhere in the Soviet Union and I wondered, "Do they not have the slightest curiosity about this white-haired stranger checking his tape recorder and camera, consulting his notebook? Do they not wonder who he is and where he comes from and what he thinks of their country?" Only bureaucrats and journalists ask what you think of the Motherland.

The woman snapped out an order – "Bring this man a bun" – quickly the waitress brought a bun on a plate and, my, she did have a wonderful smile. Even tentative smiles are appreciated in the Soviet Union. One sees so few. I still wonder why.

"I will say who I am," she said. "I am the manager of this shop. You can call me Dorothy. That is a name you will know."

Dorothy?

"My country has a famous writer living in your country. His name is Saroyan. Saroyan is a very good name in this country. His first name is Joseph. Joe."

"No, William. I am very well acquainted with Saroyan. He is dead now but he wrote some very fine stories about Southern California. I think there were three or four movies made of his books. He made a lot of money . . . "

"Then his father's name was Joseph."

"Joseph doesn't sound like an Armenian name to me, but Dorothy doesn't either. And Saroyan lived in the United States. I am from Canada, north of California."

She laughed. "I know that, you foolish man. It is only Canadians who wear those badges on your coat. I have seen some. Now you tell me why is that so, and I will tell my friends a Canadian told me. You are the first one I have talked to. I know the flag. Hockey."

"I wear this pin so that Soviet citizens will know I am not an American. Simple as that."

"You are wrong. They still think you are an American," and she called over my shoulder to the next table of women and words flew back and forth, then she said, "Three of them think you are an American and the other, she thinks you are from London."

"Tell them I am a Canadian, please."

"I did. They still think you are American or from London. Foolish old women. Out all day looking for a tin of this, cherries, maybe, or a little dog carved out of wood. Maybe some cheese or a plate or a cup, something the stores got in. They don't want to shop. Their sons and daughters-in-law send them lots of money; these workers on the state farms, they're the ones with the rubles. We in the city, no. But they come in from the farms and they buy American dollars or German marks and the men go to the hotels. You know what these fine gentlemen want? A chance to talk to American schoolteachers on a tour. I say to one I know, 'Hey, you kid, why not our own girls? They go out alone now, you see that. Why these girls from far away?' He tells me, 'The American girls, see how white their skins are.' I say, 'You fool, they are tanned, this is the summer, they are dark like us here.' He says, 'Under their tan they are white. American girls. Big you-know-whats.' I say, 'Russian girls from

Moscow, they are white.' He says," and she makes the ages-old gesture. The high sign, the first-finger salute.

"What is Canada anyway? Rocks and ice like Siberia?"

"Well," I said, "much of it, but much of it is like the Soviet Union. Part of where I come from, British Columbia, is very much like around here. Hills, mountains, the same kind of life, wildlife. Wine growing. Farms. Big orchards, little towns."

"But no boss man from Moscow telling me how I should run this little shop," and this time she gave the ages-old gesture on her own behalf. We both laughed, and I asked where she had learned to speak English.

I had already figured it out, but she said, "You are the one. Armenian people, we have our own ways, and we have our people in California, the grapes, and we see each other a lot. Many times. I have been to California and then to my cousin's house where he grows grapes and has a big car – it is called a Buick [pronounced "Bwook"] – and lots of kids. He comes over here. We drink, we fight. All this time we are eating a lot and having fun and trying on the dresses and underwear they bring us. Last time it was two suitcases. Two for my family and another for the Russian customs fellows and women, but they just let them go through. That is a good laugh."

"Slick as a whistle, eh?"

It happened again. From her smock she took out a pencil and shoved an order pad at me and said, "Write that down. What does 'slick as the whistle' mean?"

From then on, every time I used a Canadianism she would point and say to write it down, causing the conversation to bounce along, I scribbling, she laughing, and once, clear as a bell, she said, "*Tabernac*, I get you another glass, mister, you are earning it."

Curious, I asked, "Where did you pick up that word? *Tabernac*."

"Oh, somewhere, I had a few lovers when I was in America when I was younger. There, I think. What does it mean?"

"It is a French Canadian curse word. You don't hear it much."

She thought, then made a motion of dismissal.

She had been impressed with the United States. In her heart, she said, Disneyland would always be the place where she would die – a strange way of expressing herself. Would she like to live there? No, it was too crowded. There were too many cars, ignoring the obvious fact that outside the door were some of the craziest drivers in the universe. I pointed and made the cuckoo-twirl signal around my right ear and she snorted, making a zzzzzzzrrr! noise and a fast, swooping motion with her hand. "Crazy fast," she said. "There, they have big and terrible accidents, seventy miles an hour. In Yerevan, crazy, okay, you are right, but little accidents."

No, trips were good enough, and she liked bringing home treasures – "these little things our people can't get" – and she pointed to her nether regions. Ah, lingerie, and, yes, she nodded, "and perfume and a VCR for my son and all these things the bosses get but we can't buy in the store unless we break the window and steal the only one they got out in that window."

To put it precisely, that was often the only way one could obtain a prize piece of merchandise from many Soviet stores I had seen.

Was managing this small café a good job? Yes, she said, and the people who came in to visit and sip tea and have a small meal, they were the best part of it. Did it make money? Oh, yes, it made money. She had been asked to manage a large cafeteria in a factory, not once but in several factories, but then it would be just a job, she said. She liked talking to people and she kept the staff low. I had noticed this. There was the girl behind the counter and a very old woman who was mopping the floor. Why was that? Didn't she want to make more money, as she would have. No, and she winked, and said the café had good hours that suited her and her staff worked hard and it made money and, then came the gesture leading away from her wink, the rubbing of thumb and forefinger and a pushing gesture down into her large bosom.

She told me she made 240 rubles. The Soviets are rarely reticent about telling a stranger how much they make, probably because all work pays the same salary, so everyone knows within a few rubles. A sales clerk made 110 rubles, which accounted for their intolerable rudeness, and our counter clerk made about 90, which did not account for her cheeriness and singing as she zipped about the café in perpetual motion. Dorothy made a better-than-average wage, and there is always money to be made on the side.

"What if they should catch you?" I asked. "Maybe someone will inform on you, tell them something."

Leaning over, fixing me with those black eyes, she said,
"Never. Not them. I know too much about them and they know
nothing about what I do. If they want to make trouble for me,
I could just say a few words. Just a few words, many kinds of
few words. These words would send these puff-bellies back to
their holes. I know too much. I talk to people from all around
here. They tell me too much."

"You tell me, and then we'll both know."

She patted my arm and said, "No, no, no. These are things
we keep among ourselves. Our little things of ammunition.
What you have when some puff-belly wants to show what a big
man he is. Our secrets. Everybody in Yerevan has their own
secrets and we keep them to ourselves. They are our protection.
For myself, my family, the kids, and I look after the girl over
there and the old woman you saw and her husband. My work
book is clean." A work book, which all Soviets carry, is like a
passport in which all jobs ever worked at are listed, as well as
reasons for leaving, dismissal, advancement. The history of a
person's work life.

"The book is my protection. If some boss tried to get smart
with me, we would go before this committee and they would
look at what I have done. My record. They know I could manage
a big cafeteria. They think they know why I do not want to do
that. A cafeteria is too big, too many bosses, too much to do,
and too many people stealing and too many with bad work
habits. Then there is the drinking and the making of bad spirits
by the cooks. This rotgut of the cafeterias, everybody knows
about that. Did I say stealing? There is a lot of that. You could
run ten, maybe fifteen little cafés like this one with what is
stolen from a cafeteria at a factory, maybe 2,000 workers.

"I just want this little place, my three employees. I have tea
and buns ready for the workers at seven in the morning and I
close at five and that is good with me. In between, I run everything myself. The state gets its profit and I get mine and we do
fine, I know. This is a good job. Everyone is happy here. I talk
to a lot of people. They are always telling me stories, what is
happening. I know everything and I remember it all, everything.
I just sit here sometimes when we have locked the door and I
have my coffee and I say to myself, 'I know everything, so I
have everything and nothing can hurt me or my family or my
little family here.' This is a good feeling. Let them be Siberian

tigers out there on the street or at Party headquarters. I just sit here and think, 'Everything is good, so why should I care and what will I buy for my wonderful husband for dinner tonight?'

"You see, all the clerks from the stores in this neighbourhood come in here. Marina, she works in the meat shop, she needs 10 rubles quickly. I lend her 10 rubles. I say to her, you keep it, and when there is some good meat, you save me a piece. She is my friend for a long time. She comes in and she says there is a good chicken she has put under the counter for me, or there is four cutlets she has for me. Then, Leonid, he's a Russian boy who is assistant manager of our department store; he is in here a lot and he wants to take his girl for a drive. I lend him our Lada, oh, and he is so happy. He comes in and he says, 'Dorothy, that was wonderful. I asked her to marry me and she will. You are invited to the wedding, but it will be in Rostov, not here, so if there is anything you want, just tell me.' Okay, that is fine. If there is something I want, a recording, a bicycle chain for a friend like I did just last week, I can get it. Maybe not right then, but when one comes in. Leonid comes in and says it is ready. We help each other. I can do something for you and he can do something for me. This is the way it works. The *blat*. The–" again she rubbed her thumb and forefinger together. "It works. We have to help each other against them."

I knew if I could have talked longer I would have hit the mother lode for, in a small way, she was the neighbourhood's centre. Our talk was interrupted constantly by people stopping by to say a few words, and many studiously avoided looking at the foreigner. She made no move to introduce me – why should she? – and I could see that information was being exchanged. Favours given, favours promised. Where to find a deal. Who to find to make a deal. In a way, perhaps like a neighbourhood Mafiosa, Armenian style, with no malice, no menace. Just the *blat*. You scratch my back, I'll scratch yours, and we'll both be happy and wealthier.

I had to go. Through an hour of talk I had expected her to ask me at least one question. 'Who are you?' Or, perhaps, 'What are you doing here?' But no. She showed not one iota of interest in me or my background. It was eerie.

❦ *A Capitalist Under His Hat*

"I have a young friend, a poet, twenty-six, and he comes to my apartment and sometimes he brings me two buns with spun sugar on the top, and I tell him of the three years I spent in the Gulag. He goes away and every time he comes again he brings me a poem. He is young, and the things I tell him are not in the books he read in studying and he is very sad when he leaves. He is a good young man, the son of my friend who died, and he knows I am alone in this world. He would someday get his poems in a book. We are all poets. There is a deep soul in all of us and I read his poem and I can see the sadness in his heart but I can see the bravery and the courage, too, and I say, 'Don't wait. Don't be patient. Don't bow your head any more. Write your poems and there is a day coming, not far away, when it will all be better and you can be a famous man and we will be happy for you. You will find your dream and speak for all of us who have suffered.'

But I say, 'Now you must speak for yourself. For your friends and for what you feel. That is the way of a poet. To tell others how you feel because the poet, he has in his hands the mirror of his people, and when they look at your poems they will be seeing down into their own hearts.'

Here is a poem he left me the last time he came and we had buns and tea and we talked and he asked me why I was in the camp and he is trying to understand. I have translated it into English for you. He writes in Armenian, which is the language of poets, and in the shadow of Mount Ararat where he dreams, he makes these poems. This is the one, so you can see how he is thinking.

> How long can you sleep at The Congress?
> How long can you stand all the _____?
> Why don't we speak our minds?
> Why don't we kiss in the daylight?
> Where did you leave your school friends?
> Where did your innocence fly?
> Where? How? Why?
> Which of your masks would fit better?
> Which of your hands can grab more?

But have you ever tried to relax
And go through the land of no more?
When did you last see your mother?
When will you reopen your heart?
What is your menu for next day?
What is the dream that you've lost?

Yes, it is a very expressive poem. It tells of his frustrations. With The Congress, the deputies who meet in Moscow and do nothing because the laws have already been made. Now, they are changing. With *glasnost* and *perestroika* and the force of the will and ideas of millions of young people who are not afraid to talk out loud any more, there will be many changes. They cannot keep the young people in their pockets, hidden from the sun, any more. They think too much, they see too much; they want all they should have and when they get it, then it will be there, too, for their children. The children, that is why all these things are for. Change in our country comes very slow. After the revolution the leaders and Lenin saw that change they tried, the fast change, the new rules and regulations and the freedom, they saw it could not come like that. Quickly.

Now it is coming. You can see it. There are things that are happening now that would have been horrifying ten years ago. Sorry, I do not mean horrifying. I speak English not much any more and it is only some books I have had from long ago I read in English. Once, long ago, I was very good and was a translator and met with English friends in cafés and we talked much. Then it was a language I could love and the great English poets, I used to read them and Shakespeare, the greatest poet of them all because he can make poetry out of prose.

That missing word. Yes, I knew you would ask about that word. I did not translate it because I did not think it was good in the poem. This is the way the young people are today. They want to shock the old ones. No, I do not mean it that way. It had a purpose, just as every word in a poem has its own purpose. Its own meaning. The word he used sounds at work better in his language but I could not find the way it should be in English. It would mean, let me see, the word I used to hear my English friends use many times. The word, I know what it means. In English it would mean 'bullshit.' That is why I did not think it would be right in this translation. It takes it away from the strong meaning of the poem. He is not a boy who would shock me. It is me who thinks that is the right word, but I did not want to write it down for you when you said you would visit me.

I was not always like this. I was hard and I grew up as a child in the poorest district of Kharkov. This was in the thirties years when our country was in very bad condition and there was the world in despair and also poor, but the Soviet Union was the worst. There had been the revolution in 1917 and everyone thought it would be a new country the leaders would bring forth. It was not so. The dictator Stalin was ruler after Lenin and he made ruin of the agriculture and put all the peasants onto the state farms, and they did not have their little pieces of land and there was no reason for them to work hard. There were poor crops and much theft and much, much corruption and the people were starving badly.

This is when I was growing up with my mother in Kharkov. I was born in 1923 and my sister told me she did not know who my father was. It was a great shame and the neighbours and boys in the street would make great fun of shouting at my mother and my sister. My sister, she was only five but she remembered, and my mother was twenty-three when I was born. No father. Just a man she met who was kind to her. This is what she told me. A kind man.

Hard times. Mr. Dickens's novel. I have read everything of Mr. Dickens. He knew the soul of the working man. He is like some of our great Russian writers, dear men, so strong and writers the world has never known since. Hard times for my mother, my sister Lu. This was before the war when my sister was brought home by an officer of the soldiers who had a camp near us. I was only fourteen and my mother made me go to a neighbour in the apartment house. She said to stay away and in half an hour I came back and my mother was crying. She said I must never do what my sister was doing. There was the army camp and she told me that my sister had been selling her body. This was prostitution, and it was an illegal thing to do. I suppose it still is. Women will always be hungry and soldiers will always be lonely. My mother cried and my sister, and she was eighteen years old and very beautiful, she told my mother she would not do it again.

The next day my sister and I were walking in the park where the roundabout and the swings were for children and she said that this is where she did it at night. She worked at the sewing machine factory during the day, and at night when she was taking night classes to be better, this is where she met the soldiers. She said my mother was a hypocrite and that the tears and crying was for her benefit and not for me. My sister told me my mother knew what she was doing. Lu gave my mother the money. Then it all was clear to me. This is why we had food. My mother could not work because of her hip when she had fallen off a tram car, and the money was for our food and rent. My sister said it was the shame of the captain coming with her and telling her, the neighbours watching in the hall, every one of the old women, and that was why she was ashamed. Not for the other.

I think now, for a few kopeks. Maybe 20 or 50, a few minutes, that was all, but it bought bread and sausages and beets and potatoes for us, and my sister did not stop. The army officer thought Lu was too beautiful to do this thing, prostitution, and he wanted to warn my mother. She already knew.

There is great tragedy in every family, I have known tragedy and every family, something touches them of an evil nature, or the evil that other people do to them. It is very sad. That is the way of life. Now, I believe things, our lives, will be better. They are not unhappy now. It is better than before. There is this new feeling, there is spring in the air and the skies are blue and the sun, it will shine more on my country and our problems.

Women should be in control of the world. People would be happier. There would be peace. Everybody says we must have peace and why is all this talk of war? The men say we must protect our country from the Americans. I do not think they want war. Just their leaders, they say the same: to have this peace, we must prepare for war. In my readings, that was something the old Greeks said when the mankind of this world was very new.

Everyone has this cult talk. I do not understand it. There was the cult of Stalin. He could kill by his orders one thousand men and women a day for nothing, for every day of the year, and nobody said nothing. We were all so afraid. Do you not think there was a cult of Lenin? Of Khrushchev, yes, I knew something about that fellow. He liked to get attention and he was an actor and the Americans loved him. Yes, he banged his shoe in the United Nations and the world's peoples remember him for that foolish thing. It was not his shoe. He carried slippers to make his feet comfortable and he had them in his pocket. This is what he hit on the desk, his black slipper, but he is known as the crazy Russian with the shoe. Brezhnev, what a foolish old fool. He gave himself the Lenin Prize for Literature for writing a history of the war. He did not write it, and he was not in the war. This is history. Napoleon said history was fiction that everyone agreed upon. Something like that. So much for history. Andropov, a good man but he died too soon. Now we have Gorbachev.

This is an amazing person. So young. Fifty-six, I think, but we really do not know anything about him. Yes, he has been a politician and a bureaucrat since university, I believe, but this man has good ideas. It is good he is Ukrainian, too. They have a solid looking at life. He can talk to the worker in the Kiev Aircraft Manufacturing Works and the fishing captain in the Barents Sea and the wood cutter in Siberia and the student and the housewife and the old war veteran. He has touch. There is no cult with this man. He wants work. Jobs, productivity. Action. This man is a capitalist under his hat. You will see.

He is trying his best. The possibilities against him are very high. This is the chance to take. I'm sure. Something he is doing no leader has done before. There is openness in the newspapers and freedom we have never seen before. What is happening today in this country would not . . . it would have been impossible five years ago. It gives people new hope. You see? It is the beginning, only the beginning. Much has to be done. The necessity for this is urgent, these reforms he plans, and they must be brought forward at a rapid pace.

I am talking about the *glasnost*. The political and economic reforms are important. I think they are more important. We must have democracy. I know everyone thinks that is impossible because never, never, never has the . . . all the peoples of the Soviet Union except for the Baltic States, never have they known democracy. They must have it. The control of the Party must be broken. We must be free. Elections, we must have them and anyone, man, woman, if they can get on the ballot, they can run. It cannot be Party rule. We, if we still do not have this, will be finished before we are begun.

I talk, I have many influential friends. In the sixties I knew many of the great writers and intellectuals. I was in the war driving vehicles and after the war I worked in Moscow. I had many friends of importance and I knew what was happening. I met good writers – Vinogradov, all the ones who worked for *Novy Mir*, the great literature magazine, and yes, I knew Medvedev and the great man Solzhenitsyn. The Nobel Prize, remember, he won that and they would not let him take it. He was not that great a writer, you know, but he was a symbol. He had been in the camps and he was a brave spirit and his pen would not be quiet. He drove the Politburo insane and usually he did not know he was doing it. Yes, I knew many and those were angry days in the sixties and seventies, but at the end I was getting tired.

I was respectable by day in my good job and I was one of the chiefs of the *samizdat* operation at night. This is how the books of many fine writers were read. The Moscow Writers' Union would say no, this book cannot be published. They were under the finger of the bureaucrats. We would get the manuscript and it would be typed and copies made, and then people in ministries and offices would duplicate it. This way, these stories of the camps and oppressions and hardships, they were read by thousands of people. It was very efficient and the KGB and the ministries tried to stop it. Ha! I say this, they could not. We were resourceful and cunning. We knew. One step ahead. Very tiring. Weary, most of the time I was weary. Then I had to say, 'You must stop.' Exciting periods, then, and much good was done. There was great oppression in the land in those days.

That was when I was sent to the work camp in the East. Three years. I was lucky. A soft sentence.

Maybe I will write a book about all those desperate times. I can remember foreigners from America being sent to visit me, a friend in New York, someone I knew who lived in Chicago, they would send people to see me. Intellectuals. American intellectuals. Such babies. Not weaned yet from the breast of soft living and wealthiness. They would say, 'Oh, how wide and clean the streets are.' They would say, 'Russian girls are so beautiful and they wear colourful clothes. They have style. We went to a café last night and the caviar and champagne was so good.' They did not look below, to see the cockroaches and the gummy sausages we had to eat and the cheap wine and beer and taking one hour on the underground to get to work and the smell of the people because the water system had broken down again and there was no water to wash in. These things. The jokes we told them, each with a little tale in it, of the bad days, they would say, 'You have no reason to be bitter. Everything looks fine.' A famous New York novelist who is a fool, this is what he said. To write good novels, and they are good, and then to walk around the Soviet Union with his eyes closed for two weeks, that is . . . he was disgusting.

Aaaaaaah! I talk on too much. An old woman. This pretty gift from an old admirer, this bracelet, it gives me a bit of spirit, but I do not think I will be in this world when we celebrate the victory. The long fight, the battle, the struggle. It has been endless. I will not have the spirit to give on to our young people. They must be taught to fight for freedom.

This apartment, nice, you would call it. Pretty. The trees by the windows. Those rugs, from Afghanistan a long time ago. The samovar, an uncle gave it to me. The rugs on the walls in our Armenian tradition, from Uzbekistan. A hard country place but a friend took me there ten years ago and we had a wonderful visit with the poets of that republic. Each poem was a battle sword waved around the head. Fierce, joyful, but old men now. Once their moustaches bristled with anger of youth. That is a thing that is of the past.

Our writers used to be our heroes. We have few now. That one, we would say, he will rise like Mount Ararat, high, shining there in the sun, the snow. Then corruption. The Writers' Union: 'You do with us or you do not do at all. You are in our power.' They want us to write songs, stories, but what kind? Gush. Dirt. There are Russian words to express the kinds of poetry they write now. We need strong young men again . . . ah, the kind I used to know. We would make fire and put it out with our tears of love.

Writers and poets should shout. This is the time of action, a new revolution. No guns, please. No powder making the air smell. No sound, no noise of guns. This is not what we need. The revolution has come and Gorbachev will say he has won, the nation, Mother Russia, holy of all, is a better place and I will not be around to say, 'Where is the sound of fierce shouts and glory for the new years to come?' Sad.

There is *perestroika* now. I am an intellectual. I slept with intellectual men. All old men now, nothing to do. Some fought, others didn't, and now the good fight is to begin, the young writers and poets have nothing to say. We have raised a race of nothings. Intellectuals lead revolutions, leading the workers and the peasants forward. This time, no intellectuals. Only old women like myself. Come, into battle."

Only in Armenia

Things I saw I could never figure out and I'd just think, "Oh well, this is Russia," although in this case it was in Yerevan, the capital of the autonomous republic of Armenia which, to further complicate things, is no more autonomous from central control than the province of Saskatchewan or the state of Iowa is. However . . .

I was standing on a main street, the usual swirling and grinding of traffic, buses, honking cars and trucks, and I saw a man walking towards me with a three-quarter-size bathtub. It was not crated, just a white bathtub, and it looked like the tub was walking by itself since all I could see was his legs from the knees down and his head poking around the side to keep his direction.

He stopped and I thought, "He's waiting to get a taxi, but how will he get that thing in the taxi?" Then I realized it was a bus stop.

Buses seem to run at three-minute intervals; one came along and it was jammed, not unusual even though this was only mid-afternoon. He'd never make it. No driver was going to let him on, but the others clambered aboard with boxes and bundles, mostly old women and students. Then he edged himself and his cargo through the door. I waited, expecting – in fact, hoping – he would be turned back, but no. I could see him squeezing along the aisle, or rather the large white bathtub making slow progress. The bus pulled away.

I thought, "This cannot be," and it was so unusual I mentioned it to my guide. "Why wouldn't he take a taxi? He could have wedged it in the trunk. I'm sure of that."

"He wanted to take it home on the bus," he said in the casual manner they have when they explain something that a foreigner considers utterly improbable or even insane. "Taxi costs rubles and bus only kopeks."

"But wouldn't he be causing a lot of trouble? Inconveniencing other passengers? Aren't there rules, regulations? Look, you just don't take a big bathtub home on a crowded bus. You don't even take it home on an empty bus."

"This is Armenia," he said, "not North America."

If he had answered, "It all depends," I might have understood because this frequently heard rejoinder answers a lot of unexplained questions, at least to the satisfaction of Soviets trained to deal with foreigners. What he was telling me was they do it their way, we do it our way, and I said, "Suppose a man came along and got on a bus with a big piano?"

"He wouldn't. The piano wouldn't go through the door of the bus."

"But supposing, just supposing he could get it through the doors of the bus?"

He replied, "It all depends."

Damn it.

☙ *The Right Woman Came Along*

"Listen to me. This is the way my father told me of our revolution. The war was with the Germans and our armies and soldiers were brave but there was a shortage of rifles and artillery and slowly and then faster, the Germans became the victors. They had not won the war but they were winning the battles and there was great problems in the kingdom.

My father was born in 1890 in Odessa where his father had a shoe factory. He was educated and he, his name was Nikolai, he saw what was happening. This was before the war. Nikolai was wealthy but he saw how poor the Russian people were. He felt very unhappy about this. This was in 1914 and there was great commotion among the poor as the intelligentsia were saying there must be a change. There must be democracy like there was in England and America. People must have their own destiny. This is where the Bolsheviks came, before the war. The Tsar, our king, the cousin of the English king, he had to be set down and the people would rule.

This went on for a long time and more and more people heard of the new movement and the Tsar, the government, they had what was called the Okhrana. That was the same as the KGB, the secret police organization today. Maybe it was worse, maybe it was not. But it was cruel and many people were called spies and revolutionaries and put in fortresses, the kremlins, these prisons in the big cities, and tortured and killed. This was their way of stopping the revolution which had not started. It was terror. Every night. The special police would capture innocent people. My father saw it all but he was never touched. He had revolution in his heart, not in speaking out about it. He, Nikolai, my father, had got this factory from his father and uncle who had died. He knew that the city was not safe for him and, when the revolution came, he would be just another rich man. He had to do something. He was afraid and he gave money secretly to the underground organization. This would save him, he was sure of that.

Then, okay, let me go back. The war. The Kaiser was the German king and he had spies in Russia who spread the word that England and France did not care about Russia. They just wanted our Motherland to keep fighting so the Germans in Russia would not be moved to fight the English and French armies in France. Do you understand? It was the same as in the Great Patriotic War. The English, Mr. Churchill, wanted a great military effort by our armies on the Eastern Front against the Germans so the Nazis would not conquer England. History is a merry-go-round. It comes back to the same place.

Things went badly for our armies. They had no shells for their guns and no bread for their bellies. The Bolsheviks, they went among the people in the cities, the hungry and the afraid. They said we will give you peace and bread. Bread, bread, good bread. The cry of the masses in the cities everywhere was *'Khleba!'* They would march through the cities, too many for the soldiers to kill, and call out for bread. *Khleba.* Bread. *Khleba.* They were starving. Then there came the flash of fire to the powder keg in Petrograd, which is Leningrad today. This began the revolution and it was the workers, the machinists, the railway workers, the tram drivers, and the regiments, they won. They overthrew the government and the word went to other cities. The people had won.

My father was happy, but then a friend, a worker, this foreman in his factory, came in the night and told him that he and my mother would have to flee. The committee was going to arrest him although some of the workers said he was on the side of the workers. These committee men had been sent from Moscow and they did not know my father. That night they got in their motor car with just a few things and went to the sea-coast and got on a ship and it was going to Egypt and that is where they got off. They were safe.

The rest you know. The Germans, they had been keeping Lenin in Switzerland. He was the boss behind the revolution. The chief Bolshevik. He was half Jewish, very smart. An intellectual. The Germans brought him to Petrograd and that was when the government began.

There were many problems. The Soviet Union then was huge and only in the cities the people had an understanding of politics and revolution. The soldiers stopped fighting, which was under the Kaiser's plan, but then what to do with them? The newspapers were controlled by the government. Anyway, the peasants did not read. Russia was an illiterate country. They were for more land for themselves as they were cunning and greedy and hated the landowners. The Bolsheviks promised them land. The people in the cities, they were sophisticated, many of them, and they wanted peace and now there was peace. This was in 1918. They wanted bread. There was no bread. There was nothing. The country was broken down. Using Lenin and his intellectual friends, the Germans had won the Russian war. Now, this is when the real trouble began.

To understand my country, you must know what happened next. The Reds, they were for the revolution. The Whites, those were the armies commanded by generals and officers who were privileged classes, rich, of noble Petrograd families who ruled the country, they did not want revolution. There would be a Red army here in this part of the country controlling it and over here, a hundred miles away, a White army. All over Russia. Siberia. The Ukraine. Like Odessa, it was held first by the White army after the October Revolution of 1917 and two years later the Red army came in and killed off the rich and the middle class and . . . oh, it was a terrible time. Tens of thousands of poor young soldiers who did not know why they were fighting other Russian young soldiers, they all died and tens of thousands of mothers mourned and wore black clothes forever.

Other countries, Japan, the Americans, England, oh many, they sent guns and men to help the White armies but it was no use. The people would conquer. In 1920, three years after the storming of the Summer and Winter palaces beside the Neva River, that mighty day, the Reds won. The people had won. Now the revolution could go ahead with democracy and much food for all. It tore my country apart and there was nobody who knew how to make it together again. Lenin always was writing decrees. Do this, do that. If you do, the revolution will be strong. He did not say if you do not do this, do not do that, you will be shot or sent to prison camps. People did not know what to do and if they did it wrong, they were in trouble.

I was born in Cairo because they fled in the night from Odessa. We went to Montreal because there were many Jews there. We lived in a room in a big house on Drummond Street and my mother's jewels and rings were taken to the pawn shop and we lived. There was a depression then after the war, my father told me, and he could not work but he finally got work in a clothing factory. He became a foreman.

It was in 1924 and Lenin had died and Stalin was the chief. One night a man came to the door of the apartment on Guy Street where we lived and my father sent me to the bedroom and I could hear talking. The man was a Russian agent living in Canada. He had reported on all the Soviet people living in Montreal and they wanted my father to go back and run his old factory. The workers could not make it run efficiently. Now, this was something to think about very seriously. My mother wanted to go very much. She loved her country and used to cry and cry because it was so far away and they were exiles. My father thought, as he told me many years later, he wanted to go very, very much but he thought that he would get his shoe and boot factory working efficiently and then the Bolsheviks would kill him. He was not wanted any more. But his great love for his country overcame his fears and in 1927 we got on a ship in Montreal and went to London and then on another ship to Leningrad. That was the new name. It was the summer and the city was beautiful. Very busy. I was only nine and dressed in my little grey suit with my little military hat, and my father and I both carried small malacca canes and we were elegant.

The city was very poor. There were many poor people about. We went to the Astoria Hotel for a few days and my father used to sit with foreigners in the lounge rooms. There were many foreigners from England and France and South America and Spain there, he said, and they wanted to do business with the Soviet Union. They would wait and wait and then they would get a note and they would catch the train to Moscow. My father said Moscow was where the business was done, but the businessmen wanted to stay in Leningrad because it had good hotels and good food and good women.

The Astoria Hotel was very proud, an old hotel by the Neva, and the old porter who would take me for a walk every afternoon. He was there in the revolution. He said that the day after the Leninist group took control, after they had bombed open the doors to the armoury and got the guns and did their work, the soldiers took over the Astoria Hotel. He said they were like animals. Drunk. These were not the elite guards who protected the Tsar . . . I should say that in those days Petrograd was where the court of the Tsar was . . . he and all of his were killed at a town called Ekaterinburg. It is in the Urals. It is now called Sverdlovsk, a very large city. These soldiers were peasants and like animals, the old porter said. He gave them everything they wanted. Food. Drink. Women. Money. He said if he had even blinked, they would have shot him.

Then the new officers the men had appointed, from the regiments, they took over the Astoria Hotel and many of the soldiers were shot. I don't know. This may be history or just this old man's story. I remember, I was nine years old, and I can see him acting all this out, the shooting of the soldiers by the officers. It was a time of great agitation and there was one man who was the leader. Stalin. We had him for many years.

These were desperate times. We were in Odessa. My father, it took him three years and he was able to get the factory working properly and he did everything by the rule. Every day he made a report to the city government and the police and every day they told him he would be able to get better material to make good products. It was a struggle. It was in the 1930s when there was a depression and it was very bad. In the Ukraine, hundreds of thousands of people died. It was very sad. People said Stalin was sincere and a great leader and then the next day the army would come and take away the grain they had harvested and sell it at high prices to the people in the city. There was great famine, great suffering. Even in Odessa, where there should be food, there was great suffering.

People would die and the family hung a rag on the door of the cottage and the truck would stop and take the body. They went into big graves and there was no place, no worship place, a cemetery, where you could go and put up a cross and go and visit it. Besides, a cross was the sign of Jesus and religion, the Christianity, and nobody would put up a cross. The cross was in their hearts. You could touch your breast and touch that cross and make a little prayer for the dead one.

When I was eighteen and going to the scientific institute in Odessa my father spoke to the commissar. My father was boss but the commissar was from Moscow and he was the chief. My father took orders from this man who was a politician. He was a member of the Party. My father was, too, and I was in the Pioneers and then the higher-up rank, Young Communist League. He said he needed me in the factory to learn the business. The commissar said there would be a discussion about it. I was put in the factory. Very young. I made 40 rubles a month. Good pay. My father made 90, I think. My mother and my two sisters were at home. This was an apartment we had.

Odessa was a shipbuilding city and there was some work and the workers needed good boots. The commissar would say to my father, 'Here is the letter from Moscow. You are not making enough boots. Make more.' My father would tell him, more hides, more boots. No hide, no boots. Where are the hides? My father would say, 'The hides are in Genoa or in Barcelona.' The hides to make the leather, they come as donkey hides from Algeria and Morocco, which I think was French. The commissar would say, 'Get the hides.' That is how my father and the commissar went to Italy, to Spain, and bought the hides. The commissar, he was a fat man from Moscow and all he wanted to do was have drink and women.

They went and my father did not come back. The commissar came back with no hides. My father had run away. He had cancer and he knew he would die in the Odessa hospital.

There was no medicine. My father, he wrote us once and we got the letter through an English ship captain who came to Odessa and he said the war was over in Spain and he was dying of cancer. This was his letter of goodbye.

That was the end of my life. The war was coming. There was already the war with Finland. I was not punished for what my father did . . . I am sorry but this is hard to tell you. He was a good man. He did his welcome best to tell us not to worry. I was questioned many times and I told them I knew nothing. The commissar was taken away and I think he may be killed because he had been drunk when my father broke away from his attentions. They put me in military school and then they took me into a transport section and that was when the war had started.

It was an important job, this arranging of transport and keeping the trucks going, and I was an officer. I never saw the fighting. That is why I am telling you this today. I was rear troop movement. Matériel supply. To the front. I was always watched but I did my work cleanly and with good taste. It was very difficult for me.

After the war I was a captain and I went back to Odessa but I could not find my mother and sisters. The girls were too young and a man I met on the street said they had been sent to a work farm. I stayed in Odessa and the factory was still there but all the workers were gone. My father's superintendent, he invited me to his home among the bombings and he told me to forget about my mother. There was no hope for her. That was a long time ago, my friend. A long total of many memories.

Stalin was still there. He was the great hero. He had won the war. He did not, this terrible man, he did not. He sacrificed Soviet armies to his pride. He killed so many thousands of people without guilt . . . yes, innocent, thank you . . . so many hundreds and hundreds of thousands. His brain, I think, was being eaten by the worm of cancer. Our surgeon doctors did not recognize this sickness. He had control and the democracy my father used to tell me would come, it never did. It got worse. Finally he died. Now we know what this terrible man did.

Myself? Yes, I was still young. I was thirty and there were my papers and medals as an officer but they did me no good, you understand. The Motherland was full of officers. I was given a job in the railroad. It was good work. There is a pride of keeping the trains running, they are so important. I worked with men, not these stinking bureaucrats.

There was great shortages in these times. I would tell a few men I trusted. 'Break open that car.' I had the papers in my office and I knew what was in the cars. I said, 'There is food in that one. Take ten boxes and bring them here tonight.' Each man in my section, they would be there and we would give each of us the food. Maybe tins of beef. Maybe herring. Butter. Once I made a mistake. The three men were caught by the police and one was shot in the prison and the others got sixteen years in the East. This did not stop us. They did not inform on us. This was the way we lived.

This is the truth. The state was turning us into the criminal mind. To steal, that was the way to survive and sell the things we stole. Nobody ever knew. We were like a gang of brothers. Everyone was very secretful. There would be 300 boxes in a car, we would steal carefully – take ten and nobody will know. I would give my men a new seal to put on the car door. In Moscow or Smolensk or this city or that city, these food cars, they would think the stealing came from where the train was loaded. We did this. We had to, this criminal act.

Then I was sent to Yerevan, this beautiful city. There was great stealing in the rail system and they said I would have to stop it. They said there had been no stealing in my section, so they said, 'You will be able to stop the stealing there.' This was the way they thought.

I was happy to do this. We had been making money on the black market for nine or ten years and to do this and not be caught, and to not have an informer among the people, that showed the brotherhood and the loyalty and love we showed for each other. Some of the men were getting to be pensioned and new ones would come in and then it would end. These young men, they would say, 'Why does Vasily and Igor and Nickolai, these guys, why do they live well with food and have good clothing? They must be doing something.' You can see. Our little operation was going to go badly. This was the year 1965, I think, and we had been smooth too long.

We had a meeting at a tavern where there was lots of drinking and lots of noise and I told them, 'I am going to the South. They have put me in charge of things there in Yerevan, in the yards, and I will have an office. I am tired of all this; it has gone all along too long and too fine. When I go you can keep on, but you will have a new boss and he will be watching. He can join you or he can inform on you. If he gets to know our operation you will be in a camp for ten years or working as a slave. What will happen to all those kids of yours? Quit now,' I told them. 'Just stop this. You have all plenty of money. Our secrecy has been a good thing. We are brothers, but the cousins are coming and they will trap you.'

I was sent to this city and I was very happy. It was so beautiful and warm and I did not dream there could be such a nice city. I did not want to leave it and I made many friends and I thought, 'I am fifty and I have worked hard and I will get a wife.' This was not easy. There was a suspicion of foreigners among the Armenian people and I would find it difficult, my new friends said to me. 'Friend,' they said, 'just wait. We believe you do not have to be like our hot young men who chase the girls and want to marry and have babies. The right woman will come along.'

She was Armenian but her father was Russian, a dead engineer, and she was a doctor in Moscow and she was visiting her mother. Her name was Galina. This was eight years ago when I was soon retired, and I was riding my motorbike and I hit a dog and ran into the wall of this building. Near the circus building. She was walking by and she said I had a broken bone up here in the arm, up here. Yes, the collar. She took me in her father's car, a big one, to the hospital and I thought to myself, 'I am going to marry this one.' She was forty-nine years old then. I thought, 'When I get out I am going to find her and tell her about myself and then we will see.' It happened this way. The next day she came to the hospital as to see how I was doing and she brought me some cakes and a book. I didn't even know her name.

That's how we got married. She went back to Moscow two weeks later and then she came back on a permit to work in Yerevan and I was at the airport and our friends, her friends, my friends, were waiting at the apartment. We got married in the apartment by a clerk and then we went to her church and we got married there. Two old people. Now, I mean. We moved into her mother's fine apartment with all the finest of furniture of her grandfather and I sent to Odessa to my cousin the news and then I went and got my father's very fine furniture, which was his father's, and that was that. Her mother died and we now have a very happy life. A big apartment and trees when you look out the windows and there is much money. I have mine and she has money and if she wants to work, she does, and it is only two days a week in the hospital. That is what we like.

We go travel. There have been four cruises on big ships, on the Volga and the Black Sea, the Mediterranean Sea, to Rome and many other places. We can see the world if we want, there are no holdings on us. Any place, go, any time. This is a different place. It is Armenia and I feel very happy with it. There are mountains and wonderful food. The food, when I think of looking back of those days in the city of Odessa and my father changing food from the captains of ships for shoes and boots he took from the factory, and during the war, so little bread and cabbage soup with maybe a few herring heads and tails in it and tea, only tea and no sugar, and now, the rich food we have. I think we live for food but we do not get fat. We exercise. Swimming. Jogging, in my fine American shoes. Five kilometres every day, with Galina by my side and people smiling at us.

The terrible days are gone, and it is wonderful to have money. I never tell her where it came from. My secret. This is a wonderful country. It is the most of all in the world when you are living with Galina in Yerevan, and whoop-de-do-da. No politics, no trains, no bureaucrats. A young girl just twelve years younger than this old goat, hand in hand and very happy. This is the world of goodness."

Return to Moscow

❦

*Every Georgian Is a Poet . . . A Little Cloak-and-Dagger
Business*

*Before flying to Siberia, I touch down in the Soviet capital
again. With no interviews arranged for me, I am on my own.
My guide Andrei, whom I call The Expediter because he gets
me on and off those creaky, worn-out planes and in and out
of hotels with a minimum of fuss and bother, is not equipped
to act as translator. I ask a Moscow-based engineer, "Is your
life better than it was four years ago?" Ten minutes of Russian
dialogue later, Andrei turns to me: "Yes, he says it is." Some
translation.*

*My best interviews come from just talking with people who
come up to me on the street, in cafés, subways, the hotel
lobby. These are real conversations, ranging wherever they
want to take them. But they don't approach when The Expediter is with me. They know Officialdom when they see it.*

👐 *Every Georgian Is a Poet*

"I miss our Georgian bread. It is made with goat cheese and you can eat it with honey and it is like candy. One of us, when he comes back from a visit in the mountains of our own country, he phones somebody who is in our network and says he has brought back a box of our bread and we get together with our wine and eat and there are grapes and yogurt and honey and little Georgian cakes and we die with laughing and singing our own songs.

Yes, I said network. There is nothing sinister in it. No affairs against the state. Not here in Moscow. I am talking about Georgians. We are our own nation. We were a nation many centuries before there was a Russia. A Soviet Union, that is just perhaps two pages in the history of this country and the book is 100 pages. You understand what I am speaking to you about. In a foreign land as Moscow is, we of the South know each other. There may be 200,000 Georgians in The Centre and there could be 200 people in each network. Nothing bad. The people in each network are from one small town or some villages in Georgia and we all know each other. Another network, that might come from villages in the west of Georgia, where the great orchards are. Another dozen might come from Tbilisi. It is just our way of keeping together. Our faith, you would say. Our songs. Oh yes, and our dances. This all comes under the term of it being a culture.

Together we are all Georgians, but we are plenty of little peoples, little groups, and this we call our network. Other groups might call themselves other names, just as a soccer team calls itself the Stars or the Dynamo team. Something like that.

Everybody lets everybody know there is to be a party. Some of us, we have big apartments. Three rooms. The children are sent to another apartment for the happy occasion, the night, and the rest come. There could be forty or fifty come from our network. They are everyone, men and women, young girls to dance with, and we have professors and men who drive tractors and old women who work in the laundries. There might be five boxes of food because maybe three people have been to Georgia. Yogurt in big jars. Plenty of wine and cognac. Georgians do not drink beer and not much vodka. This is the way it is. Beer is not much in our country. It is unpatriotic for a countryman to drink beer when we have so much wine. You have heard of Georgian wine? There is much drinking of it. Singing our songs. Wild songs. That is why we are such fierce fighters. We used to, our young warriors, go into battle singing. Drunk sometimes, too.

No, you do not understand. Not drunk because they were afraid. In the old days when they fought the Turks and the Armenians and everyone else who wanted our wonderful country, they would fight in the day. The night before, they would drink to celebrate the battle which was to come. They would be in castles or big camps on the mountains and on the high hills and they would be on their ponies and then they would charge down on the enemy. Swords. Guns. Spears we called lances.

We are fierce. We have big strong men. It is the good food. The good wine. The strong women who give us strong children. It is good to put a sword into the hands of one of our little boys, and maybe he is six years old. It is heavy but if he holds it right ... if he knows the right balance of it, we say he will be a warrior. That makes a father very proud.

We do not fight that way now. That was in the history of our country when we were free. Now we are not. It is very sad. Many Georgian songs weep for the freedom we had and how strong and fierce and how many invaders were chased back through the passes in the mountains.

At our parties, it is in this big room. The biggest room in the biggest apartment of one of the men in our network. Mostly relatives and friends, you see. You have to belong. That is your entertainment. The Georgian in Moscow, any big city, he is different. They look at us and say, 'That's a Georgian. Stay away. He's bad.' Because we are big men and strong and our women are beautiful. Our skins are darker and you will never see a real Georgian with eyeglasses. We never need them. You never see a Georgian with no hair. How do you call it? Yes, bald. Funny word. No bald Georgians. We are as hairy as our ponies. As feathered as our famous turkeys. As thick as our famous sheep in the mountains. As keen in the eye as our famous cowboys who ride the mountains protecting the sheep against the wolf.

The party. Yes, the party. One man is always the leader. We don't elect him. He is just the leader. He may be an important man on the floor where they make the steel in a factory. He may be a professor at the academy. He may be a journalist. But he tells us, when everyone is there, he will make the first toast. When the next person makes the toast in brown wine, the cheap wine, he points him out. When we drink the spring wine, it is the same. He says what song will be sung, and who will lead in the singing. He is the leader. He will say when the women should bring in the wonderful food and then we feast.

We love to feast. Our feasts are famous to us. Our beautiful women bring out the legs of young lamb which have been brought to Moscow from our mountains farms. There is yogurt with honey and there are figs, big figs. You know figs? They make a good wine, too. Very strong. Pomegranates. Peaches. Cream. Coffee. All this and the kebab meat, all brought in from Georgia by our visitors. This is a feast. And we drink more wine.

Every Georgian is a poet. Our leader will say, 'Robert, sing to us of our homeland,' and he will get up. I should say he may be swaying by this time and the room is hot and the laughter, it is loud, and all this, it may affect him. But he tells us a poem. It may be of the glorious battles we fought so long ago to protect our homes and our beautiful women. It may be the sun rising over the mountains, the warm wind coming down from the hills. The green trees lining the roads and the young boys tending their sheep and goats and turkeys. It will be, maybe, of the great leaders we had. The beauty of the old castles in the moonlight. These were the refuge of the people when our country was invaded and the priests took them in. We are still a religious country. We believe in it. It has helped us. More young women are being married in the eyes of God. This was not the way it was. I was married in a church that the army closed down and beat up in 1931 and now, again, it is being used for religious things.

Our leader, maybe he is swaying now, so much wine, and he gives a toast and then he talks about our resistance. Georgians are unhappy, as you can see everywhere you look with the Russians in our country. They stage protests or this and that. It does not matter which, the shortage of gasoline, the shortage of good clothes, the slowness of building the underground in Tbilisi. Anything. The Russians think we are protesting the subway or the honking drivers but we are protesting *them*. There are riots that are never in the journals. One thousand, 3,000 people, they don't really riot, but they march with flags of the old days and banners. Yes, yes, yes. It is not much, but we do want to do it. Blow off steam, as you call it.

We have poets read their poetry. Everybody in Georgia is a poet. The shepherd boy on the hillside, he makes poetry. The truck driver, my cousin, he drives long distances over the mountains and nearly dies from the black diesel smoke, so what does he do? What does this crazy Nikolai do? He makes poems about Baku diesel smoke. It was funny, as you call it. To Nikolai it was a protest. The woman in the glove factory, my neighbour when I lived in the deep South, she was a poet. She was very good. Just this woman at her machine eight hours a day and making 120 rubles, poor soul, sorry about that, and she was a poet. A poetess.

You know. My English is not good. They do not teach English in my country like they do in Leningrad, where the intellectuals are, or in Moscow, where the scientists and the fat bureaucrats and the army is. They teach it. Yes, we do have good schools, but too many of the teachers are sent in from Russia. That is something else we do not like. In a Georgian village where nobody speaks Russian, they will send in a Russian teacher or a Ukrainian teacher. This is crazy. So, if you were like me, on a merchant ship for twelve years, you studied English. New York, Boston, Shanghai, Vancouver, Buenos Aires for grain, your Halifax and Montreal, these places, I bought English books. I have bought hundreds of English books. There was English when I was in school. That was not enough. I could get by, as you say, but with an English dictionary I could read these books better. I read Norman Mailer and I liked him and your Pierre Berton and Shakespeare. I have all the plays of Shakespeare. A very wise man. So many others. John Updike is another favourite. Then Plato and many French writers and the poems of Robert Burns and

Robert Service. He is the best. He is not an intense poet but he speaks from the heart. If I had ever met him, I would have said, 'Mr. Service, you have the soul of a Georgian.'

We can get English and American magazines and ones from other countries. I speak English and Russian and I can also speak German but not as well. I can go to Armenia and do business if I wanted to go there, but they are all crooks and embezzlers. It is their way of life. The things we have together is our distrust of the Russian boys.

Then comes more feasting and drinking and we have gula kababi and that is meat, spiced meat, inside our famous flat-bread I mentioned to you about, and khinkali, which you would like. It is more meat, lots of spices, and it is folded in dough. The women have made them for hours and they come in on big red- and gold-coloured platters, up this high. Even higher. Everybody eats, drinks more wine, and then somebody says we should have some beer. This is Russian beer, not bad, and it clears the throat. Then more wine. Cognac. Somebody says when is this going to finish. It is two in the morning, but then somebody says not until the sun comes up. Nobody works then. Another day off at the ministry. Sorry, factory boss, but I was very sick.

There is more drinking and the old women, they fall asleep, their kind old heads on their chests. The younger women, they want to dance and there is dancing. There is nothing crude about it, no hugging, but there is not much room so there is little dancing.

Somebody yells, 'What is the news from the world?' Everyone laughs. I point to Grigori, my good friend, and he has steel teeth. I say he should open his mouth and see how many radio stations he can find in his mouth radio. There is a short-wave radio in the apartment and there is silence and the owner of it, he tries to bring forward 'The Voice of America.' Sometimes it can be done, but then there is nothing on it, and besides, most people do not understand English. This is the radio station for the American soldiers in Europe.

Then we sing. We sing low because it is very late and there is a chance a neighbour might have a telephone and would call the militia. The police. They would come, these stupid farm boys . . .

I ask you, is it the same in your country? The authorities want the police to be farm boys so they will not be smart and will learn exactly all the rules and laws and not use their noodles to think in all situations. If there is something they do not understand, they call their superiors. Then people can be in trouble. There is a rule and a law for anything. If we had a party and I invited you and you were on your feet, but you wouldn't be because nobody can drink like a Georgian, but if he saw your feet on the floor and found you were from America, then there would be trouble. It is even a law that peoples of the Soviet Union cannot talk with foreigners. If you ask me for a fire for your cigarette outside the Intourist Hotel right by Red Square, that would be an offence. Nothing might happen to us, but it would be on our record. Times are changing, as Bob Dylan sings, one of our favourites, little Bob Dylan, and soon this may end. It is foolish. How are we to know about the world if we cannot see it? On "Vreyma" television, nothing. Plenty of things about fur farming by the Yakuts on the taiga and the crop of wheat in the southern Ukraine and fishing in the Barents Sea and who is visiting our glorious leaders from the glorious republic of Bulgaria, but nothing of America and Canada or the world.

When I was a sailor I found all the peoples of the world were polite to me and my friends. If our ship was in New York Harbour, in Brooklyn, Pier 38, the places where foreign ships went, we were always welcomed in the streets. Italians, Greeks, American people, they were always nice. Our commissar on the ship, he would say not to talk to the Negroes. I will tell you, I met these Negroes when I was a sailor. I was a radio operator. We were in harbour and I was not needed for the work of loading the goods. I met them and I talked and drank with them and I liked them. In Moscow, here, we do not see many Negroes. Only the foreign students and they look so unhappy. They are here to learn Russian methods and go home. Yes, home where they go is not good, I think. I am told that.

You ask why I am in Moscow? I was sent here. I was a student and then I went to the academy in Tbilisi and got my papers and they said I would be a translator. Yes, because I am a linguist. I know several languages. My mother says I am the only one in our family, all our family, all over our western part of Georgia who can speak these languages. It is because of the books I got. It is very easy for me. I work hard and I do my job and I get my money and I live with three other translators. The government gives us an apartment. A good one. So these other guys, they have many books in English and German, too. German is easy for me to understand. The long words all pushed in together. You can read it easy. Speaking the German is more difficult but reading and translating it into Russian is easy. I do scientific texts and then they go to another translator who is a scientist and he does it better then. He is paid more. I get 210 rubles a month and my rent is 9 rubles. That is thirty-six rubles for the apartment for four of us and so we have lots of money. When I write to a cousin and he says he is coming to Moscow, to sell flowers or pork or grapes, in bags he puts these things, and flies by plane and then we have a feast.

I will marry again. I was very sad when my first wife died. That is when I went on the ships to forget. I was twenty-one years of age and then for ten years I saw the world and then I became a translator and that is when I was sent to Moscow. Aaaaaah! Moscow.

I will be going back to my country in a few years. Maybe two years. I have had my papers to my superior for two years already, but there is not much hope soon. I want to go. My heart is there. The poetry of my country calls me home and my heart longs for talk and laughter and good food from the little farms. There is no food in Moscow. No pork, no beef, no fish except in those glassine bags with the water and the blood swishing around in them and they are bad.

In Georgia there is much food. People all the time here in Moscow talk of food. 'I bought a duck in the market yesterday on market day,' a man says. How much did it cost? 'I went crazy,' this neighbour said, 'and bought it for 20 rubles.' I said, 'You are crazy.' He said, 'I would have paid 30 rubles.' That is what it is like. In Georgia you can buy all the food and fruit and everything, chocolates, tarts, buns, good bread, no problems. Here in Moscow, food is an obsession of life and they think it is wonderful because they have the Bolshoi and you are lucky to get a ticket from your director. And the politicians and important people and their ladies, all you hear them talking about is food. That is funny. They are the ones who get the good food, the excellent food in their special stores and their special privileges.

I laugh because I know when I visit my relatives in their villages by the Sevan Lake I know I will eat the finest foods in the whole Soviet Union. There will be big red strawberries. They are the best in the world. I will drink Georgian tea, the best in the world. That is the truth. There will be fruits and lamb shashlik and special sauces from our berries and our wonderful bread made with maize and honey and goat curd. There will be the finest wines from the region of Kakhetia, and these wines are famous around the world. You should try and get this wine. It is like heaven. This is the wine made by the villagers. Not in the big refineries, the wineries where everything is done by machinery. Each grape in Kakhetia is tenderly picked and packed in jars and buried and it ferments in the warm earth. I can have for a ruble three or four huge oranges and there are pineapples. These are not things you can buy, even in Moscow or in Leningrad, where the snobbery of the people makes me sick. I have been there. They make me sick with their literary airs and noses. They sniff you.

When I go home they have a big feast for me and a lamb is killed and roasted and we sit and I tell them how lucky they are to be in our own country. I go to a cupboard in my cousin's house and I take out my uniform of Georgia. Even if it is summer I put on my big sheep hat and my robe and I wear the sword of my great-great-grandfather, a Georgian sword, and I am fierce. Look at me, this big moustache and my dark skin and my black hair, black, and I am tall, two metres high, and I stride in and sing a song and everybody claps and I clap my hands and we begin to eat. I am the leader. This will be a meal that lasts three hours and much wine, jars and jars of it, and all the good food, and I tell them about Moscow and the places I have visited. Then I say, 'You are Georgians. It is the best country in the world. I have seen the world.' We are drunk by this time and dancing and eating and our blood is boiling and we yell and hit the table and hit each other in the chest and we cheer, we roar and they cry out, tell us more.

I am drunk and I say this. I say, 'The collective farms are not Georgia because every man and woman of us and our children, too, and the old men who are more than a hundred years old, we are all free people. Let the Russians come and build their high apartments and their electric-hydro plants on the Kura River and let them build their lorries and military vehicles. They can build the highway and their trucks can go on them, but we still have our goat tracks in the mountains that we know about and nobody else does. Let them have their circus. Let them have their shrine to the killer Stalin who betrayed the Georgian people. Spit on him, if you want. But spit on all the Soviet leaders, too. Stalin was only a man. He left us, but he was still a Georgian in the tiger of his heart. Let the Russians say they have made us a great country. They did not put the Kura River in place or the mountains, not Mtatsminda, where you can look down on Tbilisi at night when it is lit up with all the Russian hydro. Houses in Tbilisi and Gori, they are 600 years old and good and they don't fall down. Georgian people built those homes and they will never fall down. Be proud you are Georgian. It is the world's most important place and fourteen armies, that many countries, attacked us since Christ was born and each time we knocked them back. Be proud of Georgia. You are Georgians.'

Then everybody cheers and I once jumped on the table and danced and kicked things off it and then, I should not tell you this. I became unconscious. Too much wine. But you can understand. Aaaaaah! It will be good to go home again and build a house and live the way God made it in his ways for our people to live."

A Little Cloak-and-Dagger Business

"You speak English?"

We were standing in a line at an ice cream stand opposite the Intourist Hotel in Moscow. He was a tall, thin fellow dressed in a chocolate-coloured suit, a lighter brown shirt, and a dark red tie. He carried a briefcase–bureaucracy, minor level.

"I want to talk to you. Will you listen, please?" Immediately I smelled a rat. A small rat, perhaps, but nevertheless.

"I will buy my ice cream and then you buy yours and then you follow me down the street." He motioned to the left, away from Red Square. I thought, "Here's a new twisty character." He did not appear to be one of the dissident Jews whom foreign correspondents had told me about who want to catch the ear of the foreigner. Perhaps he just wanted to talk. To practise his English.

I followed him, and we went through the underpass and at the top, standing there, he flicked his thumb, indicating I was to walk ahead. I sauntered along, looking in windows, taking my time. In a few minutes he passed me and said, "Follow me again." This little game went on for a few minutes until he turned into a side street and walked partway down it. Then he stopped and said, "It is okay here," when I caught up to him.

"And now, my friend, I would like to ask a favour of you," and I thought, "Oh-oh, here it comes," but there seemed no way to back out. "It is my sweet little wife's birthday tomorrow and I want to buy her something special. Very special. Something that will make her happy."

"Vodka?" I said.

He laughed. "No, perfume. Just a bottle of perfume. They have them in the hard-currency store, the shop in your hotel. A little bottle, this high," indicating with his fingers a bottle three inches high. "French. They make the best."

"But no vodka?"

"Vodka, we have it all times, always. No problem for us."

Extremely curious by now, I asked, "How can you get vodka? Those line-ups, 300 people in them. Where do you get it?"

"Ah, you are a curious fellow. Like all foreigners. Okay, my friend, it is this way. You see, I work in a ministry, one son in a shoe factory, one son is a cab driver. My wife and daughter work in a place that makes women's clothes–but we have our ways," and he made the universal sign for pay-offs.

"Just about every morning the phone rings at six o'clock and it is a friend of mine. He works in a place, an office, and he knows what stores will have bottles of vodka for sale. He also tells me when it will open. Maybe eleven in the morning. Maybe at twelve o'clock. Any time. So we go, in our car, and when we get there there is just a little line-up because people haven't found out by then. Each of my family, my wife, my two sons, and my daughter-in-law, we buy a bottle of vodka and then we drive to another store and then the line will be long and we have to wait a long time, maybe an hour. Two hours. But then we have ten bottles of vodka. Then we go back to the first store and the line will be very, very long, maybe 500 people. They will wait a long time, maybe three hours. So I go to the end of the line and I say to a fellow, 'Why do you want to wait in line for three hours for some vodka, comrade? I will sell you vodka, right out of this store. Only 25 rubles. Right now. Is this something you want? I have it.'

"I know for sure he will buy it. Maybe there is also an old babushka. Her husband makes good bonus in the factory, and she will hear me. Maybe it is an army officer and he wants to get a bottle and get back to his office and drink it with the boys. Maybe anyone. My son does the same thing. He just goes up to someone, maybe this guy looks like he is in a hurry, a bureaucrat, and he doesn't have the ticket to buy it in the shop in his ministry, and so, that is how we do it."

He looked around behind us. "We should move along now. We have been here long enough. A militia car might come along. Walk down to that corner and turn right and stop at the next street and go down it. I will go around the other way and meet you."

All this cloak-and-dagger stuff. But as I walked I did some calculations. "You're making about 800 rubles a month just on vodka," I said when we met again. "You guys are rich."

"Expenses, my friend. Each week we have to give one bottle to the boss where we work. That's five bottles. Three to the fine fellow who phones us where the stores will have vodka. That is eight. Do you see. So, much less."

Then something clicked, and I said, "No! Wait a minute! It wouldn't be 800 rubles. I was figuring on five bottles a day you buy and then sell. But you do it twice. So, looking at it that way, it is 1,600 rubles."

He laughed. "Well, my friend, does it matter? But that is why I want a nice bottle of perfume for my wife."

"How do you get away with it?"

He rubbed his two fingers together again. "Money. It is wonderful. Vodka. It always talks. Always. Your country, this country. Today, 500 years ago, money talks. Look at your government people. Look at ours. We have a word, words for it, so do you. It means grafters. Everywhere. Everybody does it. This is how we live."

"But buying perfume for you is illegal as hell," I said. "Every visitor is warned: no exchanging money, no 'doing business.' "

"Come along, my friend. We will walk back the same way. You in front and I will be waiting outside. I have my eye open and I'll talk to the taxi drivers. They will know if anyone is watching. You go in. It is a small bottle with a gold and black label. Just give the girl 20 dollars and wait around for five minutes and I will come along. You will give me the package down the street there, in behind that big bus for tourists. That is all."

As we walked back I was silent. He said, "I know what you are thinking, but it's okay. The store gets the dollars. That's all they want. The girls, ah, those girls, they get a few rubles a week. You are just helping our system work, my friend. I am a good Russian. All I want is a birthday party, a good Russian dinner, some vodka, and some friends of friendship to come in for company, and for my little wife a present."

"Okay," I thought, "what the hell. The experience is worth it," and I went in and bought the bottle. Then I thought, "My 20 dollars! How is he going to pay me? In rubles, of course. Ah, I'm leaving for Irkutsk tomorrow and I'll need rubles." Rationalizing, I said, "Everybody does it."

I went out on the street and over to the bus and he was waiting and he took the bottle. "See the porter at the counter in the hotel," and he was gone. Striding off across the wide boulevard, he turned at the far side and waved.

Stunned, I thought, "Skunked. Trapped by a smart shyster. Oh well, we live and learn. It could have happened in Mexico City or Istanbul. Anyway, it's a good story."

But I went to the porter's desk and as I approached, one of the men reached out and handed me a roll of bills, tightly wrapped in paper. No expression. A stone face. I went back to my room and I didn't give a damn if the secret TV camera was eyeing me – if there was one – and counted the rubles. Sixty. Three rubles for a dollar.

I laughed. Nothing was illegal. I had bought the perfume, all legal. The state had its hard currency. They're happy. No money had changed hands between me and Ivan Ivanov, or whatever his name was. The porter had done nothing illegal, just handed me something wrapped in brown paper. The three-for-one exchange was illegal – but technically legal – the Soviet government unofficially sets the black market rate.

But how did the porter know who I was, and why I was approaching him? And how did he know he was to give me 60 rubles? Who gave him the 60 rubles? Wheels within wheels.

That's what bothered me. It still does. When I told this story later, I was told, "Forget it. It's just the way it works. The porter would get a couple of rubles, too. The politicians do the same thing, except with them, it is just plain stealing. You dealt with a city slicker, didn't you? You should see the games that the peasants play. They make those Muscovites look like dummies."

There's one satisfaction. The woman described as a "sweet little wife" got her bottle of cheap French perfume.

Of course, the whole cloak-and-dagger business made no sense. Why play silly games? Why not just ask me to go in and buy the perfume? I would have. But I *had* played the silly game.

The sad thing, really, was that a Soviet citizen could not go in and buy the perfume with rubles. But if he had bought dollars on the black market, which is a crime, he could have walked in by bribing the doorman. The clerk at the perfume counter would have known he was using black market dollars, but she would have sold him the perfume, no questions asked.

What was it that Churchill said about the Russians?

NINE

Irkutsk: Deep in the Taiga

Siberia's Seven Simeons . . . Working on the Railroad . . .
Baseball on Ice? . . . The Youngest Officer at the Front

So this is Siberia? I have left a windy, chilly Moscow for the
sunshine of Irkutsk. This centuries-old city of 700,000 is sit-
uated on the broad, smooth-flowing Angara River that drains
Lake Baikal. Once a stop-over on the Silk Road between
China and Europe, it is now an R-and-R spot for men working
in the Far North.

I sip a beer with some husky Ukrainians who've just flown
in. They tell me that they are making 600 rubles a month
deep in the taiga, and they're saving money like fury. Why?
I ask them. "To go back to Odessa or Kiev, buy a taxi, find
a wife, and prosper in the black market."

During my four-day stay, I watch old men in their fishing
punts on the river; there in the morning when I wake up, there
when darkness falls. What do they catch? "Little ones, not
much good." But out there they escape the cackle of old wives
in the kitchen, my guide adds. "Some are old soldiers. They

remember the Great Patriotic War." Andrei has only heard
stories.
    One old veteran tells me he was the youngest officer at the
Front. I like him very much.
    I have not yet visited one sports complex, and the trip is
nearing the end. Then, in far-off Irkutsk, I get my chance.
True, it's an old converted factory building, but the director's
enthusiasm makes up for a lot. Some baseball mitts and a
Little-League-sized bat catch my eye. Baseball? In Siberia?
Why not? They practise on the ice . . . Only in the Soviet
Union!

Siberia's Seven Simeons

I was in Irkutsk, thousand of miles east of Moscow and that
afternoon the local Novosti Press Agency guide, a tall, lean,
and soft-spoken fellow named Sergei, asked if I would like to
visit a group of jazz players. Seven brothers who had gained a
measure of local fame. At this point I would have accepted an
invitation to watch a dancing bear.
    It was a short ride to the Ovechkin home, a small bungalow
enclosed by a high fence with a door painted yellow. Other
houses on the gravelled and potholed street had fence doors
painted pink and blue and mauve.
    At the door, we were met by the Ovechkin brothers. All
seven. The youngest about eight and the oldest twenty-one, a
serious young man with a pencil moustache. Friendliness was
in the air. Like most Soviet youngsters they had taken English
as a second language, but like so many, they were reluctant
to speak it although they understood some of what I said.
    The brothers lived together; their mother Ninel lived with
two daughters in an apartment. The mother worked in a soft-
drink kiosk, although Soviet authorities later described her as
a bootlegger – hardly an unusual occupation in the Soviet
Union. I asked about the father, and was told, "He is gone."

The house was small and old, with low ceilings, but sturdily built, and with the large woodstove it would be cosy during the long Siberian winter. The furniture was old but serviceable. The second oldest boy was the cook, called The Muffin Man, and we sat around the large table and ate, drank coffee, and talked. This puzzled me. The large cookies they served had just been baked recently as though they were expecting us, but they had no phone and could not have been warned we were coming. So, it had been planned anyway. Or had it? In the Soviet Union, one never, never knows.

Louis Armstrong was their god. On god's right-hand side was Oscar Peterson, the Montreal jazz pianist, and when I said I had met him once, they were very impressed. I mentioned I had heard that he had had operations on both hands between the thumb and index finger to increase his span on the keyboard, and before this was translated, they all pointed to The Muffin Man, their pianist. He held up his hands outwards. He had the same flat span, but he hadn't needed any operations.

As with other musicians and jazz fanatics I had met, their passion was Dixieland, first, last, and always, and did I enjoy it? Yes, I could listen to it, but I preferred the Beatles, Country and Western, and the light classics. They had heard of the Beatles but knew nothing about them, and Country and Western was foreign territory. They told me they had put on concerts in and around Irkutsk, had had their pictures in the local paper and in a couple of magazines, and in a small way were celebrities. They had even gone to Moscow for a concert and there was a trip to Japan coming up.

I perked up my ears over that one. This was extraordinary. Seven boondock kids and they were off to Tokyo to play with some of the world's top jazz groups? The Soviet Union sends only the very best to international festivals or on tour to earn foreign currency. A trip of this kind would be no dollar earner.

What was this all about? Some arcane type of politics was behind it, otherwise the brothers could not survive. My guide hinted that local politicians had a hand in it.

Anyway, they had come a long way. But going where?

The front room was about twelve by fourteen feet. It was lined with a type of silver foil, a contrast to the other two rooms, which were plastered with Western posters of Dixieland stars.

This silver room was where they practised at least three and often five hours a day.

I noted the piano, the set of drums, and an electric guitar, a trumpet, a saxaphone, and a trombone. The eight-year-old played a dime-store guitar that was not hooked up to their antiquated electronic gear. He was just along for the ride because his chording made no more noise amid the general blare than a robin's feather would have falling on a thick rug. I'm no expert but looking at these instruments, and studying the photos later, I could see that they had survived their alloted timespan. Old, certainly, and no attempt had been made to keep them polished. The piano was decrepit. The drums were battered, although the drummer was expert.

It was loud. Loud! The smallness of the room and the bounce-off effect of the silver foil perhaps increased the decibel count. But it was Dixieland, no doubt of that, and it sounded great. By my uneducated terms they were "with it." They played three pieces and by then my ears had started to vibrate.

Back in the larger room we ate muffins, drank tea, and talked. They were a cheerful bunch. I genuinely liked them. The oldest, he of the Mississippi gambler's moustache, wanted to see a Canadian dollar. He was insistent. He wasn't asking for money. He just wanted to see what one looked like. I joked and asked if he wanted to see the picture of Elizabeth II on it. I doubt that they knew a single fact about Canada–except that Oscar Peterson lived there.

My Canadian and U.S. currency was in my money belt and I didn't want to take it off, so I said my money was at the hotel.

Just before we left, with good will flowing, my guide asked if I had any Canada pins to give them. Yes, I found six in my pocket. Alas, one short. The youngest, who had been out of the room, came in and saw he was left out. Quick as a blink, he pointed to the expensive Canada Maple Leaf pin in my lapel. He had me! I unscrewed it and screwed it onto his sweater and his grin spread from ear to ear. The winner! His brothers only had ordinary pins.

Then we left, and as we bumped down the road I looked back and they were standing together, at the yellow gate, waving and smiling. I stuck my arm out and waved goodbye to The Seven Simeons, their professional name.

Five months later during dinner I was listening to the CBC six o'clock newscast, and heard that a Soviet airliner had been hijacked on a flight from Irkutsk to Leningrad. Nine people had been killed and others injured, the plane had been destroyed by a bomb, and a group of brothers who were jazz musicians in Irkutsk were responsible. It rang a bell immediately and I said, "Hell, I spent an afternoon with those kids!"

I could not believe it. Of all the people I had met, talked with, visited with, they would have been the last I would have thought would pull such an insane stunt.

Bit by bit, the story came out, and Western correspondents said the Soviet authorities were more up front with the details than on most stories. The Soviets said the Simeons' mother – who was a Hero Mother of the Soviet Union because she had borne eleven children – had masterminded the plot. A woman selling soft drinks from a kiosk plotting to hijack an airliner and force the pilot to fly on to London? Moreover, it must have been difficult to get eleven passports to fly from Irkutsk to another Soviet city because all travel is restricted. How had they arranged internal passports?

The newspaper stories said the two oldest boys had sawed-off shotguns. Extremely unusual because it is a criminal offence for a Soviet citizen to have a firearm. Only members of hunting clubs can have them, so they must have stolen them. Since there are no security checks at Soviet domestic airports, they could have smuggled them aboard. Apparently they all took seats at the rear of the TU-154 airliner and near the end of the journey they passed a note to the stewardess telling the captain to fly on to London.

Anyone who knows Soviet flight schedules knows their airliners are fueled only for the distance required to fly between A and B, and sometimes I experienced the wings tipping as the pilot drained the last of the fuel from the wing tanks into the engines. They play it close on Aeroflot, a practice I consider exceedingly dangerous. There is no reason for it . . . or is there?

The airliner would not have had the fuel to fly to London, so the pilot told the family he would land at a Finnish field, north of Leningrad. However, he alerted one of the many military fields around Leningrad, landed there, and then the carnage began. All we know is that a Red Army security force attacked the plane, an action that brought forth criticism from the authorities, an extraordinary admission in itself.

No one will know what went on, but one of the boys with a shotgun killed the mother, indicating that indeed she may have been the ringleader. Perhaps he did it out of compassion, for she would have been executed. Then apparently there was more shooting and four more of the family died as well as one stewardess and three other passengers. How many were wounded as the soldiers burst into the cabin is unknown. Soviet military fields have no unloading platforms, so a portable staircase would have had to be pushed up to the door.

And then there was a dynamite explosion at the rear of the plane and it was destroyed. Where did they get this "bomb"?

There were 101 unknowns involved. What happened to the other three boys and the sisters? Had the youngest, his eleven-year-old brother, and the twelve-year-old been involved? Why did The Seven Simeons attempt the hijack? Had the trip to Japan made life in flat, dull Irkutsk too much of a come-down? Had my stories of the incredible wealth of Western rock stars got to them, made them want to share some of the glory?

Then this sensational story dropped out of sight, and in November 1988 the Soviet Embassy in Ottawa phoned and asked me if I would shepherd a free-lance journalist around Vancouver for two days. Sergei Ostrumov, whom I'd met in Irkutsk, was sharp and personable and the fact he was travelling alone was clear evidence that things were changing. *Glasnost.*

He was overwhelmed by the city, its richness, its beauty, its people. We lunched in the lovely Brockton Point Café in Stanley Park overlooking the First Narrows entrance to Vancouver harbour and he scanned the elaborate menu and said, "I don't know how I will ever tell my readers about Canada." He had shown me his ration card, which allowed one person a pound of meat a month, so much coffee, so much butter and sugar.

It was then I asked Sergei about the hijacking. "The oldest, Dmitri, was sentenced to eight years," he said. "They said his mother forced the brothers to do it. It is very sad; I don't want to talk about it."

I thought, only eight years for hijacking and murder? Surely this did not fit in to either *glasnost* or *perestroika*. What else was going on over there? My guess is the Soviets knew they had botched the thing so badly they wanted it swept under the carpet.

Dmitri was the one who had wanted to see the Canadian dollar bill.

Working on the Railroad

"I wanted to be an engineer. I had graduated high school and there was a year before I had to go for my military service of two years. My mother asked me what I would do. She said, 'You have eight months. Let us think.' She was a supervisor in a factory that made sweaters in one part and underclothes for women in another. Two factories. She said it does not matter what you do, but she did not want me to do something unproductive.

That was my mother. She had red hair and was very aggressive, very strong, and she was in charge of the underwear section of this big plant. I think there were nine hundred women and girls who worked for her.

This story is not about my mother. It is about me. She said, 'Ilya, until you go into the army you will work for our plant.' That is what I did. I began learning how to fix the knitting machines as they were very old and the job was never done.

I worked there seven months and we had fun with the young girls. They were from the country and got special permits to come from the farms and work in the factory. There was a special place they lived, three tall buildings with little flats and they had a little stove and a fridge and three tiny beds. If you wanted to visit one of these girls it was complicated. Very difficult thing to do. The girl had to ask her two friends to go to the theatre or into Moscow downtown and walk around. Then there was in all of the three buildings old women. The policemen. The old women who sat by the door. You had to give her 2 or 3 rubles to get past her. The Tiger, the girls called her. She'd let you in for two rubles and she made a lot of money. The girl I liked was Ekaterina. They watch the animals when they are children and they grow up very fast. Katya was seventeen when I would visit her and she had been there four years, since thirteen. She was hot. My mother found out and said it was all right. 'We are all human anyway,' she said, 'but do not get a disease.' I told her I was the only one and she laughed and said something like I did not know much about girls.

Then came my army time. My father, he was just a clerk and he could not go to someone and say I should be put in a special group. There was nobody to bribe because he couldn't find anyone. My friends, some of them, three, they went into special sections where army life was better. I went where they sent me. There was a camp. Boys from all over. Muslims, a Northern boy who had trapped sables and his family was rich, and he looked Japanese or Chinese but he was a native. Ukrainian boys from farms. Georgian boys who spoke bad Russian and I'd ask them why not and they would say they had no teacher who spoke good Russian. A few Estonians and Latvians who thought they were better than anyone and talked their own language among each other and once I asked what they were doing and one said, 'We are speaking German.' I said German? He said, 'Yes, because one day the Germans will come and free us from you awful Russian beasts.' There was a fight over that one and when a sergeant asked me what had happened to my face I told him I had fallen over a box. There were Russians, most of us, from the cities and towns.

Our sergeants were beasts. At times I thought there was no hope for us. If the enemy did not kill us the sergeants would. They had flat bayonets and they would slap us with the flat side. If you smiled and thought, 'Go ahead, you piece of shit, go ahead and kill me,' they would know what you were thinking and get you again.

I asked a sergeant who had come from our district, I said, 'Why do you treat us this way?' He said it was to make men and soldiers of us. I asked him, 'If you treat us this way, how can we be soldiers when we hate the army so much?' 'That is the way it works,' and he asked for a cigarette and took the whole package and said, 'Now, cockroach, that will make you hate the army some more, won't it? The army needs good haters. Stay on, be an officer. You have the right goods for it.

Education, smart. You'll make a lot of money and you won't be killed. You'll have a rich fat life with white sheets on your bed and the colonel will call you in one day and say, "Ilya, you have passed the test. You can join our club." Then you will become rich with bribes and selling army supplies to the mayors of the towns and the civilians. Use the trucks to do your dirty work and have all the nice girls and Armenian cognac and maybe you will be a colonel. A colonel is the most important man in the army.' He meant the colonel was high up in the bureaucratic hierarchy but not too high where he could be exposed. You can blame the ones below, and the ones above will protect you because they have to. They are the ones up to their noses in the bribery and mud.

We learned to drill and march and weapons training and the ones from the country, the boys, they learned manners, I think you call it. How to eat right. How to behave. To take orders. They would be taking orders all their life. Some, some I could see would make good soldiers. Everyone is willing to die for his country and so was I, but these boys were more. They . . . well, we all had a great love for our country. It is the greatest country in the world. It always has been. But these boys, you could see that they believed just that much more than we did. They would be the ones to go willingly to Afghanistan and die. Born to be soldiers, and happy for them, because we need good soldiers and airmen and sailors, men who will die with happiness for this wonderful country. I was not that way. This is our Motherland but I didn't want to be a solider.

They sent us out to the potato fields that autumn and it was in the rain and our boots were poor. Soldiers digging potatoes, I thought. Then I said, 'Why not? They have only got our bodies for two years and they haven't got my mind.' Besides, every Russian child knows that the Soviet Union lives on potatoes. Our most important crop. The potato is everything, for humans and cattle. No potatoes, starvation. So I'd tell the others this and say we were doing our duty to our country. I thought about my grandfather, who had a lot of money because he was a veteran and got a big flat after the war because he was a hero and he rented two of his rooms to other people and they paid him 30 rubles each and he had a little car the government gave him.

He would tell of the battles during the war. We never believed him. He had wounds, awful ones, on his left arm and on his body, but old grandfather Sergei would have had to fight twenty years in a four-year war to have been in all the battles. But it was fun and I think he had only been in two battles, Stalingrad was one. That was enough for any soldier. He just told the Battle of Stalingrad twenty different ways. He'd stand and wave his arms and shout, 'Just six of us left,' meaning only six left of his section and the Germans coming and they were going to die. And then they would fight them off and kill them and the battle would go on next morning. I was just a kid and I thought this was a wonderful thing to do for our country, saving it from the Nazis, and our great leader Stalin in the Kremlin saying this army will move here and these tanks will be in front of them and there go the Nazis, running for their lives and dying in the cold and what a great victory.

That was Old Sergei's war, and my army life was not like that. The old shacks we lived in and the terrible food and waiting for letters from my mother and feeling them to see if they were soft, which would mean there were some rubles in it to spend in the canteen. It was terrible that first winter and we were not allowed to go into the towns and our boots were rotting and it was cold in the barracks and the fuel, it was coal and dirty and everybody smelled and there were fights. We would get drunk on moonshine. The sergeant would call us out at four in the morning and we'd rush out, no coats, just guns, you guys, and we'd fire at the sky but just pulling the triggers, no bullets, and someone would ask what we were fighting and the sergeant and the officer would laugh and say planes. The enemy. It was just stupid. Bureaucracy in my mother's factory, bureaucracy in our regiment, silly, dumb, stupid.

Then we got on a train and six days later we were in Georgia. Three hours by plane but six days by train, eating out of pots, cabbage soup and tea, and those terrible Georgians. They hated us. We could not go into the city, not even near the farms to see if there were girls. But there were mountains. It was the first time I had seen mountains and I thought they were the most beautiful things. We had been in the taiga in the cold, little trees and mud and ice and snow, and Georgia, it was warm. It was spring and we could see the farmers. I thought,

'These people are savages. Look at them and their beards,' and I didn't know they were a different people. They said the Armenians were worse and would cheat you more if they had the chance.

When we went to the battle training ground we drove down their roads through the mountains and they . . . I still can't believe this and I am telling you it all. They had turkeys, and there would be 200 and three men looking like savages would be herding them. Three men and two dogs. Their sheep. My mother knew about wool, she was in the business of using it sometimes with the cotton for the garments, and she would not believe these sheep. Their cattle, how could you get any meat off these miserable things? I thought, 'Is this what we eat at home?' Meat off these stinking things, and when we passed there would be people in the orchards and there were orchards in the smallest places where you didn't think anything could grow. These people were like Arabs but some of them worked in the camp and they told us they were happy and rich. Some didn't speak Russian and the Georgian boys were so happy to be home and they would sneak out at night and come back and they would have a tub of yogurt and mixed with honey and there was wine in it and it was the best happiness of a feast we had. We would give them 2 rubles each, maybe 40 rubles, and they would bring back these confections . . . confections? Yes, and they said these big farmers had cars and big houses and nice furniture and this is how they got rich. Forty rubles for a tub of confection.

Then it came the time of Afghanistan but we had been in the mountains and we weren't trained. In the place we had been before, it had been digging potatoes and the second camp was in the taiga where it was all woods and trees and water and then the third camp, Georgia. We trained a bit but we also helped the engineers work on the roads and there were two times somebody had burned the railways, the bridges, and we had to help with them.

This was a good time for me because we had other things to do and they found I had some rheumatic fever in the right side, so I did not have to do the strong work. There was a doctor in the hospital and he found out that it was my dream to study my English more. I was given a job helping this doctor and his nurses and he said we would only talk English. He knew of my dreams. He would not allow me to talk Russian and he said the ones of us who spoke and could write in good English would be important to our country in a few years. 'Don't speak Russian,' he said. 'Only English.' He called it the language of the world.

I studied the English books he gave me. They were English novels. Conrad, who was Polish but who wrote lovely English, was my favourite and I read *Lord Jim* and other books many times. There would be no trouble for you to understand the joy I felt when I learned of your taiga up north among the wolves and the natives, and that was in a book called *Never Cry Wolf* by Farley Mowat. He is a Canadian and much loved in this country. If you said 'Farley' to an educated Russian he would know what you were talking about. A little man with a red beard. I have seen his picture.

Then it was time to end the army days and leave my doctor and this is when my life entered an interesting pattern. You have heard of BAM. It was one of Brezhnev's crazy things. A railroad through the nothing of our country, nothing, just trees and rocks and lakes and mud and no people, no places, and it went from Baikal to nowhere. The whole of a land bigger than Europe would be open to settlement and coal mines and the great fields of wheat which was not there, the coal and the oil and the gas, which nobody knew was there, and let me see, everyone was saying the railroad was to be the wonder of the world. What a wonderful world when a railway more than 3,000 kilometres was being built! The project that Lenin dreamed about. That is what they said. No such thing he ever said. I think it might have had a great deal to do with our coming war with China, but that is not ready yet and I don't think it is wise to fight a country with a billion people and five can die for every one our country can lose. But the railway made no sense and the economists said it did, oh yes, it did, it will make our country strongest in the world. Look at a map. There are none with this railroad on it, I don't think, but go with your finger from Lake Baikal away to the east there and see if there is anything. Nobody writes on the map, 'There is nothing here,' but they should. Other wise economists said it was foolish but Brezhnev said it must go and all those boot-lickers said, 'Yes, yes, Comrade Chairman, we will put the road through.'

This was the plan. From Baikal, go forward until you reach something. Build a few hundred kilometres at a time. Be sensible, some said. We can't afford, we are unable to pay these huge costs. Afghanistan was coming up and people were unhappy with life and the Americans were draining away our blood by forcing us into the momentous arms race with nuclear cannon and men in space and satellites to watch the world. They said, 'We can't live with what we have, our poor economy. Why do we need such a railroad?'

I am being honest with you. They said, 'We have the engineers and does not the Soviet Union make more steel than any other country?' Engineers and steel and country to use them in and then it was all settled. But hey! Who will build it? 'Get the Ukrainians, they are big and strong and they love money more than anyone.' They got the Ukrainians, but not enough. 'Get the political prisoners.' Thousands of them, sorry, you poor fellows, but they were not strong.

Then somebody said, 'Get students. There are two million in universities and institutes and trade expressions in our country. Pay them. The summer. Pay them.' But they couldn't get many because, my friend, it is not the dream of a city boy or girl to work all summer out in Siberia.

The bosses said, 'Pay them big,' and do you know how much a commodore of a Russian jetliner makes? He makes 1,000 rubles a month and he is like a king. He makes more than a fat and stupid bureaucrat. 'Yes,' I said, 'yes, I'll go,' and others did, too, because it would be big money and no place to spend it on. They did it this way. One hundred kilometres, this is what we will do. Each unit of students, they will do twenty kilometres for a summer. The work must be done. It must be said that work did get done. It went on for several years. I think I was there about the fourth year and much had been done, but slow. Very slow. The students, they enjoyed it. I did. Fresh air and sitting around the fire at night, laughing and drinking and dreaming of what we would do. One would be a professor and another would be an astronaut and schoolteachers and managers and . . . a lot of loving went on.

[This reminded me of another man I met who said he had worked on the BAM and when I asked what it was like he curtly said, "Much fucking."]

We ate very well and the harder we worked, the more money we marked up in the books, and we could see we were making money. We didn't mystify the inspectors because we couldn't. They could see what was done and if the unit had done it well. They also knew the kind of land we were working in and the terrible difficulties and that if we were slow, then it was not our fault. And we were slow. Supplies didn't come through. A machine would be needed on Saturday and it would come four days later. The bugs [mosquitoes, black flies] were very painful and we had some horses and one died from the bugs. Some people left because they could not stand the bugs.

So we worked hard and sang and talked about how great we would make the production export of Eastern Siberia and the Great Pacific Region and I think we were patriotic, but we were doing it for the money. The Ukrainians and farm people not from the city worked harder, and all they wanted was a lot of money and go back to their home and get a taxi and make money off the tourists and be in the black market. We learned not to put our trust in the Ukrainians or the Baltic ones because they were not to be trusted. As a soldier I learned that.

I do not know how much work we did that summer. I mean, I don't know how much all the units did. I know it cost billions of rubles and I think it is finished now. It is finished, but it is not used. The coal, I think, and maybe the pipeline but we never hear of it. It is called a great failure and I think it was because in that strange land there was nothing. No crops, no people, no places. It was Siberia. That was three months and two weeks of very hard work and with the bugs and strange people you had to know, but I made 3,000 rubles. That was a magnificent thing. My father makes 180 rubles a month and my mother makes 220 rubles, so in three months I made so much more than they could dream of.

I went to my second term of university and lived in an apartment with two of my friends and we had a happy time. I could read all the English journals in the library and there were English books and I was quite famous. I mean I knew lots of girls and some would say, 'You don't have to take me to a café, let us go back to your apartment right now.' Even at three in the afternoon. We went there to study, of course!

The next summer a friend of my mother's sister, my aunt, got me a special job as assistant purser on a cruise boat. All tourists. I was, too, a waiter for the evening meal. The Americans, the gratuities! 'Here, do something with this,' an American would say and give me 10 rubles, if I had done something special, 10 American dollars. You cannot understand what that means. That is 40 rubles or walk into a hard-currency store, they don't care, and buy something with hard currency. Cassettes, chocolates, razor blades, gin. Gin. Scotch. Magazines. Even *The Guardian* from England. I made very good money but not like the BAM

Another year and then my happy student days were over. My good English helped me because they knew that engineers can go anywhere, and go to England and America and if you speak English so well as I am, you have a better chance. So here I am in Irkutsk, waiting for my chance now. There will be a project soon, maybe in a year for me, and I will be an engineer who is an interpreter, a translator.

Soon I will get married. There will be two children. One must be young to have fun. It is not easy for us later. There are hard times ahead and the future, nobody knows what will happen. Happiness for the world, I hope."

Baseball on Ice?

And now I will tell you about how I taught the Siberians how to play baseball, North American style.

It was in Irkutsk, on a cold and grey morning, and, as usual, Novosti Press Agency did not have an appointment set up for me. Did I want to visit a sports complex? I jumped at the chance. Something had puzzled me during the previous three weeks. If the Soviet Union was such a sports-minded nation, where were the sports fields and where were the students who would be playing on these fields? Even though I had read and been told that education was king – or tsar – in the Soviet

Union, surely there was room on the curriculum to squeeze in an hour's play. Repeatedly I asked my guide Andrei and he would grunt and say, "In study, school."

The three schools I had visited were in downtown Moscow and Leningrad were indistinguishable from factories or office buildings; strong brick or stone and very old. At one of them the teacher proudly told me, "This was built in 1908 and during the war it was a hospital. It served our country well during the Great Patriotic War." But no room for playing fields or gymnasiums. I was sure the budding Soviet atheletes who constantly wiped the West off the scoreboards at the Olympics and other international competitions did not attend *these* schools.

Of course, they were not for the elite – the sons and daughters of politicians, bureaucrats, scientists, writers, and colonels and up in the armed services. They had their own schools. "You should see some of the equipment they have, the very latest," marvelled one Canadian teacher I spoke to later, and his wife replied, "Yes, but it did seem to be odd, you know. Nobody was using it." Defensively he replied, "But yes, there was a lot of it."

I asked where this sports centre was and the local guide, Sergei, pointed across the broad Angara River, flowing smoothly out of Lake Baikal from the south, and said, "Over there."

"Over there" was a tangle of railyards, through which ran the famous, or infamous, Trans-Siberian Railroad of story and song – mostly bawdy – with a backdrop of factories belching pollution into the Siberian sky.

When I suggested we take a bus or streetcar across the bridge, Sergei went into the hotel, five minutes went by, and then we walked across to a station wagon.

Ten minutes later we were across the river and prowling down potholed gravelled roads looking for the complex. This way, that way, down this road, turning around when it ended at the railway embankment, but finally we drew up at a low concrete building and it was here that I met Alexei. Perhaps thirty-five, he was certainly one of the youngest in spirit and vitality I had met in many thousands of miles of travel. A man who could look you in the eye and smile. He had a good smile. I warmed to him instantly.

Alexei was the director, enthusiastic, proud of his work, eager to show me everything. A happy Russian.

It would be difficult to describe his sports complex. It was solid, long, low, and old; at the western end it had a second story from which an extension cantilevered over the bottom floor. The grounds were gravel and the lot next to it was a jumble of old cement blocks and rusted pipe. I later learned that one day this area would become a soccer field.

The riddle of this ungainly structure was solved when I learned that this site had once been part of a cement factory. Why it had been torn down, God only knows, because it was ideally situated to the rail lines to bring in the raw materials and a few hundred yards from the Angara River with its ever-lasting supply of water. (Lake Baikal has 20 percent of the world's freshwater supplies, a fact I found incredible considering Canada's Great Lakes and its tens of thousands of northern lakes; yet Canada is said also to have about 25 percent of the world's fresh water. The world divided the other 55 percent.)

Inside, the gym was cold and gloomy. There was a small collection of weightlifting machines, some gym equipment; a hardwood floor had been laid down and two basketball hoops were in place. I tested the floor and it did have bounce. Someone knew what he was doing, but I doubted if the Irkutsk team in the Siberian league, which did not exist, would be much of a challenge to any top-rated North American high school team. The floor was about two-thirds regulation size.

I toured the small men's and women's change rooms and asked about the showers. There would be showers, I was assured, but they were not on the agenda yet. "Agenda" is a Soviet term that covers a thousand errors, omissions, and plain, old-fashioned sins. Usually it means they are not prepared to act on something; i.e., there is no one with expertise on the matter to consult, or there is no money, or they have been waiting several months or years for the go-ahead on the project.

Yes, Alexei knew English, but as with most Russians – the estimated 10 percent who have a working knowledge–he spoke through the interpreter; even so, his infectious enthusiasm came through. "This club is not to make records in some kinds of sports," he said. "It is for young people, up to the age of thirty, those who want to come and use their mentalities, their abilities, to help themselves, to test themselves, to do better . . ."

He explained that the basketball court was also used as a volleyball court, which made sense. I noted mats that could be laid down for wrestling and a ring erected for boxing. There were also tables that could be set up for Chinese tennis.

"Chinese tennis?"

"You would call it Ping-Pong." Oh. Of course.

Boards could be hung up against the walls for archery, but he said they had only one bow and six arrows, and when I commented that no champions would come out of this club, he laughed.

They had soccer teams, too, he said, but at my puzzled look my interpreter said, "Oh, they have fields in the city they can rent for their teams to play. Someday they will have their own soccer field," and I thought, not bloody likely. Not here, anyway. But Alexei explained that the junkyard – my description – would be their soccer field. Also, they planned a swimming pool, a folly I did not dare to comment on. Canadians would consider Irkutsk sub-arctic.

Sure, this derelict building was crude, cold, poorly equipped, but still the kids had done a good job on it. The work showed imagination and, certainly, initiative, and I was positive it was Alexei's drive and enthusiasm that had made it work.

"Essentially, then," I said, "this is to get the kids off the streets."

"Yes, to get the kids off the streets. Out of trouble. To give them something to do," and adding the Soviet tagline, "so they can use their abilities to their highest level."

I asked where the kids were because there were only two others in the gymnasium, a youth of about twenty, distinctly Asiatic in origin, possibly a Northerner, as they call their natives, and a smartly dressed girl of about twenty-five who stared at me with unrelenting gaze, followed us everywhere, and never spoke. I took them to be Alexei's assistants.

He said the club was open from 7 A.M. to 11 P.M. and some came when work was over at 6 P.M. and if I had been here between 7 A.M. and 8 A.M. some members would have been working with the weights. Imagine going to an office after working at body-building without a shower?

Upstairs, there was a large room, panelled in pine and carpeted, plus Alexei's small office and a small kitchen as well as a common room where the club members could socialize.

The club's bow hung on the wall beside a .22 rifle of Soviet manufacture, and I lifted it down from its peg, sighted it out the window, and said, "Bang." Alexei spoke and my interpreter said, "He says you would never be allowed to shoot like that in competition. You are lefthanded."

I also saw a baseball bat in the corner and I picked it up and took a few swings. The astounding thing was that the bat was Little League size.

"He says they are training a baseball team," said my interpreter. "The best player from Irkutsk will be sent to the South to train for the 1992 Olympics. He might not make the team, but he will go."

I told them I had read recently that the International Baseball Association had approved the entry of the Soviet Union, making it the sixty-fifth member, and I laughed and said, "Of course, you won't be sending a team. It takes years to learn baseball. It takes a very special talent. It takes more than talent and years of practice, too. You need what I call a baseball mentality." And I thought, yes, but look how the Soviets caught on to hockey. Back in the late '40s, a hockey stick was virtually unknown in the country and yet, not to be deterred, the Soviet government sent a team to the 1956 Olympics and eventually were beating Canada at its own game. I mentioned this, and added, "But as far as baseball is concerned, you would be playing checkers and the Americans, the Japanese, the Canadians, the Filipinos, everybody else will be playing chess."

This entailed a long exchange between the two, and finally Alexei said, in English, "You may be mistaken. We will learn from Cuba."

Forgetting my manners, I replied, "Yes, Cubans play baseball very well. It's their national sport, I believe. But as the Cuban people hate the Soviet government so much, I wonder if they will really teach you. I think the Japanese or the Americans would be better teachers."

Oh-oh. Dead silence. Then I got the usual treatment, my guide saying, "You have been misinformed. The Cubans are the Soviet peoples' best friends."

I said, "Ask any Cuban," and ended the conversation on that subject by saying, "This is a Little League bat." Knowing they could not know what it meant, I added, "This is the kind of bat that children play with. Little boys of nine, ten, or eleven years. Where did you get it?"

Alexei said they had had a sports director from Irkutsk visit Japan for a two-week training course and he had brought back some equipment, including this bat. They had gone to a lumber yard and carved their own models of the LL bat. Yes, I could see on inspection it had been carved with spokeshave. On closer inspection it had been done crudely and I said, "It's not right. It does not have the right balance," and I took down the competition rifle from the wall and hefted it, balancing it at its fulcrum point, and said, "A bat needs balance, like this. It must feel good. The weight must be distributed right. Do you see? Let me see the rest of what they gave you in Japan."

A duffel bag was brought out and gloves were dumped on the floor. "My God," I thought, "the Japanese are sticking it to these poor guys."

There were three first baseman's gloves and about four fielders', all old and stiff, and I said, "You haven't got enough here for even one team. How do you do it? Take this one," picking up an outfielder's glove. "You see, it's stiff. Like a board. You've got to oil it with a light oil, and work it, make it soft. Work it, keep slamming the ball into it until you've got a pocket. Make it like it is part of your hand. Work at it. The thing's no good this way. Do it with all the others. You've got six gloves like this. Okay, make up three teams of two and have them throw the ball at each other. Downstairs in the gymnasium. Bounce the ball at their feet and make them scoop it up. Throw it at crazy angles. High, make them jump for it. To the side, the left, the right. Straight at their faces. Try and make them miss," and all the while I was diving to the right, jumping high, scooping up ground balls, smothering hoppers.

I stopped and looked at the faces around me. This was ridiculous. A rusty old man who hadn't actually played the game for years acting like a fool in a far-off part of the world where the word "baseball" was as foreign as the word "yuppie."

I laughed and then picked up a first baseman's glove. "Now this is for the first baseman. The main job of the opposing team against the batting team is to stop a player getting to first base. No first base, no scoring. See? This glove, look how long it is. It is like an extension of the first baseman's arm." I put it on and told Alexei to throw the ball off to my left, out of reach.

He did and I flicked the glove out and snagged the ball neatly in the webbing. "See?" I said. "It gives the first baseman more reach. This has to be oiled and worked and put into shape, too. And practise, practise, and practise some more. You can do it all winter and spring downstairs in the gymnasium. Keep your boys at it. Throw the ball. Here, toss me one of those balls."

I looked at it and thought, "This isn't a regulation ball." Too small. More the size of a cricket ball. I asked where they got it and was told it was from Japan.

"Well, the Japanese are playing a trick on you," I told them. "This ball is too small, but perhaps that's okay. If you learn to hit this, the bigger American ball will be easier to hit."

It was not until months later that I learned the Japanese baseball actually is smaller than the American ball.

"But you've got to practise outside, too. Get out on one of those soccer fields where there is room to run and throw the ball around. Get used to batting, but you'll need better bats. Heavy ones. If I were you, I'd send off to Japan and get a lot of equipment, balls, regulation bats, dozens of good gloves, padding, everything you need. This stuff you have here is really useless. Go to Japan. Buy the best they've got."

That did it! What I had just said was too much for my guide. "Japan! Buy these things! Barry, what are you thinking about? How to go to Japan? How to buy this goods? You say it so easy. These poor people have no money. Maybe when there comes self-financing, maybe there will be a chance to trade in Japanese market. Some possibility then." His blue eyes were blazing.

Alexei, a small smile on his face, understood every word and he looked at me and winked. Still, he wouldn't speak out in English.

I said, "Listen! You're doing deals with Japan every month. They should be good friends with you, and they are, but you have to watch out for yourselves. Take a bunch of those sables your hunters catch and see what they will buy you. You can barter them and bring back as much baseball equipment as you can carry. If you want to play baseball, go about it the right way. Christ, you haven't even got a park to play in!"

Then the most astonishing thing happened. Alexei cut in on us and I heard the word "Baikal" and in a couple of minutes my guide said, "He says they do have a playing field to practise on. Last spring they went to Lake Baikal to practise. It is warm down there between the middle of April and the middle of May and the snow is gone and the ice is good to practise on. He says they can learn to slide better on the ice, too."

Baseball on ice? I'm not one given to hysterical laughter but I came close.

(The sequel occurred when I returned to Moscow and was talking with a foreign correspondent and told him the Lake Baikal story, how the Boys of Irkutsk had travelled about forty miles south to practise on ice with small-sized Japanese balls, Little League-sized bats of their own making, and without equipment worth a damn. The story he wrote was printed in many Canadian newspapers and perhaps was picked up by American ones, leaving all baseball buffs shaking their heads in bewilderment.)

I said, "Look, the human body is a very complicated bit of machinery. The most vital parts in baseball are the elbows and the knees and the shoulders; they can be most badly damaged in playing baseball. You can't have young players out there in the cold, on the ice, using these delicate bones and muscles," and I went into a Satchell Paige type of wind-up, left leg high, body leaning backward, arm back farther, and then I went into a slow-motion pitch, ending up leaning forward on the balls of my feet, glaring at the imaginary ball speeding towards the plate, waiting tensely for the crack of the bat and the liner flashing back, possibly straight at me.

Suddenly I realized how amazing this little scene was, with the Canadian imitating a professional league pitcher, the Russians staring, me crouched and ready. I straightened my creaking back. "Well, that's how it is done. The throw to the catcher. The pitch. The fastball, curve, slider, oh well."

Nobody said a thing, and I added, "It takes American professionals many years to play the game. They start when they are six and seven years old. Well, it is their national sport." No reaction. Desperately, I added, "The best players are national heroes. Like Canadian hockey players. Gretzky, Lemieux, you know." Adding depth to the vigour of my declarations, I said, "The best players, especially the pitchers, they can make more than a million dollars a year. Much more. That's four million rubles' worth of American dollars on your black market. Think that one over."

Alexei, astonished, said in English, "For playing the baseball?"

We wandered outside into the brisk autumn air and Alexei flung his arm out and said, "That will be our baseball field."

"How long will it take?" I asked the interpreter.

It would take as long as it would take, he said, but it was on the agenda . . .

While we waited for our car to arrive, the grand plan for Soviet world dominance of world baseball was laid out for me. Obviously some thought had gone into it. Every city in each of the fifteen republics would have a team. They would play in leagues and then for the republic championship. Then national playoffs among the republic teams would be held and the best players, regardless of the winner, would be chosen for the Olympic team.

"But the 1992 Olympics is only five years away. How can you expect to field a team," and I waved back at the clubhouse, "when you don't even know how to play the game? It is an intellectual game. A manager might have to make 400 decisions in nine innings. The players, it has to be drilled and drilled into their brains how to make the right play at the right time. It is not just hitting a home run and scoring. It is like chess."

Alexei had left us, smiling, shaking hands, and my guide played his ace.

"These people don't matter. They do what they want. We already have a team. They have played in a tournament in North Korea and they lost, but they did well. They have played the Nicaraguans. They are being taught now in Cuba, where it is warm, and when summer comes they will do more training in the South. They have good equipment and the Cubans are teaching them to play well. They are playing well already."

Trumping his ace, I said, "Yes, I know. Nicaragua is a democracy, you know, and what happens there gets into our papers. All of it . . . Soviets supplying the government with tanks, Americans supplying the Contra soldiers with explosives to blow up the tanks – and Russians playing the South American teams in tournaments. It's all one big happy family, sport. All kinds of sport."

Later I thought, "Don't be too scornful." The Cubans are the world amateur baseball champions, and some of their top amateurs are truly professional. The Soviet Union has kept Cuba alive economically since Fidel Castro took over almost thirty years ago. About 40,000 Cuban soldiers have been fighting the Soviet's war for them in Angola. The Cubans will always be dependent on the Russians. Why wouldn't their best players and coaches train Soviet kids to play baseball? The director told me the master plan is to have Soviet kids start learning the game at six years of age. By the 1996 Olympics, those kids will be fifteen. They are already training in the south of the Soviet Union. Give nine years of intensive, all-year-round training under expert coaching to the kids who are already twelve and you've got a nineteen-year-old player.

Why not a Soviet world championship team? Indeed, why not?

And by 2000 A.D., why not a World Series in the true meaning: the United States versus the Soviet Union? Don't bet against it. They may not be able to install a shower head that works, but when it comes to the quest for world prestige, the Soviets can do amazing things.

Provided that they come up with enough foreign currency for uniforms, balls, bats, gloves, and no more training fields on ice.

The Youngest Officer at the Front

"I was in the war. Now, first, I must tell you how I got to it. I was fourteen and I had four brothers and six sisters and my mother, she said to me, 'Boris, you are the one I will not let go to the war.' This was in 1941 and terrible happenings were with our armies. We were being driven back by the Nazis on the fronts and we knew, in Leningrad, in Moscow, everyone knew. There was no way the news could be kept hidden.

My two oldest sisters were told to report to one of the hospitals which was in a warehouse beside the railway tracks by the Kursk Station. This was in Moscow and the Nazi armies were coming closer. One day she and my other sister were allowed to come home for two days. We lived on a farm a hundred kilometres from Moscow and they told us of what the soldiers had told her. How they were dying. I remember that day in June. We went to the edge of the woods to pick the little red wild strawberries and we sat under the trees and ate them and had milk and bread and they told me. I could not believe it. Our mighty armies and they were being beaten badly and many thousands of our brave soldiers were dying. It was a day very long ago and I remember it still to now.

When I had taken them to the railway station in the cart I went back and I told my father I was going to join the army for my country. He was a big man, a boss on the farm, and he had many problems. The peasants had been through very hard times when the collectivization came. My father was the best mechanic, he could make parts for the farm machines in the blacksmithing shop with metal and the forge. There was no welding then, you can understand, and if a part broke it had to be made. My father was good at this.

Then time passed and he became a boss and we produced grain and pigs and meat. The bosses in Moscow sent trucks and took our produce, but now my father had had the people dig pits in the ground and a lot of our produce and grain and pigs were hidden when the trucks came. For this, the people on the farm loved my father and this kept them not hungry in the winter. We knew others were starving on other farms because they would come in the darkness and my father would give them grain.

My mother said one day someone would inform on him and he said, 'No, when you are helping people and looking after your own, they do not inform.' My mother said someday it would happen and he stood up at our table and tore open his shirt and I remember him saying, 'Then they can shoot me. I will have died for my friends. For them. Not for the fat boys in the big offices in Moscow.' You see, that was my father. A great man.

He has been dead for many years and you may now ask, how do you speak English? Go ahead, how do I speak your fine language? My father. It was him. He had been on Russian ships many years before he came back to the farm and had been in many countries and he learned it. He had many books in English. The great writers of the English language. I learned from him and from the books and I never forgot. Once I spoke better than I do now. I was very good.

That day after I came back from the railway I told my father I was going to join the army. He hit me and knocked me down and told me that when I was big enough to get up and knock him down, then I would be old enough to join the army and be a soldier. He was that kind of a man. He was very hurt at that time because my oldest brother, all we knew was that he was missing in battle with the enemy and that meant he would be dead. Even then, as I know now, the Germans were taking our prisoners and our wounded and taking them back to Germany to work in their factories and fields. This would mean more German soldiers could go to the front.

I told him I was going and I would go in a week. I said I would sell my violin to get the money to go to Moscow. He looked at me, he looked at me, and then he told me to sit down. We had this small house. Four rooms and a kitchen and that was for all of us. He told my mother and the sisters to go visit their aunt and he took out a litre of vodka and some pickles and he said, 'All right, sonny, I know all about sailors. They are no different than soldiers. Barbarians.' Those were his words.

He poured out a glass of vodka for himself and one for me and he told me to drink. He said when he hit the table I was to drink and when he stopped hitting it, I would have had to finish the drink. I drank and it was the first time I had drank vodka. When he finished hitting, his glass was empty and mine was, too. Then he said to have a pickle. How do you feel, and I said it was funny stuff. Then he gave me some tobacco. It was called Turko-tabac and I had never had a cigarette before and he said to draw it in and he thumped me on the back and I swallowed the smoke. I felt it roll down my throat like a big ball. Hooomph! Oh . . . I can still remember it.

He gave me another glass of vodka and hit the table every time I swallowed, and I had another big pickle and he handed me a dish of boiled cabbage my mother made and I had to eat that. Then another smoke and more vodka and soon I couldn't see. I got up and nearly fell down. I remember he was laughing, hitting the table and laughing and saying I should eat another pickle. He made me drink another big glass of the stuff and I knew something was terrible happening to me and then another and he asked me if I felt like dying. I can just remember hearing him and his voice and laugh came from a long way. Then I stood up and fell over and began to be sick. On my mother's scrubbed floor and I couldn't do anything and then I rolled over into it. That's all I remember.

Next morning he got me out of bed and I was funny and still sick and everybody at the table was quiet. They just ate and I looked at my bread and milk and cabbage and he said, this is my father talking, he said, 'Now you know what it is like being a soldier. Get your pay and go to sleep drunk and in your own vomit. Now you have the feeling of death on you. That's what being a soldier is all about. You still want to be a soldier and fight for your country?' Words like that. I remember them. My mother and sisters were crying and he told me to drink from my bowl of milk and I did and I was sick again. Right on the table. I was humiliated.

I remember him looking at me and he was laughing and I said something like, 'Papa, you've lost a son,' and he said, 'All right, go, be a soldier but don't be a hero. They always end up dead.'

I went to Moscow that morning and the war was on heavy then and the sergeant, he looked at me and said to another sergeant I was hardly a young rooster yet and they laughed and they signed me up. I was a soldier at fourteen years and my papers said seventeen and the sergeant said, this laughing fellow told me to come back next morning and I was to get myself fucked that night because there was no place in the army for virgins.

That was how I got into the army.

Away to camp, with all the training and soon we were getting new guns and I had to fight everybody in my company to prove I was good enough. It was the way they did things. Just stand up and fight. See this nose. They broke ten of mine but I broke thirty of their beaks. It was tough and one day about fifteen of us were sent out behind to dig a new line of latrines. A few hours later the officer came out and we had nearly dug about ten of them and he was surprised and he asked me why I was not working. Just standing. I told him that if fifteen people worked at digging the holes, nothing would get done. If one person stood aside and said he'd beat the shit out of those who didn't work, then the work would be done. The officer told the sergeant to keep an eye on this one. He meant me. Then I thanked my father for teaching me how to get things done.

Two weeks later they sent me home on three days' furlough and then I'm to then go to an officers' training camp. They had all my papers made out and it was out to the East and it took eight days to get there. It should have taken a day and a half but there were bombings and troop trains, supply trains, trains carrying the young and old people and some workers away from Moscow to the East and it took a long time. Everything was in bad shape and everyone thought we were losing the war. We were. Did you know that? We nearly lost that war in the first year. Did they tell you that in the West? Those Germans were invincible at first.

I became a junior officer and that took five months, I think. About that. The same shit as in soldier training, battalion level, but they taught us one thing. Soldiers were shit, and I knew that, but we had to protect our men. All the time. When you are in that uniform, they told us, you are a different person. Your father may be a scientist, your father may be a drunk, your mother may be a prostitute, your mother may be a ballerina, but in that uniform you are an officer and you are a leader. Where you go your men will follow. You can't push from behind. You call from in front and say, 'C'mon, boys, this is nothing. We'll have them running in five minutes.' Of course, you know it yourself, that's why they trained tens of thousands of young officers. There is no better way to kill yourself.

I was sent to a tank regiment. We had no tanks. The ones we had were shit and the Germans, they had the big ones. Ours were like little rifles only good for killing hares and they were elephants. I was wounded twice but not bad. This arm, and in here, this part of the shoulder. Two weeks in the hospital for the arm, just enough to get a chance to love up a nurse and then you were gone. Back to the front.

But something happened. I'd kiss the man's arse if I knew who it was but this was 1944 and we had the Germans running hard. They'd fight, run, fight, stand and fight, good fighters. We hated the vermin but they could fight. Good soldiers. It was only after the war . . . well, all I will say is that when I see a bunch of those German tourists getting off a tourist bus

I wish I had a machine gun. But that was a long time ago, the time of the war.

Yes, yes, something happened. A genius designed a tank and it was called the T-34. That was our beauty. Now I was a fighter again and in a tank that could fight. Not a piece of tin with a gun that was no good. This was a big man tank.

Sorry, it was 1943 and not 1944. I'm old. I'm losing a year here and there. After my second wound, when I got back there was this big devil. I asked the squadron commandant and he said it was thirty-two tons. A battleship. It had a gun with a diameter this big. The .76-millimetre and then they gave us an .85. Nothing could touch us. I was in the command tank and we'd roll, right through a house if we wanted to, as big as that building over there, through the valley, up, over, down, and a stream was nothing. The only thing they had against it was that damned 105, but our infantry would wait and our artillery would plaster the area and then the boys would go through and kill off the 105 pieces and then we'd roll again. It was glorious. Remember, I was only seventeen.

I must have been the youngest officer at the front, just seventeen and a man. We beat the Germans with that .85-millimetre gun. It was like a torpedo. It could sink a ship if there had been one out there. That T-34 won the war, no doubt about it. Forward, wheel right, wheel left, aim, fire, and either it was one of theirs going boom, or a few shots and no more pillbox or one of them put a shell into a house and the thing would explode.

In January of 1945 when the Nazi boys knew it was all over but they were going to make it tough on us all the way, I got my orders. Because of my high ration of shells to kills, something like sixteen-to-one, they called me in and gave me a medal, made me a captain, and sent me back to train others how to do it. That was the end of the war for me. Of course, it saved my life. I'd have been killed sooner or later. No man lives through that kind of war.

I never got to the training camp. I was sent to Moscow, the boys in the nice uniforms, twenty-five, thirty years old. Majors, generals, and they soon found me out. Who was this kid? I wasn't even an officer in their style. I was just a kid off the farm. My records said so. My education, I had none. Village, farm education. All their little tricks, the way they drank a glass of wine, just so. You eat with a spoon and your hands in your tank, just you and the gunner, or you sit around a fire in a barn and eat a pig and rations. White table covers. I'd never eaten caviar. I knew nothing. One major asked me if I had read such and such a general on tank tactics and I said I'd never heard of him. They laughed. This was at a reception for a general. I said I hadn't, but I'd shot out enough German tanks and armoured vehicles that I figured I didn't need to read any book.

An old general who was sort of the head of the table asked me how many. I told him forty-three tanks. Somebody laughed and the general told him to leave the table. That was an officer who was finished, I bet. Off to the front with him and give up his ballerina girl friend and his servant. The general came down the table and shook my hand. That was the most important moment of my life.

Then I was released from the army when the war for Berlin was over and what was I to do? I had some money and I was okay and I thought, well, I've seen Moscow and it has a wonderful underground subway and the theatre is nice to see once and a while and the girls are pretty but too high and smart for me. I told myself, 'You're just a country boy,' and I went home to my father's farm. He was the big boss then, an important man and making the farm very productive. He cried when he saw me coming down the road in the farm wagon sitting on top of some bags of supplies and he cried and cried, and then he gasped out, 'My son. My son.' He kissed me and I kissed him and we went into the house.

There was a party that night after we'd dug the priest out of his farm clothes and they had pulled the altar out of the potato house and set it up, and we had a ceremony for the memory of the dead and prayers, and the candles lit up the house and we all prayed for the dead boys of the village and that there would be peace forever.

Before I'd left headquarters I'd gone to the officers' special store where you could buy wonderful things from America and England, and I bought gifts for my father and mother and the two sisters who were married on the farm and I bought caviar and cheese and candy and chocolates, and I also bought many bottles of vodka and wine.

I sat at the table with my father and I thought, he looks like an old man now. I think he has had a hard time of this life and I told him, two glasses. One vodka, a litre, the best in my satchel, and I filled up both glasses and I started hitting the table, thump, thump, thump, and we finished off those glasses on the third thump. I just wanted to show him I was not angry like I had been when I left that morning in the sunshine.

He remembered, and I think we both cried just a little. 'Grown men don't cry,' I thought, 'but I'm only eighteen years old.' Just a kid.

Fine. That was a wonderful party and then it was over and I was back in bed that night like always. My uniform hanging in the cupboard beside the window. I thought, 'Okay, it is all over.'

I never did much with my life after that. Worked on the farm. Worked in towns, cities, always came home again. Nothing changed for me. I can't say those were bad years or good years when I was a trooper. They just happened to me, just like they happened to a million other boys like me. You forget. I mean you remember, but the world forgets, so you forget, too. That's what life is about. Does it matter much?"

TEN

Moscow, Farewell

♨

A Bag of Broken Cookies ... "They Have Killed the Aral Sea" ... "I Dream of Seeing Greece" ... "No More Lies" ... The last Mini-Bar

Fog delays our take-off in Irkutsk, but it finally clears and we fly back to The Centre, covering vast stretches of nothingness before reaching one of Moscow's satellite airports. Milling around the terminal are fifteen young Cuban athletes, trim in red-and-white track suits. Every female in the place is eyeing them, and the young men know it. Some things are the same everywhere.

This time I'm in the Intourist Hotel, hard by Red Square. The long line of visitors to Lenin's Tomb has disappeared for the day. Tomorrow there will be just as many queuing up. Where do all these people come from?

I'm invited to a Canadian couple's apartment for dinner, and a twenty-minute subway ride to get there turns into an hour and a half: I got lost. Fortunately my hosts are late, too. I'm delighted to have a home-cooked meal; I think I cannot face another hotel hamburger topped with an egg and the inevitable tomato-and-cumcumber salad.

Furthermore, I'm sick of the rudeness of arrogant waiters who always try to cheat me. I must say, though, I can't complain about the waitresses, who are always cheery and smiling. A tip from a Dutch traveller has served me well: look for the mini-bars found in some hotels; they serve the best food in the USSR and it's cheap.

A few last conversations with ordinary Russians. One tells me she dreams of seeing Greece; another tells me she doesn't want to return home because the Aral Sea is dead, killed by the know-it-alls who wanted to grow more cotton in Uzbek.

These people are very wait-and-see about glasnost and perestroika. They want peace, they want better food, better housing–but most of all they want no more lies.

A Bag of Broken Cookies

While waiting for my guide to pick me up outside the Intourist Hotel in downtown Moscow, a waitress in uniform pushed a three-decker trolley onto the sidewalk, a feast of cookies and cakes and other delights. Within seconds a crowd began to gather.

These pastries were for sale–the extras from the dinner the night before or . . . do Moscow's hotels have their own bakeries?

The first order of business for the waitress was to carefully pick up every cookie, whole and broken, which had spilled from a bag that had fallen from her overloaded cart. She put that bag aside. Then the selling began. This was not a queue in a straight line, English style; it was more like a blob. Fashionably dressed women beside roughly dressed labourers, a pair of perfectly turned out army officers – the best-dressed males in Moscow–beside shopgirls, a couple of drivers from the taxis waiting in the street, the hit and miss of a Moscow street where the crowds flow endlessly. About twenty had gathered. Others passed by, looked, and then continued on, as if to say, "That girl has only so much to sell and when it is my turn it will be all gone."

There was no pushing, no shoving, no pulling of rank by the officers – who had been joined by two policemen – and each seemed to know precisely who was ahead of them, in order of arrival. As the small cakes, four or six or eight, elaborate pastries of every variety were bought, the girl put them in newspaper cones, flashed her fingers over her abacus, took the money, made the change, and stuffed the bills into one pocket of her smock and the coins into the other pocket.

This young girl, perhaps eighteen, was the boss. A woman pointed to some goodies on the second tier but the waitress shook her head. No! We will clean off the top shelf first. A shrug of the shoulders. Her word was law. This was the way it would be done. The second tier quickly vanished, then the third, and I watched the two army officers fill their briefcases with the pastries and cakes.

Now, the only thing left, the pièce de résistance, was the brown bag full of the broken cookies. Many people were left, and she spoke rapidly, probably saying, "Comrades, this is a bag of good cookies. Here, look at them," and she fished one out and held it up. "Good, but some are cracked, some are crumbled. Do you want to buy them?"

Without hesitation one man stepped forward, paid his money, and hurried off.

Was this capitalism at work? A hotel selling off its unused desserts and pastries from last night's dinner? Why didn't the staff take them home, as they would in a North American hotel? This was a lucrative business. Why didn't a second cart appear? There were far more buyers than there were pastries. A large amount of money could be made, especially if this unusual form of business went on all day, the bakers turning out the goodies as the crowds ebbed and flowed past this hotel all during the day and late into the night. And Red Square was hardly more than a stone's throw away.

❦ *"They Have Killed the Aral Sea"*

"When I was a young girl they told us in our school, 'There is only one truth,' and there were two of us, my dearest friend and me, and we would ask, 'What does that mean?' and all the teachers would say, 'It means there is only one way.'

We know now that this is not true. It is in every newspaper and magazine and on the television and now they are saying, 'Maybe that is not the way it is. Maybe there is a lot of ways to do things,' but I will tell you something from my heart. Our way has been wrong. For many years it has been wrong, and if you ask me I will tell you one way that was wrong and everybody in our region knew it.

I am talking about our beloved Aral'skaye More, which in your language means the Sea of Aral. I lived beside it with my mother and father and my three brothers and two sisters and we were happy. This was when I was a girl and I remember it and it was such a huge sea, maybe 300 kilometres long (180 miles) and very wide and in the moonlight it was like a huge place of white water and very beautiful. Our beloved Aral-'skaye was very huge and it had, it was full of fish and there were villages and little towns of fishermen and their families around it and everybody made a good life of it.

That was maybe thirty-five years ago and then somebody in The Centre, the central planners, these men said, 'There is much water there and it is clean and it will be good to make water to go into these things called canals from big engineering pumps and it will make cotton grow in the deserts of Uzbekistan.' This is what they wanted to do. They did not want to buy cotton from Iran and India any more. Why spend good money to those awful people when we can grow cotton in Uzbekistan?

So this is what happened. The big rivers, they built dams on them and pumped the water away into canals so the water would not run into our sea. They did this for years.

My father, he was a manager of a fish factory and a member of the regional Soviet and I remember him saying, 'They take our water from our great lake where there are thousands of fishermen, and this will destroy it.' Nobody would listen. I was just a girl but I knew what he was saying.

My father and his friends were correct in their saying this. The Aral'skaye More is now a useless thing. This great sea of water is no more; now a person can walk for miles and miles and still not reach the water. There is just some in the centre of this lake, and that is a tragedy. I think they told us it was the one, two, three, four, the fourth largest inland piece of water in the world. Very large. Big ships used to go on it. Hundreds and hundreds of fishing boats. There were the fish factories around it and everybody worked and it was a good time.

Oh yes, the irrigation was a success and there was so much cotton the bureaucrats, they would say to my father, 'Here are the figures. Look at this production of ours. Go, look, see, the cotton fields, the biggest in the world, the best cotton. Look at the other farms. Look at the grain and vegetables. Look at the new towns and how happy the other people are. Why are you such a bad person? Look at what our plans have done, look at Uzbekistan and Kazakhstan and Turkmenia. Industry is there now. People from other regions. We have created something that the world has not seen before. A new land.'

You understand, I am making up these words, but they were like what my father told me. Now, I will tell you something. They have killed the Aral'skaye. The fishermen are gone because the millions of fish are gone. It would take more than a day of hard work walking to get to the water and it is full of chemicals, which come in off the cotton and vegetable lands. The wind when it blows hard brings in the sand of the parts of the Uzbek deserts that are not irrigated, and there is more. There were two great rivers. The Syr Dar'ya River and the Amu Dar'ya River. All Russians were proudly happy with these great rivers. Now they are hardly any more. The sea is finished and one day the cotton fields of great size will be finished, too. The government killed the sea, the rivers, and the regions will be desert again and what will it all have been for?

This summer I went back to the place I was born and then to Ozek where my mother lives now, comfortable on her pension and little house. She says our mighty lake is gone. No water, so it is hotter. The air is full of blowing things, awful things. The people have no reason to stay there. I ask about the people and she says many die because chemicals from the fields get into the wells and they die of disease of the liver. That is too bad. I ask her and she says, 'Oh yes, people work. A little.' I say where, and then she told me something I did not believe. There is a big fish factory but there are no fish. You must understand that. What do these great thinkers in The Centre in their big offices do? They say, 'We will bring you fish.' Baltic herring. Please, do not laugh.

They fly in these huge airplanes with herring from the Baltic. Then they are cut up and cleaned and put in big flat tins and taken back to the big cities and sold. I am not an expert with figures, but I know that if you fly fish thousands of kilometres and then fly the tins back to the marketplace, then the cost of the fish . . . why, nobody could pay for it. It would be double the price of fish from Estonia and Latvia. But I know it is the same price. I have seen all these cans. They are paying millions of rubles to do this. Why they do it, I cannot say. I think these Russians have their pride and they do not want to say they made a huge mistake and killed off the sea and the fish. You can see it was total stupidity. They won't admit their mistake. Why should they? They are the bosses. If we complain, they say, 'Go away, you little person.'

But my mother says now they will be making plans to make things as they were when I was a young girl. It will not work out. Their drawings and figures are useless. They have hurt nature and nothing can be done. Why could they not have learned from other nations who knew these things? But will they be punished? No, my friend, I will tell you that the planners and the engineers, they are all wearing medals and marching in parades as heroes of this thing, that thing. Everything. We honour our idiots and our fools.

Greed. Ignorance. Oh, excuse me, I get very angry. Our great sea, our pride, and when I saw it, what did I see? Blowing sand, and my mother says not to drink water from the wells. Chemicalized, she said. All for some cotton, and they destroy a land that was home to thousands and thousands of good people for hundreds of years.

My mother, she is old and she takes these events as they come along. But I am glad I married a Moscow man and went to The Centre. It would have hurt me very much as this happened.

Perestroika, this thing will not help the lake. *Glasnost,* that will be fine because people will talk, write to the newspapers, say it on the radio, and this will not happen again. It will not happen again, naturally; any fool can see that. There was only one sea like it."

☙ *"I Dream of Seeing Greece"*

"All the time in my life since I was a little girl I have wanted to visit the land of Greece. When I was a child my uncle had a book on that country and I saw it and I thought, 'I will go there.' And now I am thirty-two years old and I have been married once and now I am free. I still want to go. I live with my mother and I can leave my job for a month and she will look after the needs of my children and their good times and their food.

My mother does not work now. The doctors said they could fix her hip but they made it worse, so she does not work. Every morning at ten o'clock she goes out and buys the bread and milk and maybe she can get a chicken. Then we have feast, but usually it is sausage. There is a very big factory for sausage that is out near one of the districts, but the farms do not bring the meat in, so, well, we make out. But the children should have more things to make them strong. Lunch at the school, cabbage soup and bread and a cup of juice. That's no good.

You must not use my name or my address when you tell this. It would be bad for us. They would know.

My Valentina is nine years in age now and she asks all the time, 'Where is my father?' I tell her he has gone away and will not come back. I do not know where my husband is. He was a drunkard, and one day I came back from the store . . . I worked in a store in the GUM and he was gone. He has a brother in Irkutsk, and I think that is where he is. I won't write and find out. He was a bad man. I should have had an abortion, but instead I married him and it was bad. My little one, he is just a child, he is six.

My little boy does not want me to go to Greece for a holiday. I tell him, just for a month. I say that I would not leave him and his sister. Little children, they don't understand. I say I would stay with a friend.

She is my best friend. We went to the same schools as children, and then she met this Greek man and they became in love and she married him, and then in nine months she got her visa and she went to work and live in his country. She went when she was nineteen; she is twenty-nine now and she is very happy there because it is like our Sochi and Yalta. The sun shining and everything like that. All her letters, they say, 'Marina, you must come and visit me. You will live in my house and we will drive to the cafés and markets and swim in the ocean.' I dream of it.

It would please me if you told me you were what they call a good-luck charm and I touched you and when I went home, my mother would give me a letter. It would be from the visa department and the letter would say I can go and visit my friend in Thessaloniki, to her white house with the trees so green all around it.

But I go and they say, 'Why do you want to go to Greece?' and I tell them as honestly as I am able to. I say it is my greatest dream. I want to see the land of the very old Greeks, the tall men who fought wonderful battles and had philosophers. I tell them I do not want to stay there; I tell them if I could not live in my homeland I would want to die. I *would* die. I want to hear the Russian voices around me. My heart, my greatest heart, that is my country. We have been through the bad times and now with *perestroika* we know everything will get better after some time of living the new way.

I cry to them, 'I do not want to live anywhere else but in my country because I was born here.' My grandfather, my mother has his medals because he was killed in the war. He was a major in the artillery guns and was very brave. I do not know what my father did but he was an officer, too, and his medals are in my mother's lacquer boxes where she keeps her precious things. He died when I was a child.

I dream of seeing ancient Greece and sit on those old stones, but those men of the Party, those fat men in their suits and shirts and green ties who have had two bottles of vodka at lunch before they see me, they look at me and they are saying, 'Why does this young woman bother us?'

All they think of is themselves and their vodka at lunch and they say, I think they say, 'We did something nice for two people this morning. We let them go to West Germany to a conference on a delegation.' Then they think, 'It is now time to do something bad for some peoples,' and they take my document and they write on it, and that means No. Why? They are like that. The Party. They are the bosses. They do not know what it is like to be young and have dreams.

I ask them, 'Why? I am doing no harm. I have the money. I have my children and I would never go away from them.' The first fat face, the one in the middle, he looks at me and says, 'You get out of here.' Then I know it will be another six months and I will try again. I will be an old woman by then.

That is why we hope for *perestroika*."

❀ *"No More Lies"*

"You are leaving this country, this Russia, tomorrow? Come, sit, have coffee, tea, with me and we will talk.

Look at me. Look at these hands. They have carried a machine gun and that was when I was eighteen and in the war. My friend, I will tell you something. It was just about over for my Motherland, and later it would have been the world. Germany would have made peace with Winston Churchill. That would have been easy. The Soviet Union would have been destroyed, and wouldn't the Ukrainians and the Georgians, the Latvians, the Estonians, the Armenians, wouldn't they have jumped and clicked their heels with happiness. They would have been free again. The Germans would have seen that happen and Churchill would have had his greatest happiness. The end of Russia, the Soviet Union.

Yes, Hitler nearly won. It was close. After it was all over, why didn't we all start to rebuild our country again? Why do we put up with this talk that we are recovering still from the war with the Nazis? The West Germans recovered and are one of the world's richest countries now. So are the Hollanders. They got knocked around a lot. But we still blame the war.

Now things will be changing. We have *glasnost* where people can write to the newspapers and say these things and our General Secretary, now, I think he is smart fellow. A peasant boy, don't you know. They are cunning. Smart. He is a smart politician and he will get the country running right. I feel that. I have much faith in this man. I think he is a good man. Let us forget Lenin. That was seventy years ago. Let us think about Gorbachev and what he can show us to do about this country of ours. I think this is our last chance.

Have you ever seen a cow in a swamp? It goes mooo-mooo, and fights and sinks deeper. Then it dies while all the people stand around and say, 'Oh, that poor woman. Her best cow is dead.' But if a man comes along with a rope and gets it around that cow's horns and neck, then he tells everyone, 'Get on this rope and when I say pull, all of you pull.' You think the cow is going to die because the rope is tight but then zzzssshhhttt! Out it comes, faster and faster, and then the old woman who owns the cow she is hugging the man with the rope and, okay, that's the way.

Our hands will be sore from the rope and our shoulders stiff from pulling. The cow is going to have a sore throat for a while, but we've got the cow out of the mud. And the man who came along with the rope, the man who knew how to get it on to the cow, that was this man Gorbachev.

He makes too many speeches but he has to, because so much has been done badly for so many years, but the speech he could give to those dumb village people should be, 'You shouldn't have let that yard be so close to the swamp and you, woman, you should have watched your cow, but you see what can be done. Everybody works together and we save the cow.'

That is what you call peasant talk. Straight talk. He says things we understand. They tried so many years to fool us. To lie to us. It was always that things would be better and it is all America's fault that things are so bad. What was it all about? It was our fault. Now we know that. The young people will be taught they can do things, not the old way, which has always been wrong but, you see, the new way and it will be right.

We will work harder and stop thinking of the old ways, all those old terrorists and thieves and crooks and bullies that we had before. Now, we have Gorbachev. Let him live long and do his duty to our country. He is our only hope. Right now. We must help him. No more lies."

❦ *The Last Mini-Bar*

Westerners who visit Russia on a tour do not see the real Soviet Union. They are led by the nose from wake-up knock to breakfast table to museum to monument to factory before the big red Intourist bus drops them off, glassy-eyed, to await dinner. Their meals are served in special rooms, or at tables set up in corners of the vast hotel dining rooms where waiters serve one course after another almost at a dead run.

And, as Soviet cities close down at 6 P.M. for tourists, except for concerts, there are only the hotel rooms and the talk of home town, Canada, and the growing dissatisfaction, the increasing unease, the sad knowledge of opportunities missed, and the desperate and determined effort to convince each other that this expensive tour is educational, and interesting.

For the traveller alone in this vast, indifferent, and confusing land, just eating can be a problem. Alone, you will not stay usually at the major Intourist hotels reserved for tour groups, especially in the hinterland; so the tricks picked up make life a little better. The bigger hotels have a buffet breakfast and I hoarded, learning quickly the impossibility of getting lunch. Most buffets are remarkably well stocked, with several types of juices, mounds of hard-boiled eggs, plates of bread of several flavours and textures and all of them good. There is a pancake similar to a blintz, sometimes wiener-like sausages, ham that is very like our wartime Spam but edible, milk with a chalky flavour which you assume is the 4.4 percent butterfat content they boast of, plus fruit, tea, coffee, and a table of sliced carrots, cabbage, and cold beans. Plus more. All in all, rather startling. A feast amid famine.

My problem was solved early by an English woman sitting opposite me at breakfast who brought two huge piled-high plates to the table and proceeded to finish one off in grand style. Then she took out two self-sealing plastic bags and put in four eggs, two sandwiches made of Spam, vegetables, fruit, more bread plus the little packages of jam. She looked over at me: "My lunch. Perhaps my dinner, too. You never know here." Then she handed me two of her bags and said, "All I can spare. Wash them out every night and you'll make them last. Fill another plate and fill up your bag. You'll thank me. Don't worry–everyone does it."

In Leningrad, Tallinn, it was so, and in Irkutsk a gift of 99-cent pantihose the first morning made my little waitress my friend for life and she filled my bag from the kitchen, so I survived. Things did not go all that well in Kiev and Tbilisi and Yerevan and other cities where the buffet was unknown.

The first morning in Yerevan – remembering Tbilisi – I entered the dining room for breakfast and began my usual routine of tapping my water glass. The five waiters looked over at me. I had a car booked in forty-five minutes and at 8 rubles an hour, 18 dollars Canadian, I needed a fast breakfast. In Tbilisi I had virtually cracked the glass, tapping on it. Now I really swung the knife at the goblet and it shattered. This brought action as well as a simultaneous hush over the room. "I want breakfast and fast," and snapped my fingers three times. The waiter hurried away. He brought back, well, take a small eggroll and divide it in half: that was breakfast, plus a tiny saucer of a reddish-orange sauce for the eggroll and a tiny cup of coffee. I showed two fingers and said, "More," and gestured to my belly. He shook his head.

I stood up and walked across to a table of satellite Soviets – Bulgarians, Polish, I did not know or care–and from their laden table I selected bread, rolls, a plate of butter, jam, sausages, eggs, and smiled at them. Nice morning, isn't it? There were now three waiters at my table, all jabbering, as I sat down and began my breakfast.

I wished I could have told the departing diners, who studiously avoided me, that the rate I was paying for that tiny roll and the coffee would have bought me a sumptuous breakfast in the finest hotel in Canada.

Later, after I described this incident to a Soviet friend, he said, "I'm not saying it happens in Moscow but in the republics, the Southern ones, the waiters pay the manager 20 percent of their wages. If there are ten waiters he makes a lot of money.

But he lets the waiters run the dining room and the kitchen, and the food that comes in, it is sold by the waiters to their friends."

"Out the back door?" I asked.

"That is a good expression!" he said.

But in Kiev I met another traveller from a foreign land, a Dutchman, and when I mentioned the food, and he laughed. "You have not discovered the mini-bars in these hotels? That is where you eat. Not in their dining rooms. The food is terrible . . . "

"And the service is worse," I added.

I decided to check out the mini-bar, which was on the eleventh floor, so at noon I went up and sure enough, there it was, about the size of four hotel rooms opened up, with two smiling women at the counter. The food was plentiful and I had two hard-boiled eggs, a salad, a plate of bread with jam, a slice of cheese, and strong tea and I think it was just over a ruble. The service was immediate and the women friendly, especially the youngest, who chatted incessantly in Russian sprinkled with English, German, and French words. It didn't matter. I just pointed and she smiled and giggled.

From then on, I ate there, as it seemed to be open round the clock.

The next afternoon I put in two hours with one of the most boring intellectual bureaucrats I have ever encountered, and doubly so because he came into the huge conference room, sat down, spoke, and my guide interpreted: "He says he will now say a few words."

I'll admit my guide tried valiantly but this fool rattled away like a Gatling gun, giving my guide no chance whatsoever to interpret. After fifteen minutes I shut off my tape recorder and settled back and smoked about a dozen cigarettes. Another interview blown.

When it was over he was all smiles, pats on the back, and he gave me two albums of Ukrainian folk music and two books he had written, 10 percent text and 90 percent cartoons.

There was no way I was going to carry two record albums around the country, so that night I took them up to the mini-bar. The young girl was there and I handed her the albums. I knew were priced about 4 rubles in the record shops, and I indicated they were a gift. Her face went solemn, she looked at them, then at me, and I held my hands to my chest and flung them out towards her, indicating they were a gift from me to her. She smiled, laughed, and that was that. No big deal. She probably made 60 rubles a month, working twelve-hour shifts four days a week, and I hoped she could sell them. Perhaps buy a pretty dress. If she was married, perhaps a toy for her baby. Or a bottle of wine. I didn't care.

On my last day in the Soviet Union I visited the mini-bar on the twentieth floor of the Intourist Hotel deep in downtown Moscow. It served liquor and it had small tables with tiny chairs with foreign businessmen overflowing them. The conversation was low, secretive, furtive. What international plots were being hatched there? None, but a lot of skulduggery, by the feel of the place.

It was about three o'clock in the afternoon, and there was only one table free, so I threw my camera case on it to reserve it and ordered a small cake and a Pepsi. As I sat down I was joined by a young man, about twenty-five, who said, "May I join you?" as he swung his chair from another table.

We chatted and he said, "Cognac? Armenian," and I said yes, sure, and he brought four to the table. God knows what he paid if the Pepsi and the cake cost me 3 rubles.

I had taken in his Western suit but I couldn't figure out where he was from. He laughed and said, "Guess again." I hadn't even tried to guess. That was the way it went in this mini. The very atmosphere demanded it.

As it turned out, he was Russian, he obviously had access to money, he bought expensive American clothes, English shirts, he drank good cognac, and he was up to no good. I figured he wanted something from me, but what? But no, he didn't.

"Just touching up the corners of my English." He grinned. "I like to talk to people like you. Very interesting. And you make living so simple. I can come into any tourist hotel in Moscow and I do. Five rubles to the doorman, even 3 or 2 would do, but next time they'll remember me and when I walk out with something from the hard-currency store they just wink. These doormen, they're old men. Some are veterans. Harmless, but they all have their tricks. They can't live on their salaries, so being a doorman in this hotel, for instance, that's a good deal. Five rubles is one day's pay for them, about that. I can make 1,000 rubles a day if I want. How'm I doing?"

I replied, "You don't need any help from me." But I mentioned drugs.

He didn't tell me how he made 1,000 rubles a day, but he said, "Oh, my friend, we never discuss that kind of thing, and besides, it is very, very illegal. Very dangerous. I am a timid fellow. Look at my hand shaking," and he held it out. It looked steady to me.

We talked for about fifteen minutes, mostly about cars, then he rejoined two beautiful women and a man at his table.

That was the last mini-bar I was in, quite a bit different from the friendly ones, high above the cities with good views and a different clientele. This one had a feeling of quiet menace about it, a feeling I had difficulty shaking off as I walked to my room. Things happened there which I didn't care to know about.